A HESSIAN

OFFICER'S *Diary*

OF THE AMERICAN REVOLUTION

Translated from an
Anonymous Ansbach-Bayreuth Diary
AS ORIGINALLY WRITTEN BY
Johann Ernst Prechtel
AND PRESENTLY IN THE HUNTINGTON LIBRARY
SAN MARINO, CALIFORNIA

AND

The Prechtel Diary
A COPY OF WHICH IS IN THE BAVARIAN STATE ARCHIVES
MUNICH, GERMANY

Translated and Edited by
Bruce E. Burgoyne

HERITAGE BOOKS
2008

HERITAGE BOOKS

AN IMPRINT OF HERITAGE BOOKS, INC.

Books, CDs, and more—Worldwide

For our listing of thousands of titles see our website
at
www.HeritageBooks.com

Published 2008 by
HERITAGE BOOKS, INC.
Publishing Division
100 Railroad Ave. #104
Westminster, Maryland 21157

International Standard Book Number: 978-0-7884-0107-7

Contents

Illustrations

PREFACE

This volume, containing translations of two versions of the Revolutionary War diary of Johann Ernst Prechtel, is presented as part of my continuing effort to provide source material bearing on our country's history to those persons not fluent in the German language.

Prechtel was a first sergeant, later a lieutenant, in the Ansbach Regiment of the Ansbach-Bayreuth contingent of "Hessians" hired by England to suppress the revolt then existing in the American colonies. His diary covers the entire period of employment of the Ansbach-Bayreuth forces, 1777-1783, with special emphasis on his own regiment and descriptions of the mutiny by the troops while still in Germany, of the voyage to America, observations on American localities visited, his military activity, captivity, and the return voyage to Europe. He also notes the dates and places of the many desertions from the ranks of his unit. His description of the Battle of Rhode Island, the Yorktown siege and surrender, and prisoner of war status in Virginia and Maryland are of special historical importance.

I first encountered reference to the Prechtel diary in James Linwood Carpenter's "The Yorktown Prisoners", a master's thesis submitted to the College of William and Mary in 1950. On page 60 of this excellent account, Carpenter cited Harold Clem's "A Hessian Prisoner's Memoirs of Frederick in 1782-1783", published on pages 59 and 60 in volume XLVII of The Maryland Bulletin in February 1947. Clem had translated a few passages from the diary of Lieutenant Johann Ernst Prechtel of the Ansbach Regiment. The original was noted as being in the Bavarian Archives in Munich, Germany.

Several years later, while conducting research for my translation of the diary of

Johann Conrad Doehla, another Ansbach-Bayreuth diarist, I visited the Maryland School of the Deaf at Frederick, Maryland, and then learned that the Maryland Bulletin was a publication of that school. I obtained a copy of Professor Clem's article and decided the Prechtel diary was probably worth translating in its entirety.

When I visited the War Archives of the Bavarian State Archives in Munich, I encountered a frustrating situation. The Prechtel diary was bound in such a manner that it was impossible to read words on the inside edges of the pages, toward the spine. The diary was so thick that the book could not be fully opened. That night, in bed, the thought struck me. It was not an original binding. As it stood, the diary was a worthless volume which no one could profitably use. Why not remove the binding, copy the pages, and then rebind so that the diary could be read. I approached Dr. Heyl, the archivist at the War Archives, with this proposal and he agreed to do so.

Although Professor Clem had written that this was the original Prechtel diary, it was obvious from reading the notation on the diary supplement made by the 1910 archivist, Captain H. Helmes, that it was a copy. I had barely completed my translation of the diary, however, when I was asked by Dr. Mary Robertson, archivist at the Huntington Library in San Marino, California, if I would be interested in translating an anonymous German diary written during the Revolution, which was in the Huntington archives. To my surprise it quickly became apparent that the Huntington diary was the original, or at least pre-dated the Munich version, of the Prechtel diary.

The first two pages of the diary in the Huntington Library are badly damaged and the initial, significant entries concerning a mutiny by the Ansbach-Bayreuth soldiers could

not be read. However, the remaining portions
of the diary, which only cover the period
through Cornwallis' surrender at Yorktown in
October 1781, reinforced my belief that it was
the original Prechtel diary.

I decided to combine both versions in a
single volume to provide an easily comparable
contrast between entries made spontaneously and
those rewritten, eliminated, or expanded, when
the author meant the contents to be read by
other individuals. My preparation of the
combined accounts finished, I wrote to the
Nuernberg, Germany, State Archives to get
another manuscript to translate. As the title
indicated only that it had been written by an
Ansbach-Bayreuth soldier, I was not sure what
to expect. Knowing there were other "lost"
Ansbach-Bayreuth diaries, I had hopes it would
be one of them. However, it turned out to be a
"true copy" of the anonymous diary owned by the
Huntington Library. The handwriting was clear,
sharp, and beautiful, and the initial entries
were easily legible, filling in the entries for
the damaged pages of the Huntington diary.
There were also two excellent maps, one of New
York area and one of Philadelphia area. Both
have been included in the following volume.

As noted earlier, I have translated the
Doehla diary, which was published in 1990 by
the University of Oklahoma Press as A Hessian
Diary of the American Revolution. In the
Preface of that volume, I indicated that the
editor of the German publication of that diary
had known of five other Revolutionary War
diaries, written by Ansbach-Bayreuth soldiers -
Private Stephen Popp, Lieutenant Heinrich Karl
Philipp von Feilitzsch, Musician Georg Adam
Stang, Captain Friedrich Wilhelm von Roeder,
and Captain Johann Friedrich von Sichart. The
von Roeder and von Sichart diaries have
apparently been lost, or at least have not yet
been made available to the public.

My own research indicates that a diary by Lieutenant C. F. Bartholomai, in several different versions, and one by an anonymous officer, whom I believe to be Captain Christian Theodor Sigismund von Molitor, are available in The New York Public Library. I have already translated all the available diaries, except the Popp diary which was previously translated by Joseph G. Rosengarten and also by Reinhard Pope, and hope eventually to be able to provide students of American History access to these comprehensive, first person accounts of the American Revolutionary War.

EDITORIAL PROCEDURES

Although many entries in the Munich version are identical to those in the Huntington version, I have given entries from both versions in order to allow the fullest understanding of the author, and to make comparison as easy as possible. I have tried to use the wording, phrasing, and sentence structure used by the author whenever possible. However, there are times when changes must be made to make the meaning of entries more easily understood and it was often necessary to divide long, involved sentences into two or more English sentences.

In general I have used the spelling of proper names as they were given by Prechtel, or the copyist, but when a current, accepted alternate spelling was known, I have used it. In some cases, variations of spelling of names has been indicated and I have used a letter e after the vowels a, o, and u to indicate an umlaut in the German spelling. I have used Erhard Staedtler's Die Ansbach-Bayreuther Truppen in Amerikanischen Unabhaengigkeits- krieg, 1777-1783, (Nuernberg, Germany, 1956) for additional identifying information on individuals.

x

The spelling of ship names, because most probably were only heard and therefore recorded phonetically, seems to have caused Prechtel considerable confusion. In the Huntington version he wrote Renno several times and finally Renaunt for what I believe was meant to be Renown. He used Rennobel once for what I believe must have been Raisonable. In the Munich version spellings are all changed to Renown. I have used the names as I believe they should have been.

While the shorter Huntington version is presented very much as written, the Munich version has been shortened by eliminating lists of the names of nearly all officers who served in the English, German, and Loyalist units in America. Also, lists of English ship names, and names and pay scales of English naval and marine officers have been omitted.

In several places in the German text the author, or copyist, has used an asterisk in parenthesis to indicate a note. I have retained these entries as written. Other footnotes, for the most part, are to clarify meaning in the text or to correct inaccurate entries. However, because I believe the men, even former enemies, are more important than the events in which they participated, I have entered some footnote information which will probably be more important to geneologists than to historians.

Finally, in listing military titles, I use the term medic instead of the more correct translation surgeon when company medical personnel are meant. Also, I translate the term Stabscapitan as staff captain, and only use the expression captain lieutenant, preferred by some translators, when the German text uses that expression.

ACKNOWLEDGMENTS

I hope that the number of errors in my translation is within reasonable limits and must accept full responsibility for any which escaped my attention. However, as always, I must caution the serious student to use my translation for easy reference but, if possible, to return to the original document to verify my translation.

In addition to persons mentioned in referenced works, I owe special thanks to Drs. Heyl and Braun of the War Archives of the Bavarian State Archives, Munich Germany, for making the Prechtel diary available to me; to Dr. Mary Robertson of the Huntington Library, San Marino, California, for making the anonymous (original Prechtel diary) available to me; and to Drs. Fleischmann and Friedrich of the Nuernberg State Archives, Nuernberg, Germany, for the "true copy" of the Huntington version of the diary and for the use of the two maps which accompanied it.

The University of Oklahoma Press allowed me to use material from <u>A Hessian Diary of the American Revolution</u>, (Norman, 1990), and the Historical Society of York County, Pennsylvania, approved the use of several of Lewis Miller's caricatures.

Finally, this volume would never have been completed, nor even considered, without the steadfast support, encouragement, and assistance of my wife Marie.

Bruce E. Burgoyne
Dover, DE

INTRODUCTION

Organization and Commanders of the Ansbach-Bayreuth Troops
Employed by England During the American Revolutionary War[1]
- - - - - - - - - - -

The English Army Colonel William Faucitt, who had negotiated the treaties in 1776 to hire the "Hessian" mercenaries for service in North America, was sent to the continent in late 1776 to hire additional armies. As minister plenipotentiary, Faucitt presented his credentials at the court of Brandenburg-Ansbach on 14 January 1777, and on 1 February a treaty was concluded with that court. Under provisions of the treaty the Margrave of Ansbach-Bayreuth agreed to provide two infantry regiments of five companies each, a 101-man jaeger company, and a 44-man artillery complement.[2]

These units generally referred to as the Ansbach-Bayreuth troops were the 1st or Ansbach Regiment, also known as the Eyb Regiment, commanded by Colonel Friedrich Ludwig Albrecht von Eyb, the senior Ansbach-Bayreuth officer with the troops; and the 2nd or Bayreuth Regiment, also known as the Voit Regiment, commanded by Colonel August Valentin von Voit von Salzburg. The Jaeger Company was commanded by Captain Christoph von Cramon and the Artillery by Lieutenant, later Captain, Nikolaus Friedrich Hofmann.

Colonel von Eyb returned to Germany in May 1778 and thereafter Colonel von Voit commanded the 1st Regiment which was redesignated the Voit Regiment. Von Voit also became the senior Ansbach-Bayreuth officer in America. The 2nd Regiment was redesignated the von Seybothen Regiment at the same time as Colonel Johann Christian Franz von Seybothen took command, having been promoted to colonel on 6 February 1778.

The Jaeger Company was joined by other jaeger companies during the course of the war. The 2nd Company was added in 1779, the 3rd Company in 1781, and the 4th and 5th Companies in 1782. The 6th Company was formed in 1783 although the men probably were mostly recruits meant for the infantry regiments which had been captured at Yorktown in 1781. Lieutenant Colonel Christoph Ludwig von Reitzenstein became the unit commander when the Jaeger Regiment was formed in 1782.

Each 570-man infantry regiment consisted of a nine-man staff, one company of 113 men, and four companies of 112 men. Staff members were:

1 Colonel	1 Regmental QM
1 Major	1 Drum Major
1 Chaplain	1 Provost
1 Auditor	1 Assistant Provost
1 Surgeon Major	

The Colonel's, or Du Company, appears to have been organized with:

1 Staff Captain	1 Medic[3]
2 1st Lieutenants	1 Fifer
2 2nd Lieutenants	2 Drummers
2 Sergeants	1 Tent Attendant
1 QM Sergeant	95 Privates
5 Corporals	

The Major's Company had the same organization, except there was no staff captain.

The other three companies were organized with one captain, one 1st lieutenant, and two 2nd lieutenants as company officers.

The 101-man Jaeger Company appears to have been organized with:

1 Captain	5 Corporals
1 1st Lieutenant	1 Medic
2 2nd Lieutenants	1 Tent Attendant
2 Sergeants	78 Jaegers
1 QM Sergeant	

The Artillery unit consisted of:
1 Lieutenant   1 Tent Attendant
4 Bombardiers   30 Cannoneers
8 Conductors
Company commanders of the 1st Regiment were:
    1st Company – Colonel von Eyb until June 1778, then Colonel von Voit
    2nd Company – Major Christoph Ludwig von Reitzenstein until December 1781, then Major Philipp Friedrich von Seitz, who died aboard ship while en route home after the war
    3rd Company – Captain Stain
    4th Company – Captain Christian Philipp von Ellrodt; from December 1777, Captain Christoph Friedrich Joseph von Waldenfels; from June 1779, Captain, later Major, Philipp Friedrich von Seitz; and from December 1781, Lieutenant, later Captain, Christoph von Metzsch
    5th or Grenadier Company – Captain Ludwig Heinrich Vollrath Erckert until he died of wounds received in storming Fort Montgomery in October 1777; then Captain Christian Philipp von Ellrodt.
    Company commanders of the 2nd Regiment were:
    1st Company – Major, later Colonel, von Seybothen
    2nd Company – Captain, later Major, Friedrich Ernst Carl von Beust
    3rd Company – Captain Friedrich Ludwig von Eyb
    4th Company – Colonel von Voit von Salzburg; from June 1778, Captain Christian Theodor Sigismund von Molitor; from June 1779, Captain Georg Heinrich von Quesnoy
    5th or Grenadier Company – Captain, later Major, Philipp Friedrich von Seitz; from June 1779, Captain Christian Theodor Sigismund von Molitor.

Company commanders of the Jaeger Regiment
were:
1st Company (1777) – Captain Cramon until
he returned to Germany in December 1778, then
Captain Christoph Friedrich Joseph von
Waldenfels
2nd Company (1779) – Captain Friedrich
Wilhelm von Roeder
3rd Company (1781) – Captain Friedrich
Wilhelm Ernst von Reitzenstein
4th Company (1782) – Captain Carl Christian Ernst Tritschler von Falkenstein
5th Company (1782) – Captain Ernst Friedrich Wurm, who died 7 February 1783, then
Captain Friedrich von Kruse
6th Company (1783) – Captain August
Christian Friedrich von Koenitz.
In addition to the 1,285 men originally
supplied under the 1777 treaty, subsequent
treaties in 1779 and 1782 raised the total
treaty manpower to 1,559 men. Yearly recruit
shipments were made to replace losses due to
deaths and desertion. Therefore the total
number of men who served in America in the
Ansbach-Bayreuth units eventually reached 2,353
men. Of this number, 1,183 returned home and
1,170 either died, deserted in America, or were
given their release from the military so that
they could remain in America.

ABOUT THE AUTHOR

Very little is known about Johann Ernst
Prechtel except that he was born in 1737,
possibly in Ammendorf. He sailed to America in
1777 as the first sergeant of Major von
Reitzenstein's Company of the Ansbach Regiment
which is an indication that he was probably a
career soldier, but nothing more of his early
life can be learned from his diary. He began
the campaign in a position of considerable
authority and, although not a member of any

noble family, was able to advance to officer
status and to come out of the war as a first
lieutenant. A shipment of clothing and other
necessities sent to the Ansbach-Bayreuth troops
in captivity at Frederick, Maryland, was seized
and detained in Chester County, Pennsylvania,
by the local authorities. Public Record Office
document PRO 30/55, number 7133, contains a
list of items seized, which was prepared by
Georg Daig, Pay and Quartermaster of the
Ansbach troops, and dated 15 March 1783. This
list has two references to a Lieutenant
Brechtel (sic), which give some information
about him. One entry indicates a new sword
valued at five pounds, five shillings, Pennsylvania currency, was being sent to him. More
significant, and most surprising since there is
no mention in his diary of a wife, the list
ends with a note that a small sewing chest with
caps for Lieutenant Brechtel's wife is missing.
     According to Erhard Staedtler, Die Ans-
bach-Bayreuther Truppen im Amerikanischen Unabhaengigkeitskrieg, 1777-1783 (Erlangen, 1955),
Prechtel was married to Margaretha, nee Wirth,
and they had one daughter, Anna Elisabeth, born
23 April 1764. It would appear that Prechtel
took his wife to America with him.
     After his arrival in New York in 1777,
Prechtel served briefly in the garrisons at
Staten Island and on Manhattan. He then sailed
up the Hudson River in October of that year as
part of a force sent to relieve pressure on
General John Burgoyne. Burgoyne, advancing on
New York from Canada, surrendered before the
relieve force reached him. The Ansbach-
Bayreuth regiments returned to New York and
were then sent as a reinforcement to General
Sir William Howe's command in Philadelphia.
When Philadelphia was abandoned by the English
the following year, the Ansbach-Bayreuth Regi-

ments returned to New York aboard ship and
therefore were not involved in the Battle of
Monmouth Courthouse, fought by the other troops
evacuating Philadelphia, who marched overland
to New York.

In July 1778 the Ansbach-Bayreuth regiments were sent to Rhode Island. Prechtel, who
had been commissioned a second lieutenant on 28
September 1777, was in command of a small
detachment attacked by the Americans on 27
August 1778 and seems to have conducted himself
well. He also seems to have fought in the
battle on 29 August 1778. This was a day-long
engagement between the English forces on Rhode
Island and the troops commanded by the American
General John Sullivan, being withdrawn after
the failure of a combined French and American
plan to capture Rhode Island.

When Rhode Island was abandoned by the
English in October 1779, Prechtel and the
Ansbach-Bayreuth regiments returned to New York
and garrison duty in that place. Finally, in
May 1781, the Ansbach-Bayreuth soldiers were
sent to Virginia and became part of General
Charles, Earl Cornwallis' command. Cornwallis'
surrender at Yorktown in October 1781 resulted
in the Ansbach-Bayreuth regiments being made
prisoners of war.

Officers to accompany the men into captivity were chosen by lot and Prechtel's lot
sent him with the troops, first to Winchester,
Virginia, and then to Frederick, Maryland.
When the war ended these men marched back to
New York from which port they were embarked for
Europe. Prechtel closed his diary with the
cold, unemotional, statement that the regiment
"marched into the barracks at Ansbach with
music playing."

We are not even told if he was glad to be
back home, and only Helmes' notation on the
supplement to the diary indicates that Prechtel
might have served later with the Jaeger Corps.

CONTENTS OF THE DIARY

Like Johann Conrad Doehla, Prechtel filled his diary with a rather simple and direct account of daily activities and events, but Prechtel gives more detail about the things which he describes and his recitation of places and events is much more accurate than Doehla's accounts of the same situations. Also, entries in the Huntington version of the diary are considerably enlarged upon when rewritten in the Munich version. In particular, Prechtel gives excellent descriptions of cities and towns in America, and in Germany, also, and provides a detailed account of the siege and surrender of Yorktown. However, as the rewriting proceeded, Prechtel seems to have begun to copy the initial entries rather than add new details, and at times even failed to copy all the details of the entries previously made.

There are serious differences between the two versions of the diary contained in this volume; most notably the omission of any reference to the mutiny in the polished version. Certainly many, if not all the non-commissioned officers, joined in the mutiny as nowhere is there any indication that the mutiny was not supported by all the enlisted men. There is also no indication that any non-commissioned officers were punished for participating in the activity nor for failure to suppress the mutiny.

Prechtel's list of officers is a valuable part of his diary and his notations of promotions and punishments, and times and places of deaths and desertions will be welcome information to genealogists. However, the greatest value is that it complements the Doehla diary. Prechtel served as an officer in the 1st or Ansbach Regiment while Doehla served as an enlisted man in the 2nd or Bayreuth Regi-

ment.   Each noted activities and personnel
actions primarily within his own regiment.
          Standing alone   the Prechtel diary is a
document of considerable interest.   However, as
both the   original and   a later,   more polished
version are   available, the student of history
is given the rare opportunity to see how first
person accounts can be used to alter our
knowledge of past events, Furthermore, when
the Prechtel diaries are read in conjunction
with all the   other Ansbach-Bayreuth diaries,
still known to exist (and as noted elsewhere I
have translated all but the Popp diary which
was previously done), the serious student of
history and the   history buff will have the
complete history of the Ansbach-Bayreuth role
in the American Revolution as recorded by the
actual participants.

PLAN
der Gegend und Stadt
von
PHILADELPHIA

Scale of Miles

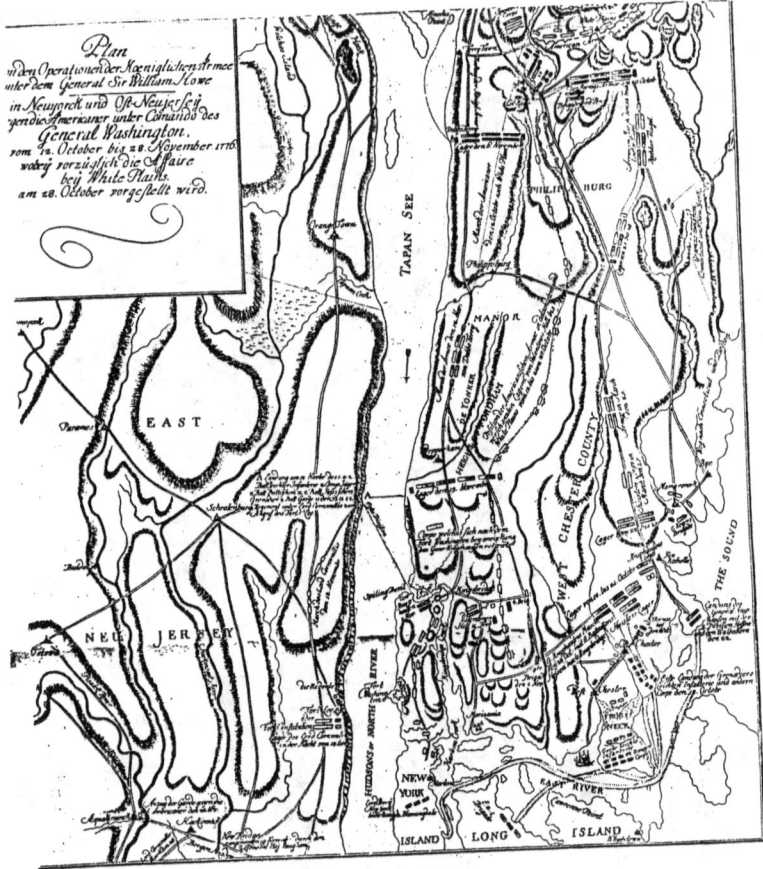

Old. Budding. in South
WaterStreet, ein Heß.

Der alte Lochner, Heß 1802.

Adt v Stengel mir fr. 13. 1777.

AN ANONYMOUS ANSBACH-BAYREUTH DIARY

1777-1781

(As originally written
by
Johann Ernst Prechtel)

Owned by the Huntington Library
San Marino, California

AN ANONYMOUS
ANSBACH-BAYREUTH DIARY

(As written by Johann Ernst Prechtel)
1777-1781

[The top of the first page is missing and the first legible, dated entry is 9 March.][1]

9 March - We went to Ochsenfurth, where the regiment was embarked.

10 March - During the morning both regiments rebelled. [The rest of the page is too faded to read.]
[The top of the second page is missing.]

11 March - His Serene Highness arrived at Ochsenfurt.

We departed from Ochsenfurt this morning at eight-thirty.[2]

On the Main River we passed Gossmansdorf, Winterhausen, and Hazfeld on the left, and Klein Ochsenfurt, Sommerhausen, Eibelstadt, and Randersacker on the right.[3]

12 March - Continued.

13 March - Again.

14 March - At Hanau we transferred ships and because of unfavorable winds, had to remain there.

15 March - On the march we passed Dittelsheim on the left and Dirckenheim on the right.

16 March - We departed from Mainz at seven o'clock in the morning.

17 March - On the march we passed Koblenz where the Mosel enters the Rhine.

18 March - At five-thirty in the morning we shoved off.

19 March - [No information entered and no space left vacant.]

20 March - Because of very unfavorable wind, we remained the entire day at Imhack.

21 March - We departed at six-thirty in the morning.

22 March - We departed at five-thirty in the morning.

23 March - We departed at five o'clock in the morning.

24 March - [No information entered and no space left vacant.]

25 March - A muster was held at the parade ground in Nijmegen during the morning. Then the oath to His Majesty, the King of England, was administered, and the English Colonel [Charles] Rainsford took over the regiments.

We departed from Nijmegen at one o'clock in the afternoon.

26 March - During the evening we arrived at the Tiel.

27 March - We departed Dordrecht and below the city the regiments boarded English transport ships.[4]

28 March - Remained there.

29 March - We sailed at seven o'clock in the morning. His Serene Highness began his return to Ansbach prior to our departure.

30 March - On Easter Sunday. We remained at sea because a storm struck.

31 March - We sailed on Easter Monday.

1 April - We saw land again and passed the French city of Calais on our left and the English harbor and fort of Dover on our right. Today we caught sight of the white cliffs of England.

2 April - We anchored near Portsmouth.

3 April - We remained at Portsmouth.

4 April - We remained here.

5 April - We remained here.

6 April - We remained here.

7 April - We departed at eight o'clock in the morning.

8 April - We entered the ocean.[5]

9 April - Sailing on the ocean day and night.

10 April - A storm arose during the night.

11 April - It continued all day and night

and the storm was very strong.

12 April - The troops were all seasick.
13 April - We had good wind.
14 April - We had good wind.
15 April - We sailed with good wind.
16 April - Good wind.
17 April - We had poor wind.
18 and 19 April - We had a storm.
20 April - We had the best wind.
21 April - We had very stormy wind.
22 April - Contrary wind.
23 April - Contrary wind.
24 April - A good wind arose this morning.
25 April - Good wind.
26 April - Good wind.
27 April - We had no wind.
28 April - Good wind.
29 April - Good wind.
30 April - Contrary wind.
1 May - We had good wind.
2 May - We sailed day and night with a
fair wind. In the afternoon we saw, to our
right, the Portuguese island of St. Michael, at
a distance of seven German miles,[6] and
throughout the night there was frightfully
stormy weather.
3 May - We traveled with a good wind.
4 May - Contrary wind.
5 May - Good wind.
6 May - Good wind.
7 May - Contrary wind.
8 May - Calm.
9 May - We traveled with good wind.
10 May - We traveled with contrary wind.
11 May - A very good wind.
12 May - Good wind.
13 May - Good.
14 May - Good.
15 May - We traveled with poor wind.
16 May - Good wind.
17 May - Good.
18 May - We traveled with a good wind.

Today was the holy Whitsuntide.[7] At five o'-
clock in the evening, Peter, the servant of
Lieutenant [Justus] von Diemar, lowered himself
with a rope from our ship Myrtle, into the
sea. Shortly thereafter the troops saw him
swimming in the water. Due to the exceptionally skillful maneuvering by the ship's
captain, a boat was instantly lowered into the
water. The mate and four seamen reached Peter,
who was still alive and swimming in the ocean
at a distance of about four rifle shots from
the ship, but he died.

19 May – On Whitsuntide Monday, we traveled with good wind.

20 May – On Whitsuntide Tuesday, we traveled with good wind and made 116 English miles
in 24 hours.

21 May – Wednesday. We traveled day and
night with good wind and made 121 miles.

22 May – Thursday. We traveled day and
night with good wind. Sixty miles.

23 May – We traveled day and night with
good wind. 86 miles.

24 May – Saturday. We traveled day and
night with contrary wind.

25 May – On Trinity Sunday, we traveled
day and night with contrary wind.

26 May – The same.

27 May – Tuesday. We traveled day and
night with good wind. Because the ship's
captain expects to reach land soon, the large
anchor rope was brought out of the lower deck
and tied onto the anchor. At seven o'clock
this evening a violent storm.

28 May – Wednesday. We traveled day and
night with good wind. The storm still continued.

29 May – Thursday. The storm continued
until six o'clock in the evening, but we
traveled day and night with good wind. 177
miles.

30 May – Friday. We traveled day and

night with contrary wind.

 31 May – Likewise.

 1 June – On Sunday we traveled day and night with good wind.

 2 June – Monday. Bottom was found at forty fathoms.[8] At eleven o'clock, midday, we suddenly saw land, which created a great joy among us.

 3 June – Saturday evening at five o'clock we entered the seaport of New York. How unforgetably beautiful the landscape appeared. It is beyond description.

 4 June – Wednesday. Still aboard ship lying at anchor at New York. Today the birthday of His Majesty, the King of Great Britain, was celebrated. The cannons in New York and on the warships were all fired at eleven o'clock, midday, and at night the entire city and surrounding area was illuminated.[9]

 5 June – Thursday. We were shipped below New York and set up camp on Staten Island.

 6 June – Friday. Still lying in camp on Staten Island.

 7 June – Saturday. Still lying in camp on Staten Island.

 Note! – As shipboard life ended on Thursday, I will include a short description of an English transport ship, here. The ship **Myrtle**, on which were half of the Major's Company and half of Captain von Stain's Company, 150 men, had three masts and was two stories high. The magazines were below and the soldiers and sailors, who were separated, however, were above. The officers and the ship's captain, named William Walker, were in the cabins in the stern. Above on the deck were nine cannons.[10]

 The ship's crew, including the captain and mate, consisted of nineteen men.

Quarters Aboard Ship

 Four men were assigned two beds,[11] one above the other, and each berth had a small mattress, a small pillow, and two English blankets.

Ship's Rations, Each Time for Six Men

Sunday - Four pounds of meat, two pints of peas

Monday - One-half pound of salted butter and cheese, two pints of greens

Tuesday - Four pounds of salted beef, two pounds of flour, one pound of raisins

Wednesday - One and one-half pounds of salted butter and cheese, two pints of peas, two pints of greens

Thursday - As on Sunday.

Friday - As on Wednesday.

Saturday - As on Tuesday, plus a quart of vinegar.

Every day two gallons of beer, and when that was all gone, one quart of rum, and four pounds of bread, consisting of zwieback. Daily a light before the soldiers.

In payment, each man had seven and one-half groschen taken from his pay, daily.

On land four men received the same ration as six men aboard ship. The women received the ship's rations free, but only a half portion. Also, the children received a quarter portion, but no rum.[12]

The fleet from Portsmouth to America consisted of fifteen transports and one warship. The name of the warship was Somerset.[13]

8 June - Sunday. In the evening an alarm was sounded by our picket in the Bayreuth camp. Therefore, the half regiment, under the command of Major von Reitzenstein, immediately moved out to the hill near the camp, but nothing occurred.

9 June - Monday. We broke camp and marched to the hill to await the enemy there. During the entire night there was a strong storm.

10 June - Tuesday. We moved back into our former camp, which was the second one.

11 June - Wednesday. We entered our third camp at Amboy, to which we had been shipped,

under the command of the Hessian General
[Leopold] von Heister.

12 June - Thursday at Amboy.

13 June - Friday at Amboy.

14 June - Saturday at Amboy.

15 June - At Amboy.

16 June - Monday. At Amboy. This afternoon there was an attack. The enemy fired on
our field watch and picket. Grenadier [Karl]
Frank, of the von Eyb Regiment, was shot in the
knee./4

17 June - Tuesday. At Amboy.

18 June - Wednesday. At Amboy.

19 June - Thursday. At Amboy.

20 June - Friday. At Amboy.

21 June - Saturday. At Amboy.

22 June - Sunday. At Amboy, under the
command of Major General [John] Vaughan.

23 June - Monday. We passed in review
before the Commanding General [William] Howe
and were placed under the command of the
Hessian Colonel [Karl Emil] von Donop.

24 June - Tuesday. St. John's Day. At
Amboy.

25 June - Wednesday. In camp at Amboy.
Today the army marched away from here.

26 June - Thursday. At Amboy.

27 June - Friday. At Amboy.

28 June - Saturday. At Amboy. Today the
army returned here.

29 June - On St. Peter and Paul Day we
were shipped back to Staten Island and set up
our fourth camp.

30 June - Monday. At Staten Island.

1 July - Tuesday. Into our fifth camp at
Cole's Ferry.

2 July - Wednesday. At Cole's Ferry.

Note! - For the daily provision on land,
six and one-quarter groschen were withheld.

3 July - Thursday. At Cole's Ferry.

4 July - Friday. At Cole's Ferry.

5 July - Saturday. At Cole's Ferry.

6 July – Sunday. At Cole's Ferry.

7 July – Monday. At Cole's Ferry.

8 July – Tuesday. We were embarked at Cole's Ferry on the ship Durand, on which there were 169 people.

9 July – Wednesday. Still lying on the water.

10 July – Still lying here.

11 and 12 July – Still lying here.

13 July – We departed Cole's Ferry at one o'clock in the afternoon.

14 July – At four o'clock in the afternoon we entered the harbor at New York.

15 July – Tuesday. Lying at anchor at New York.

16 July – Wednesday. Lying at anchor at New York.

17, 18, 19, 20, and 21 July – Lying at anchor.

22 July – We debarked at New York. We paraded through the city and entered camp at Harlem, under the command of General [Henry] Clinton. Our sixth camp.

23 to 31 July – In camp at Harlem.

1 to 11 August – At Harlem.

Note. From four o'clock on the afternoon of the eleventh, until ten o'clock at night, there was a strong thunderstorm. Hail fell the size of a man's fist and beat down the trees in the woods.

11 to 21 August – At Harlem.

Note! – Constable [Michael] Zeder and Grenadier [Matthias] Lorenz drowned in the sea while bathing at the camp at Harlem.

22 August – At ten o'clock at night our Grenadiers had to march off from the regiment because the enemy had attacked Staten Island.

23 August – In camp at Harlem. The Grenadiers have returned.

24 to 31 August – In camp at Harlem.

1 to 6 September – At Harlem. Today our Grenadiers left the regiment and moved closer

to the headquarters.

7 to 30 September - In camp at Harlem.

1 October - In camp at Harlem until the twelfth.

13 October - Monday. We broke camp at Harlem and the entire regiment was embarked at John's house, on two transport ships.[15] We traveled to Fort Knyphausen where we anchored during the evening.

14 October - We sailed at two o'clock in the afternoon and anchored on the river in the evening.

15 October - We sailed at six o'clock in the morning.

16 October - The regiment debarked and marched forward on York Land.[16] We remained on a height overnight, without tents. The Grenadiers returned to the regiment.

17 October - Without tents on York Land.

18 October - On York Land.

19 October - The regiment marched back and embarked again at the same place where it had debarked.[17] The English troops demolished the defenses on York Land. At one o'clock in the afternoon we departed.

20 October - We departed at seven o'clock in the morning, but dropped anchor at ten o'clock due to contrary winds.

21 October - We departed at ten o'clock in the morning for the region of Kingsbridge and dropped anchor there.

22 October - We departed at ten o'clock in the morning and arrived at New York in the evening and dropped anchor.

23 and 24 October - Lying at anchor at New York.

25 October - We were transferred to other ships and the regiment received three transport ships; John, for the staff, and Hopewell and Hanyriette.

At one o'clock in the afternoon, because it was the coronation of His Majesty, the King of Great Britain, a salute was fired from all the cannons on the warships. Our ships remained at anchor this night.

26 October - We sailed to Staten Island and dropped anchor there.

27 October - Lying at anchor at Staten Island. There was a strong storm with rain.

28 October - Lying at anchor at Staten Island and still rather stormy with rain.

29 October - The same.

30 October - The same.

31 October - The same.

1 November - Lying at anchor at Staten Island.

2 November - Lying at anchor at Staten Island.

3 and 4 November - The same.

5 November - Wednesday. The fleet, consisting of forty ships, departed. The troops from Staten Island were commanded by the English Brigadier General [Thomas] Wilson. The Ansbach and Bayreuth Regiments were in the brigade of Colonel von Voit. Already by afternoon we arrived on the open sea and encountered very stormy weather.

6 November - On the ocean.

7 November - Traveling on the ocean. This evening we turned toward land.

8 November - Saturday. This morning we passed the light tower for Philadelphia and entered the Delaware River. During the evening we anchored near the village of Port Penn.

9 November - Because of contrary winds we could not enter the river until two o'clock in the afternoon. We entered the harbor at Newcastle in the evening and dropped anchor there.

10 November - We departed at five-thirty in the morning and on the left bank of the Delaware River passed the village of Wilmington. Because of the ebb tide we anchored on the Delaware River. At one o'clock

in the afternoon a good wind arose and we
entered the port at Chester, where we anchored.

11 November - Lying at anchor at Chester.

12 November - During the afternoon there
was a continuous cannonade against the enemy
and against his warships lying opposite Philadelphia.

13 November - Today the firing by the warships continued and we remained lying at anchor
at Chester.

14 November - The firing from the warships
against the enemy fort increased. We remained
lying at anchor at Chester.

15 November - The cannonade from the
warships continued throughout the day and in a
frightful manner against the fort. During the
afternoon our fleet pulled back and we continued to lie at anchor at Chester.

16 November - At one o'clock in the
morning Fort Mud Island began to burn, having
been set afire by the enemy. We saw the spectacular flames. The cannons began to discharge. [Apparently the heat caused the loaded
cannons to fire.] The enemy left the fort and
retreated to Fort Redbank.

17 November - At eight o'clock in the
morning we departed Chester and anchored near
the warships opposite Philadelphia.

18 November - The troops were landed and
marched to Billingsport, where we camped under
the open sky.

19 November - We camped without tents near
Billingsport and were put under the command of
General Lord [Charles] Cornwallis.[16]

20 November - Without tents at Billingsport.

21 November - The troops marched away from
Billingsport and made camp at Woodbury.

22 November - In camp at Woodbury.

23 November - In camp at Woodbury.

24 November - The regiments marched from
Woodbury and entered camp on the river Timber

Creek. Ninth camp.
25 November - We entered camp near Gloucester, without tents. Tenth camp.
26 November - In camp at Gloucester. This
evening the sailors burned down a house at this
place.¹⁹
27 November - The army was shipped across
[to Philadelphia] near Gloucester. The last
regiments were attacked by the enemy and were
under continuous cannon fire from four frigates
lying at anchor. We arrived at Philadelphia in
the evening and the two Ansbach regiments
paraded through the city. They then entered
the barracks there. However, the officers, in
part, were quartered in the city.
28 November - In quarters at Philadelphia.
29 and 30 November - In quarters at
Philadelphia.
1, 2, 3, and 4 December - In quarters at
Philadelphia.
5 December - The army moved forward and we
entered the camp outside Philadelphia.
Eleventh camp.
6 and 7 December - In camp at Philadelphia.
8 December - The army returned at eight
o'clock in the evening and therefore we
immediately moved out and reentered the
barracks at Philadelphia.
9 to 12 December - In quarters at Philadelphia.
13 December - The regiment entered winter
quarters in Water Street in Philadelphia.
14 to 21 December - In quarters at Philadelphia.
22 December - The army was ordered to
march across the Schuylkill River and to enter
the camp there, without tents, while foraging
was conducted. Twelfth camp.
23 to 27 December - In camp beyond the
Schuylkill.
28 December - The army moved back to

Philadelphia and into the previous quarters.
    <u>29 to 31 December</u> - In quarters at Philadelphia.

1778

1 January - On New Year's Day the army moved out of Philadelphia to the Schuylkill and the alarm place, in battle formation, and then returned into the former quarters.

2 to 11 January - In quarters at Philadelphia.

12 January - This morning an English soldier, who had robbed an officer and was then caught, was punished by being hanged outside the city of Philadelphia.

13 to 17 January - In quarters at Philadelphia.

18 January - Today the birthday of Queen [Sophie Charlotte] of Great Britain was celebrated. At one o'clock in the afternoon all the cannons on the warships lying here at anchor fired a salute.

19 to 31 January - In quarters at Philadelphia.

1 to 14 February - In quarters at Philadelphia.

15 February - At three o'clock this morning the defensive watch across the Schuylkill, under the command of Captain von Ellrodt, was attacked by the enemy. The attack lasted three-quarters of an hour. Because the troops in the defenses, mostly Ansbachers, behaved so bravely, the enemy was again driven off.

16 to 28 February - In quarters at Philadelphia.

1 to 8 March - In quarters at Philadelphia.

9 March - In quarters at Philadelphia. Tonight, at twelve-thirty, Privates [Johann] Brummer and [Johann] Schard, of von Waldenfels' [Company], deserted from the defensive watch Number One at the double post.

10 March - Private [Heinrich] Katzenwinkel, of Captain von Stain's [Company], deserted from quarters.

11 to 22 March - In quarters at Philadelphia.

23 March - Two English private soldiers were captured outside the city today. They had gone over to the enemy and were caught again.

24 to 31 March - In quarters at Philadelphia.

1 April - In quarters at Philadelphia.

2 April - This evening the first thunderstorm occurred. It lasted four hours and was frightfully strong.

3 to 15 April - In quarters at Philadelphia.

16 April - Today Colonel von Voit received the von Eyb Regiment and Major von Seybothen received the von Voit Regiment. Staff Captain von Molitor received a company. First Lieutenant von Roeder was promoted to staff captain and 2nd Lieutenants von Streit and von Keller were promoted to 1st lieutenant. Colonel von Eyb received his recall to Ansbach'and 1st Lieutenant von Sichart received his release as captain.[2]

17 to 30 April - In quarters at Philadelphia.

1 May - In quarters at Philadelphia. Today a spy was captured.

2 May - In quarters at Philadelphia.

3 May - In quarters at Philadelphia.

4 May - Today General-in-Chief Howe watched the Hessian troops pass in review.

5 to 10 May - In quarters at Philadelphia.

11 May - Today Colonel von Eyb and Captain von Sichart began their return trip to Europe.

12 to 15 May - In quarters at Philadelphia.

16 May - Today an English deserter was hanged.

17 May - In quarters at Philadelphia.

18 May - Today the English staff officers gave an entertainment for the General-in-Chief Sir William Howe.[3] The entire suite passed be-

fore Redoubt Number One,[4] in a body, entered flatboats and passed down the Delaware River to the accompanyment of much music. As soon as the suite had passed the fleet, the cannons on the warships and transport ships fired together. The dinner and a ball were held in a garden outside the city and at night a beautiful fireworks display was presented.

19 May - In quarters at Philadelphia.

20 May - The army marched out and over Germantown, remained there two hours, and then marched back again and reentered quarters in Philadelphia.[5]

Germantown is about two and one-half miles long and consists of a single street.

21 to 28 May - In quarters at Philadelphia.

29 May - Privates [Gottlob] Friederici and [Heinrich] Blecker, of Von Waldenfels' [Company], and [Johann] Luck, of the Major's [Company], deserted.

30 May - In quarters at Philadelphia.

31 May - Today Turkish music was played at the regiment for the first time.[6]

1 June - Both Privates Zipfel, of von Waldenfels' [Company], deserted today at Philadelphia.

2 and 3 June - In quarters at Philadelphia.

4 June - Today is the birthday of His Majesty, King George III, of England, and because all the warships had sailed, on the frigate Vigilant, all the cannons were fired at once as a salute, at one o'clock in the afternoon.

5 and 6 June - In quarters at Philadelphia.

7 June - General Lord Cornwallis and the English [Peace] Commissioners arrived here today [from England].[7]

8 June - In quarters at Philadelphia.

9 June - At two o'clock in the morning both Ansbach regiments were embarked on sloops

at Philadelphia and, on the left on the Delaware River, passed Gloucester, Fort Redbank,
and Fort Billingsport, and on the right, Fort
Mud Island. Not far from Billingsport, the
tide was met and at nine o'clock in the morning
the anchor was dropped. We sailed again at two
o'clock in the afternoon and, on the right,
passed Chester and Wilmington, where, opposite
the warships, we dropped anchor.

    10 June - We departed at two o'clock in
the morning and at eight o'clock in the
morning, anchored near the fleet at Reedy
Point. At eight o'clock in the evening the
anchor was raised and we moved closer to the
fleet.

    11 June - At six o'clock in the morning we
transferred to larger transport ships and
remained lying at anchor.

    12 June - The anchor was raised and the
ships moved past the fleet.

    13 June - We departed at ten o'clock in
the morning but because the wind was contrary,
we anchored in the Delaware.

    14 June - We departed at three o'clock in
the afternoon, but anchored at evening in the
Delaware.

    15 June - We departed at three o'clock in
the morning. At noon a calm set in which
lasted until two o'clock in the afternoon. The
ships bumped against one another in a frightful
manner. After this calm, we soon arrived on
the ocean and most of the troops became
seasick. The wind was contrary, but we soon
lost sight of land.

    16 June - Traveling on the ocean with good
wind.

    17 June - At eleven o'clock, midday, we
saw land. During the evening a severe
thunderstorm struck. This frightful storm hit
after the fleet had reached Sandy Hook and
anchored in the bay.

    18 June - We went underway in the morning,

but a calm developed so we anchored at eleven o'clock. A good wind arose at twelve o'clock and we went underway again. We entered the harbor at New York in the evening and dropped anchor, then we moved closer to the city.

19 June - We raised anchor at evening and moved to another part of the city.

20 June - At eleven o'clock, midday, two English sailors were hanged for espionage on the foremast of a frigate lying at anchor. The signal was given by a cannon shot at which both were suddenly hanged. At twelve o'clock the ships left New York, went up the East River, and, on the left, passed both Turtle Bay and Martin's Wharf. Both regiments were landed on Long Island, opposite Martin's Wharf, and entered camp there, under the command of the English General [William] Tryon. Note. During the debarkation, Private [Johann Ullrich] Teufel, of Captain von Molitor's Company of the von Seybothen Regiment, fell into the water as he was entering a boat from the ship, and did not come up again.[8]

21 June - In camp on Long Island.

22 to 25 June - On Long Island.

26 June - In camp on Long Island. Private Teufel, who drowned on the twentieth of this month, was washed up on land from the water today and buried in the earth on Long Island.

27 to 30 June - In camp on Long Island.[9]

1 to 4 July - In camp on Long Island.

5 July - This evening Lieutenant Hofmann of the Artillery presented a fireworks display at the Bayreuth camp.

6 July - At three o'clock in the morning both Ansbach regiments broke camp on Long Island, were shipped across the East River, and entered the second camp on York Island, near Morris' fifth house.[10] At five-thirty in the evening the order arrived for the regiments to return to their former camp on Long Island.

7 and 8 July - In camp on Long Island.

9 July - Both Ansbach regiments were embarked.

10 July - Yesterday, on July 9, the three officers, Captain von Cramon, 1st Lieutenant von Woellwarth, and 2nd Lieutenant von Mardefeld, left the regiment and began their return trip to Ansbach. Captain von Waldenfels received the Jaeger Company, Captain von Quesnoy the von Waldenfels' Company, 1st Lieutenant von Metzsch was promoted to staff captain, and 2nd Lieutenants von Marschall and Weitershausen were promoted to 1st lieutenant.

At three o'clock this afternoon we sailed from Martin's Wharf and anchored at evening on the East River.

11 July - At eight o'clock in the morning we departed and anchored again at five o'clock in the evening on the East River.

12 July - We sailed at six o'clock in the morning and did not anchor during the entire night.

13 July - During the morning, because of contrary wind, we anchored on the East River. We sailed again at two o'clock in the afternoon, but anchored again. At five o'clock in the evening two enemy row galleys attacked the fleet, but as the frigate and several transport ships fired on them, the row galleys were forced to turn back toward land.

14 July - At six o'clock in the morning we sailed, although the wind was still contrary. We anchored at eight o'clock. We sailed again at two o'clock in the afternoon. At eight o'clock in the evening we anchored on the East River, to the left, opposite the vessel Providence. Because of the great depth, no anchor will hold here.

15 July - Wednesday. We sailed at four o'clock in the morning and passed Block Island on our right, where the ocean was to be seen all around us.

At nine o'clock in the evening we entered

the seaport of Newport on Rhode Island.

16 July - The anchor was raised at eight o'clock in the morning and we sailed nearer the city. We landed at one o'clock in the afternoon and entered camp near Newport. The camp was about half a mile from the ocean.

17 and 18 July - [No information entered and no space left open.]

19 July - In camp near Newport.

20 July - Monday. Both regiments were shipped over to Conanicut Island and entered camp there. The water here is about one mile wide.

21 to 28 July - In camp on Conanicut.

29 July - At eleven o'clock, midday, the French fleet advanced close to the light tower on Conanicut Island and anchored there. Our corps recognized them immediately due to the white flags. We moved out immediately and advanced about one hundred yards forward. While executing this, we received the order to retreat and to leave all baggage and tents at the ferry. We were embarked in flatboats, a part were taken to Newport on Rhode Island, and part taken in flatboats to the transport ship Becky, and carried over in it [to Rhode Island]. We entered the camp very near the city of Newport in the evening. As none of the enemy were seen on Conanicut Island during the afternoon, all the baggage and tents were recovered. Private Braun, Sr., of von Stain's [Company], with the baggage detail, took this opportunity to desert.

30 July - Thursday. In camp on Rhode Island not far from Newport. The French warships, consisting of about eighteen sail, spread out from right to left before the harbor and cannonaded the defenses on Conanicut. Our defenses returned the fire.

[There is no entry for 31 July 1778.]

1 August - In camp near Newport.

2 August - In camp near Newport.

3 August - Today six transport ships were sunk at the entrance to the local harbor so that the French fleet could not enter the port.

4 August - This evening the von Voit Regiment went on patrol very near the water's edge at the end of the island, opposite to where a French frigate was standing.

5 August - The regiment marched back into camp at Newport at daybreak. Today two more ships were sunk in the harbor, and various walls outside Newport were demolished.

6 and 7 August - In camp near Newport.

8 August - Many houses close to our front were laid in ashes today by the English. Two of the French warships approached the large fort at Newport. This evening the French ships had a good wind and therefore sailed past the local harbor. Our three forts defended themselves very well. The eight French ships fired a frightful cannonade which lasted about two hours. The ships then lay below the harbor, at anchor. The two above mentioned ships sitting near the fort went underway, also. The English set fire to an [English] frigate very close to the city and at night also set fire to four houses on a height behind our front.

9 August - The army was formed with two lines. The von Voit Regiment was in the first line near Newport. Our pickets were continuously attacked during the night. Private [Johann Georg] Lochmueller, of Captain von Stain's Company, was wounded on the right foot by a grazing shot. An English fleet, consisting of about 26 ships, arrived on the ocean not far from here this afternoon.

10 August - The French fleet, consisting of ten warships, pulled back from the city of Newport at nine o'clock this morning and passed through the harbor into the ocean. The cannonade lasted one and one-half hours. The regiment moved to the front. The English fleet had already departed into the ocean before the

French [moved out].

    11 August - In camp near Newport. This evening the camp was changed so that the right wing moved to where the left wing had been. Three enemy officers were captured by the picket commanded by 1st Lieutenant von Reitzenstein, of the von Voit Regiment."

    12 August - In camp near Newport. Today we had a very strong wind storm, with rain, so that almost all the tents were torn during the night.

    13 August - In camp near Newport. Grenadiers [Christoph] Bernhart, and [Johann Georg] Rummel, and Privates [Lorenz] Baumann and [Johann] Stadler, of Quesnoy's [Company], deserted from the camp during the day. Private [Michael] Lorenz, of the Colonel's [Company], deserted from the camp at night.¹²

    14 August - In camp near Newport.

    15 August - Today the enemy established a camp about a mile and one-quarter distance from us, and we could easily see it lying on a height before us.

    16 August - In camp near Newport.

    17 August - This morning the army moved forward and remained under arms for two and one-half hours. Private [Johann] Erlwein, of Stain's [Company], deserted this morning from the post with the picket.

    18 August - Today Grenadier [Simon] Gruber and Privates [Matthias] Rhau and [Johann Jakob] Dill, of the Major's [Company], and Private [Peter] Hunger, of Stain's Company, deserted from the picket. Private [Johann Michael] Telorac deserted from water carrying detail. At three o'clock this morning the regiment moved out and remained under arms until reveille. Our defenses cannonaded both enemy forts the entire day.

    19 August - Privates Kassel and [Johann Georg] Ulzhoeffer, of Stain's [Company], deserted from the picket. The forts con-

24

structed by the enemy were cannonaded from our batteries the entire day. At the same time, the enemy, for the first time today, fired on our defenses and camp from the new fort. Only 18-pound cannonballs were fired. A private in the English camp had his foot shot off, and a horse was killed. A cannonball fell in a tent hitting eight musketeers. Our camp therefore was changed and we moved closer to Newport, behind the great defensive position of Tominy Hill.[19]

20 August - The army moved out early, like yesterday. The cannonade from our and the enemy forts continued the entire day. The French warships, consisting of thirteen sail, returned this evening to the mouth of the sea port, and lay there at anchor. At eleven o'clock tonight there was a false alarm in camp, causing the entire army to move out.

21 August - The army moved out early, as usual. The cannonade continued heavy. At ten o'clock in the evening the regiment moved out, due to incoming musket fire.

22 August - In camp near Newport. The army moved out at three o'clock in the morning, as usual. The French fleet sailed away this morning, into the ocean. The cannonade from the enemy was not as strong today.

23 August - An English regiment conducted a patrol before daybreak, to the enemy camp. Two prisoners were brought back. The army moved out early, as usual, and during this day the cannonade from our and the new enemy forts was exceptionally heavy. Many bombs were thrown during the night from our and the enemy forts.

24 August - The army moved out early, as usual, and the cannonade was not as strong today.

25 August - The army moved out, as usual, and on this day there was less cannon fire.

26 August - The army moved out, as usual.

Privates [Johann Balthasar] Schoenell and [Georg] Ermert, of the Colonel's [Company] deserted this night from the picket, while on patrol.

27 August – This afternoon three English frigates arrived in the local harbor from New York. The army moved out in the afternoon, into line, in order of battle. There was not much cannon fire.

28 August – At daybreak the army marched back into camp. There was little cannon fire. At night one battalion of each regiment moved into the lines. At eleven o'clock at night the outer picket post, in which 2nd Lieutenant Cyriacy was posted, was attacked three times, resulting in one man being killed and two men wounded.

29 August – The battalions moved into camp this morning. Because the enemy vacated his camp this morning, our army moved out at once and fell on the enemy's rear. A battle occurred near Windmill Hill. This lasted, with small arms fire, from seven o'clock in the morning until four o'clock in the afternoon. We were exposed to cannon fire from the enemy forts the entire day. From Colonel von Voit's Regiment, two grenadiers, [Johann Georg] Ettmeier and [Johann Michael] Frueh, were killed by a cannonball. Three men from the von Seybothen Regiment were also killed by a cannonball. Ten to twelve men were wounded from both regiments. Captain [Georg Friedrich] Schaller, of the Hessian Huyn Regiment, was killed by a cannonball. Two Hessian captains were fatally wounded. The English lost seven officers from the 22nd Regiment, alone. The size of the enemy army was about 20,000 and of our corps, about 4,000.¹⁴ It was believed that the enemy army pulled back into both large defensive positions, Windmill Hill and the Artillery Defense. We remained below Windmill Hill, without tents.

30 August - In camp near Windmill Hill. We experienced the same cannonade throughout the day, as yesterday, but no one was wounded.

31 August - During the night the enemy vacated both defensive positions and was carried over to New England, and took post there. The defensive positions were occupied initially by fifty men, Ansbachers and Hessians. This occupation was soon relieved by the two Hessian regiments, Landgraf and Ditfurth.

1 September - We moved our tents closer to Fort Windmill Hill.

General Clinton arrived in the harbor at Newport with an English fleet consisting of seventy sail.

2 September - In camp near Windmill Hill.

3 September - In camp near Windmill Hill.

4 September - The old camp was left and we occupied the defenses of Windmill Hill. This evening the enemy fired cannons against our camp from the water, three times.

5 and 6 September - In camp near Windmill Hill.

7 to 29 September - In camp near Windmill Hill.

30 September - Riding Master von Dieskau,[15] of the Guards, has arrived with a recruit transport from Ansbach.[16]

1 and 2 October - In camp near Windmill Hill.

3 October - In camp near Windmill Hill. Sergeant [Johann Gottfried] Minameier, Corporal [Christian Gottfried] Baumann, and Corporal [Johann Christian] Doehlemann were promoted to 2nd lieutenant.

4 October - In camp near Windmill Hill.

5 October - Sergeant [Johann Christian] Drexel was promoted to 2nd lieutenant.

6 and 7 October - In camp near Windmill Hill.

8 October - Today about thirty men from

the enemy came to Rhode Island to obtain hay and dry wood. However, a detail of one captain, one subaltern, and fifty privates was sent out, which drove them away.

9 to 17 October - In camp near Windmill Hill.

18 October - In camp near Windmill Hill. Chaplain [Georg Christoph Elias] Erb, of the von Seybothen Regiment, preached his first sermon today.

19 to 25 October - In camp near Windmill Hill.

26 October - Muster was held today.

27 to 31 October - In camp near Windmill Hill.

1 November - In camp near Windmill Hill.

2 to 4 November - In camp near Windmill Hill.

5 November - The von Seybothen Regiment marched away from here and into camp at Turkey Hill.

6 and 7 November - In camp near Windmill Hill.

8 to 25 November - In camp near Windmill Hill.

26 November - The 1st Ansbach Regiment marched into winter quarters at Newport.

27 to 30 November - In quarters at Newport.

1 to 5 December - In quarters at Newport.

6 December - Religious services for the two Ansbach regiments are to be held here in the Quaker Church, and this began today.

7 to 9 December - In quarters at Newport.

10 December - In quarters at Newport.

11 to 13 December - In quarters at Newport.

14 December - Today the von Voit Regiment dressed for duty in new uniforms. The eleven men-of-war, which had lain at anchor in the local harbor, departed today, under the command of Admiral [John] Byron.

<u>15 to 25 December</u> - In quarters at New-
port.

<u>26 December</u> - Today there was such wind
and snow that the people on the street of the
city were almost suffocated.[17]

<u>27 to 31 December</u> - In quarters at New-
port.

1779

1 January – New Year's Day, In quarters at Newport.

2 to 10 January – In quarters at Newport.

11 January – Today the wood fleet, consisting of fourteen sail, arrived here from Long Island. Each wood ship carried 46 cords. The sick recruits, who had remained in New York, also arrived with the fleet.

12 to 16 January – In quarters at Newport.

17 January – From today on, because of a shortage of provisions, the regiments received bread made of oats and peas, and Turkish cornmeal.'

18 January – Because it was the birthday of the Queen of England, at one o'clock in the afternoon the two frigates, lying at anchor in the local harbor, fired a salute from their cannons.

19 and 20 January – In quarters at Newport.

21 January – Yesterday Vice-Corporal Schultheiss, of the Grenadier Company, had a foot amputated due to gangrene.² Six provisions ships and a frigate entered the local harbor from New York at nine o'clock this morning.

22 January – Today Grenadier [Vice Corporal] Schultheiss' other foot was amputated.

23 January – In quarters at Newport.

24 January – From today on the army received wheat bread in which Turkish corn was mixed.

25 January – In quarters at Newport.

26 January – Today Major General [Carl Ernst Johann] von Bose, of the Hessian Landgraf Infantry Regiment, and the English Light Infantry were embarked.

27 to 29 January – In quarters at Newport.

30 January – At seven o'clock this morning the fleet, carrying the troops embarked on the 26th of this month, sailed from here for New

York.

31 January - In quarters at Newport.

1 February - In quarters at Newport.

2 February - Vice-Corporal Schultheiss, whose feet were amputated on January 20 and 22, died here today.

3 to 6 February - In quarters at Newport.

7 February - Grenadier [Jakob] Kaufmann died of a high fever.

8 February - Private [Andreas] Herterich, of Captain von Stain's [Company], died in the hospital of vomiting. Letters arrived here this morning from New York.

9 February - An autopsy was held at ten o'clock this morning on Private Herterich, who died yesterday. Water was found on his brain.

10 to 23 February - In quarters at Newport.

24 February - The wood fleet from Long Island and a provisions fleet from New York entered the local harbor this evening.

25 to 28 February - In quarters at Newport.

1 to 20 March - In quarters at Newport.

21 March - Sergeant [Johann Ernst] Kling was promoted today at the regiment, to 2nd lieutenant in the Jaeger Corps.

22 March - In quarters at Newport.

23 March - Admiral [James] Gambier arrived here on the sixteenth of this month with a man-of-war from New York, and departed again today from the local harbor with a fleet.

24 to 28 March - In quarters at Newport.

29 March - Yesterday morning the wood fleet, consisting of eighteen ships, entered the local harbor.

30 and 31 March - In quarters at Newport.

1 April - In quarters at Newport.

2 and 3 April - In quarters at Newport.

4 April - Private [Peter] Meier, Sr., died today in the hospital of consumption. A fleet, consisting of transport ships on which the

31

invalids were returning to England, sailed for New York, escorted by a frigate.

5 to 7 April - In quarters at Newport.

8 April - In quarters at Newport. Thirteen men, from Captain von Stain's Company, dug up some cicuta roots, or schirling,[3] and some herbs, cooked, and ate them. Immediately thereafter all became deathly sick. Some could no longer hear nor see. Milk and liquids were administered immediately to make them vomit. Twelve men did this and recovered. Private [Johann Christian] Auernheimer, who could not be made to vomit, died after three-quarters of an hour. At four o'clock in the afternoon an autopsy was held in the hospital. The Refugees brought three prizes, worth 20,000 pounds sterling, into the local harbor.

9 to 15 April - In quarters at Newport.

16 April - During the morning there was the first thunderstorm of this year.

17 April - An enemy privateer with two masts was brought into the local harbor. It had come from the West Indies bound for New England.

18 to 21 April - In quarters at Newport.

22 April - Private Schmidt, born in Poppenreuth, of the Colonel's Company, stole one and one-quarter Spanish dollars from a shop here. Therefore he was punished by running a gauntlet of two hundred men twelve times, this morning.

23 April - In quarters at Newport.

24 and 25 April - In quarters at Newport.

26 April - A provisions fleet, consisting of a frigate and eleven ships, entered the local harbor from New York this afternoon. The new uniforms for the von Seybothen Regiment were brought with it.

27 to 30 April - In quarters at Newport.

1 to 8 May - In quarters at Newport.

9 May - Yesterday afternoon Private Klein, of Captain von Quesnoy's [Company], died in the

hospital of consumption.

10 to 13 May - In quarters at Newport.

14 May - Private [Georg Michael] Vogel, minor,[4] of the Colonel's Company, died in the hospital.

15 and 16 May - In quarters at Newport.

17 May - This morning a wood fleet escorted by a frigate arrived in the local harbor.

18 May - In quarters at Newport.[5]

19 May - The warship Raisonable,[5] which was lying at anchor, and the frigate which arrived on the seventeenth of this month, departed this morning.

20 May - In quarters at Newport.

21 May - Today the Refugees[6] made an expedition against Bristol, during which they captured twenty men of an enemy picket and seized very many cattle and sheep.

22 to 28 May - In quarters at Newport.

29 May - At twelve-thirty tonight, due to the drunkeness and negligence of the sailors, the transport ship Christiana, which lay at anchor in the local harbor, caught fire and burned completely.

30 and 31 May - In quarters at Newport.

1 June - In quarters at Newport.

2 June - The warship Renown this afternoon entered the local harbor and brought in an enemy ship with three masts and ten cannons.

3 June - This morning the regiment conducted firing exercises. Private [Christian] Schaeffer, of Stain's Company, deserted yesterday evening.

4 June - Because it was the birthday of His Majesty, King George III, of England, at twelve o'clock noon, the North Battery fired a 21 gun salute. At one o'clock in the afternoon the man-of-war Renown fired a salute from its cannons.

5 June - In quarters at Newport.

6 June - The warship Renown sailed from

the local harbor during the past night with the Refugees. This noon already these same ones brought back here to Newport forty head of cattle from the enemy and eight prisoners.

7 and 8 June - In quarters at Newport.

9 June - The Refugees returned from an expedition this morning with 150 head of cattle and three hundred sheep. However, during this expedition they had nineteen wounded.

10 June - Three regiments marched into camp this morning; the 38th Regiment to Fogland Ferry, the 54th Regiment and the [Hessian] Landgraf Regiment to Windmill Hill. During the evening a provisions fleet of sixteen sail and a frigate entered the local harbor from New York. It brought letters from Germany.

11 June - The 22nd Regiment and the Ditfurth Regiment marched into camp this morning. Major von Reitzenstein was promoted to lieutenant colonel. Grenadier Captain von Seitz was promoted to major of the von Voit Regiment and received the von Quesnoy Company. Captain von Molitor received the Grenadier Company of the von Seybothen Regiment. Captain von Quesnoy received Captain von Molitor's Company of the von Seybothen Regiment. Quartermaster Sergeant Meier was named commissary.

12 June - First Lieutenant von Tritschler was promoted to staff captain and remained with the Lieutenant Colonel's Company.

13 June - This evening there was a strong wind. A two-masted privateer sloop came in by the light tower. It either ran upon a shoal or, as it was under full sail, must have capsized, as it sank with twenty persons and no one was saved.

14 June - In quarters at Newport.

15 June - The Huyn Regiment marched into camp at Windmill Hill.

16 June - The 54th Regiment and the Landgraf Regiment were embarked today. The 2nd

34

Ansbach Regiment marched out of the line this morning and into camp. The 1st Ansbach Regiment has no tents and therefore must remain in quarters awaiting further orders.

17 June - The two regiments which embarked yesterday sailed under escort of the frigate which arrived here on the tenth of this month. As soon as they were on the ocean, the wind became contrary, so they reentered the harbor at noon.

18 June - Colonel Fanning's Regiment of provincial troops were embarked on the sixteenth of this month, also, and sailed with the others on the seventeenth.

19 to 22 June - In quarters at Newport.

23 June - Major [Karl Gottlieb] von Arnberg, of the Hessian Landgraf Regiment, fell off a chaise about six weeks ago, splintering his foot. Gangrene set in and he died today.

24 June - In quarters at Newport.

25 June - The fleet with embarked troops, which lay here for eight days because of contrary winds, sailed for New York this morning.

26 to 30 June - In quarters at Newport.

1 July - In quarters at Newport.

2 to 6 July - In quarters at Newport.

7 July - The warship Raisonable sailed from here for New London at three o'clock this morning in order to support the expedition against that place. The 2nd Ansbach Regiment had to change camps and moved to Fort Tominy Hill.

8 to 18 July - In quarters at Newport.

19 July - Private Lochmueller, of Captain von Stain's Company, last week, while with a detachment to Goat Island, where he was on watch, took a cannonball out of a 24-pound cannon, threw it away, and took the powder with the intent of using it for hunting birds. Therefore, he was punished by running a gauntlet of switches, 24 times in two days.

20 to 23 July - In quarters at Newport.

24 July - The warship <u>Renown</u> arrived in the local harbor this afternoon.

25 to 27 July - In quarters at Newport.

28 July - The frigate <u>Thames</u> arrived in the local harbor this afternoon from New London.

29 July - The deserter Private [Christian] Schaeffer was arrested on the 26th of this month at Holms' house on this island. This morning his court martial was held.

30 July - This morning the findings of Private Schaeffer's court martial were made known. Because of his disloyal desertion and his intention of going over to the enemy, he is to be hanged until dead. However, after half an hour, he was notified that instead of a death sentence, he was to run a gauntlet of two hundred men, 36 times in two days.

31 July - In quarters at Newport.

1 to 25 August - In quarters at Newport.

26 August - Private [Simon] Hopfer, of the Major's [Company], and Private [Georg] Herzog, of the Colonel's [Company], while on a command to Brenton's Point, attacked a royal marine at his post in a hospital garden. The first was punished by running the gauntlet fourteen times and the latter, eight times.

27 to 30 August - In quarters at Newport.

31 August - In quarters at Newport.

1 to 5 September - In quarters at Newport.

6 September - This evening the warship Rainbow, which had been cruising on the Delaware River, entered the local harbor.

7 and 8 September - In quarters at Newport.

9 September - Private [Christoph] Jaeger, of Captain von Stain's Company, while on a command to Brenton's Point, found the purse belonging to Private [Adam] Lauterbach, of the Lieutenant Colonel's Company, and kept it. This was punished by his running the gauntlet

eight times.

10 September - In quarters at Newport.

11 September - Medic [Friedrich] Gollwitz
died yesterday afternoon of an apoplectic
stroke.

12 to 28 September - In quarters at Newport.

29 September - The frigate Hunter[7] entered
the local harbor from New York this afternoon
and brought the news that seventeen French
warships had arrived off Sandy Hook. They had
then turned back out to sea.

30 September - In quarters at Newport.

1 and 2 October - In quarters at Newport.

3 October - The Hessian Buenau Regiment
marched from Turkey Hill and entered camp very
close to the city.

4 October - On the past October 1, both
quartermaster guards of Captain von Eyb's [Com-
pany] of Colonel von Seybothen's Regiment, en
route to Conanicut, deserted and went over to
the enemy, namely, Privates [Friedrich] Abt and
Kreger.[8]

5 to 10 October - In quarters at Newport.

11 October - Fifty-four ships, escorted by
three frigates, arrived in the local harbor.
They were all empty transport ships on which
the local army is to embark.

12 October - Loading of artillery and
provisions was carried out vigorously.

13 October - Regimental baggage was
loaded.

14 October - The warship Rainbow and a
sloop-of-war with eighteen cannons sailed out
of the local harbor this evening to cruise
against the enemy ships which had been seen.

15 October - The transport ships assigned
for the von Voit Regiment are called Mertschery
and Shipwright.[9] The von Seybothen Regiment
received the ships Silver Eel and Nestor.

[There is a word entered on this page of
the diary, in a different hand, which seems to

indicate that another ship, the <u>Albrecht</u>, may have also been used.]

16 October - Private Gollwitz, servant of the Regimental Surgeon Rapp, deserted this afternoon from quarters.

17 October - The regimental wives were embarked today.

18 October - [After the date, another hand has entered a word, which I cannot decipher.] The North Battery was demolished today. Servant Ulm, of Lieutenant Colonel von Reitzenstein's [Company], died today in the hospital. Gollwitz, who deserted on the sixteenth of this month, was captured by two residents, four English miles from here, and brought back in arrest.

19 October - Today the North Battery was set on fire. The battery on Goat Island was demolished.

20 October - More defenses of the North Battery were demolished and the magazines were set on fire. The sick of the regiment and the knapsacks were taken aboard ship. All the cattle belonging to the army were slaughtered and the army was issued fresh provisions. The dismantled enemy ships located here were made completely unusable.

21 October - The regimental horses were embarked and the fort at Brenton's Point was demolished.

22 October - The English artillerymen and the prisoners were embarked. Four English ships, including the frigate <u>Flora</u>, and the North Battery were set on fire this evening. Those provisions which could not be taken aboard ship were thrown in the water.

23 and 24 October - In quarters at Newport.

25 October - The army broke camp on Rhode Island and retreated to Brenton's Point, where the regiments were embarked in the following order: 1) the Hessian Buenau Regiment 2)

the 1st Ansbach Regiment 3) the 2nd Ansbach
Regiment 4) the Hessian Huyn Regiment 5) the
Hessian von Ditfurth Regiment 6) the 43rd
Regiment 7) the 38th Regiment 8) the 22nd
Regiment 9) the Hessian Jaegers and the
English Light Horse. Brown's Corps of
provincial troops on Conanicut were embarked at
the same time. While the embarkation was being
carried out, the fort at Brenton's Point was
set on fire. As soon as all the troops were on
board, the fleet, consisting of 130 ships, set
sail. The frigate _Blonde_ was the commodore's
ship. We left the harbor at seven o'clock in
the evening. We sailed all night with a good
wind, passing Block Island, in the Sound, at
twelve o'clock. During the retreat not a
single man of the enemy was seen.[10]

26 October - We sailed all day with a good
wind and reached Huntington, where we anchored,
at midnight.

27 October - We departed at seven o'clock
in the morning and during the morning passed
Hellgate. We entered the harbor at New York at
one o'clock in the afternoon. From Newport to
New York is 175 English miles. During the rest
of the day we remained lying at anchor.

28 to 30 October - In the harbor at New
York.

31 October - The 2nd Ansbach Regiment
landed and entered camp at New York.

1 November - Lying at anchor at New York.

2 November - Corporal [Carl] Graebner, of
the von Seybothen Regiment, was promoted to 2nd
lieutenant.

3 November - We landed and entered the
city of New York.

Promotions

The Jaeger Corps was divided into two companies, of which Staff Captain von Roeder
received one company. First Lieutenant von
[der] Heyde and 2nd Lieutenant von Diemar, of
the von Voit Regiment, were transferred to the

Jaeger Corps as 1st lieutenants. Staff Captain
von Tritschler was transferred to the Colonel's
Company. Second Lieutenant von Trechsel was
promoted to 1st lieutenant of the Colonel's
Company. Second Lieutenant Feder was made
adjutant. Three second lieutenants, von
Hohendorf, Schuchard, and Hirsch had arrived
with the recruits. The first one was assigned
to the Colonel's Company; the latter two went
to the von Seybothen Regiment. Sergeant [Georg
Simon] Halbmeyer was promoted to 2nd lieutenant
in the Colonel's Company. Corporal Beyer, of
the Colonel's Company, was promoted to
sergeant. First Lieutenant von Feilitzsch, of
the Jaeger Corps, and 2nd Lieutenant von
Strahlendorf, of the von Seybothen Regiment,
received their release and will return to
Europe.

4 November - The recruits, who arrived
here about two and one-half months ago,[11] were
divided among the companies.

5 to 7 November - In quarters at New York.

8 November - Private Gollwitz was punished
by running the gauntlet twenty times.

9 November - There was a strong thunderstorm this morning. Private [Johann Christoph]
Mercklein, of the Colonel's Company, was promoted to medic.

10 November - In quarters at New York.

11 November - Private Michael Haeufelein,
of the Colonel's [Company], was promoted to
vice-corporal.

12 November - Grenadier Hoehl was promoted
to vice-corporal.

13 to 18 November - In quarters at New
York.

19 November - Because of the capture of
the city of Savannah,[12] in Georgia, this evening
a feu de joie was fired by the regiments here
in the city, which consist of the 42nd Regiment
of Scots, the two Ansbach regiments, and four
Hessian grenadier battalions. These units

marched to the great parade ground at five
o'clock this evening. His Excellence, General-
in-Chief Clinton rode before them and had the
order given to the regiments, that they were to
march to the North River, outside the city.
When it was completely dark, a 21-gun salute
was fired at the great battery on the North
River. Then a firing [of muskets] by units was
conducted starting on the left wing. The same
feu de joie was fired by the troops at Paulus
Hook. After the salvos had been fired, the
regiments gave a very loud hurrah.

20 November - In quarters at New York.

21 November - In quarters at New York.
Recruit Seidel, of the Colonel's Company,
died in the hospital of bilious fever.

22 November - The von Seybothen Regiment
entered winter quarters this evening.

23 to 30 November - In quarters at New
York.

1 to 12 December - In quarters at New
York.

13 December - In quarters at New York.

Promotions in the Colonel's Company
Corporal [Andreas] Albrecht to 2nd sergeant.
Vice-Corporal [Johann Christoph] Schirmer
to corporal.

In the Lieutenant Colonel's Company
Vice-Corporal Schoepler to quartermaster
sergeant.
Private [Johann David] Prechtel to cor-
poral.
[Private] Gackstetter to vice-corporal.

In the Major's Company
Second Sergeant [Ludwig Theodor] Hilpert
to 1st sergeant.
Third Sergeant Schmid to 2nd sergeant.
Corporal [Johann] Blauhoeffer to 3rd ser-
geant.
Vice-Corporal Decker to corporal.
Private [Johann Sebastian] Blank to cor-

41

poral.
Private [Johann] Preiss to vice-corporal.

In Captain von Stain's Company

Second Sergeant [Michael] Hofmann to 1st sergeant.

Corporal [Johann] Flohr to 2nd sergeant.
Vice-Corporal [Johann Georg Michael] Winkler to corporal.

Private Kretschi to vice-corporal.
[Heinrich] Bauschinger, of the Lieutenant Colonel's [Company], was made a cannoneer. [Karl] Nehrlich, of the Major's [Company], was assigned to the lower staff.

Quartermaster Sergeant [Johann Georg] Beck, of the Jaeger Corps, has been recalled to Ansbach. Quartermaster Sergeant [Leonhard] Hausselt, of von Stain's Company, has taken his place. Corporal [Johann Georg Friedrich] Schmalz, of the Colonel's Company, has transferred to Captain von Stain's Company as quartermaster sergeant.

14 December – In quarters at New York.

Promotions in the Colonel's Company

Vice-Corporal Haehnlein to corporal.
Private Haehnlein to vice-corporal.

15 December – The invalids returning to

Germany were embarked. First Lieutenant von Feilitzsch, of the Jaeger Corps, and 2nd Lieutenant von Strahlendorf and Regimental Surgeon Pflug, of Colonel von Seybothen's Regiment, embarked with them.

Non-commissioned officers of the von Voit Regiment who sailed with the invalids, were:

Second Sergeant [Johann Heinrich] Wiederhold, of the Colonel's Company.

Quartermaster Sergeant [Johann Friedrich] Dorn and Corporal [Johann Adam] Weiss, of the Lieutenant Colonel's [Company].

First Sergeant [Johann] Raab and Corporal [Leonhard] Schneider, of the Major's Company.

First Sergeant [Paul] Schmid, of Captain von Stain's [Company].

42

   16 to 18 December - In quarters at New
York.
   19 December - The four Hessian grenadier
battalions, the 64th English Regiment, and a
detachment from the Jaeger Corps were embarked. [13]
   20 December - In quarters at New York.
   21 December - The troops embarked on the
nineteenth of this month sailed out of here on
the North River today.
   22 December - In quarters at New York.
   23 December - A ship with fifty jaegers,
of those troops which sailed from the local
harbor on the 21st of this month and then
anchored near Staten Island, had its anchor
rope broken by an ice flow. [14] The ship was
driven through the entire harbor and onto land
near Frog Island. It was frightfully smashed
and began to leak. The jaegers were saved and
brought on land at New York.
   24 December - Private Baender, of the
Colonel's Company, while at the outermost post
on the water at the Naval Stores watch, at two
o'clock in the morning, challenged an approaching boat four or five times. As he
received no reply, he fired at it and killed a
sailor.
   25 December - In quarters at New York.
   26 December - In quarters at New York.
   27 to 31 December - In quarters at New
York.

1780

1 January - New Year's Day in quarters at New York.

2 January - Captain von Koenitz, 1st Lieutenant von Keller, and 2nd Lieutenant Graebner, of the von Seybothen Regiment, went with a detachment of one hundred men to reinforce Paulus Hook today. In the North River, which they had to cross, there were many ice flows. Captain von Koenitz and 2nd Lieutenant Graebner were lost from sight, as no one could see where their boat, in which there were forty men, had gone. 1st Lieutenant von Keller, because of the amount of ice and an approaching storm, turned back to New York.

3 January - It is understood that Staff Captain von Koenitz arrived with his boat at Staten Island.

Note. This afternoon the regiment received information that Captain von Koenitz had arrived already yesterday evening, not at Staten Island, but at Paulus Hook.

4 January - In quarters at New York.

5 January - In quarters at New York.

6 to 13 January - In quarters at New York.

14 January - Today the East River was completely frozen so that many people crossed from here to Brooklyn on the ice. About eleven o'clock the tide came in and the river was immediately opened again.

15 January - The enemy crossed over the river, which is frozen, from near Amboy to Staten Island, with nine thousand men today and attacked our troops. One thousand men from the regiments lying in garrison here were ordered to go there as a reinforcement. They were embarked at four o'clock in the afternoon, but because of the heavy ice, could not cross and were immediately debarked.

16 January - The one thousand men were embarked again at seven o'clock this morning,

but because of the amount of ice, again failed
to cross. At eleven o'clock they were debarked
again. The enemy reportedly is on the island
in the region of Amboy.

17 January - The enemy, under the command
of General [William Alexander, Lord] Stirling,
withdrew from Staten Island. The British
troops on Staten Island were commanded by the
English General [Thomas] Stirling. On our side
four Englanders were killed, but twelve of the
enemy were captured.

18 January - Today is the birthday of
Queen Charlotte of England. At twelve o'clock
a 21-gun salute was fired at Fort George. At
night General [William] Tryon gave a dinner and
ball, to which all the staff officers were
invited. The house, where the ball was held,
was illuminated.

19 January - In quarters at New York.

20 January - The North River is frozen
over so that details can cross to Paulus Hook
on the ice.

21 to 24 January - In quarters at New
York.

25 January - During the night a detachment
of four hundred men from the regiments lying
here in garrison crossed the ice to Paulus
Hook. From there they attacked an enemy picket
beyond the city of Bergen, consisting of thirty
men. These were brought back here during the
night as prisoners.

26 to 31 January - In quarters at New
York.

1 February - In quarters at New York.

2 to 4 February - In quarters at New York.

5 February - Yesterday the English troops
sent out a command over Kingsbridge which
attacked an enemy outpost. Ninety-five
prisoners, including many wounded, were brought
back. The enemy reportedly suffered one
hundred dead, also, and the English had five
men killed.

6 to 8 February - In quarters at New York.

9 February - Private [Heinrich] Katzenwinkel, who deserted on 10 March 1778, turned
up at the regiment again this morning.

10 to 16 February - In quarters at
New York.

17 February - Private Katzenwinkel, who
deserted on 10 March 1778, was not punished for
his desertion, but because he had used the
false name Major Ernst von Reitzenstein for a
time, he was made to run the gauntlet twelve
times.

Private [Georg Peter] Beck, of the Colonel's Company, died in the hospital.

18 to 29 February - In quarters at
New York.

1 to 4 March - In quarters at New York.

5 March - The 76th Regiment of Scots and
the 80th Regiment marched away from here to
Long Island.

6 March - In quarters at New York.

7 March - Two frigates, Thames and Virginia, and a privateer sailed out of the local
harbor this morning. They are going to cruise
in the Delaware River for ships coming out of
Philadelphia.

8 to 20 March - In quarters at New York.

21 March - This evening a 74-gun ship arrived from Georgia. General [James] Robinson,
who recently left London, arrived on this ship.

22 March - In quarters at New York.

23 March - Last night a detachment of 350
men, under the command of Lieutenant Colonel
[Duncan] McPherson, was carried across to
Jersey. Not far from Hackensack they plundered
a village and then laid it in ashes. During
this affair two men from the von Voit Regiment,
Privates Herterich, of the Lieutenant Colonel's
[Company] and [Christoph] Uhlmann, of the
Major's [Company], and one man from the von
Seybothen Regiment were captured. From the
Hessian regiment, seven men from the Leib

46

Regiment, three men from the Landgraf Regiment,
and five men from the von Donop Regiment were
captured.

<u>24 to 30 March</u> - In quarters at New York.

<u>31 March</u> - Muster was held before Colonel
von Voit's quarters.

<u>1 April</u> - The following regiments were em-
barked: the 42nd Regiment of Scots, the
Queen's Rangers, the Prince of Wales' Volunteers, and the Hessian Ditfurth Regiment.
The 22nd Regiment was transferred to Staten
Island from Long Island and the 37th Regiment
was brought to New York.

<u>2 April</u> - The fleet with the embarked
troops sailed from here today.

<u>3 to 7 April</u> - In quarters at New York.

<u>8 April</u> - In quarters at New York.

<u>9 to 15 April</u> - In quarters at New York.

<u>16 April</u> - A short description of the
great tower which is built on the Evangelical
Church in this city. It is exceptionally
beautiful. It is four-sided and of squared
stones until above the bell openings. Above
this support, on each side, is a clock dial
with golden numbers. The tower then becomes
eight-sided so that between each dial a four-
sided window is made. The entire upper
structure stands on nine gold-plated balls. On
the weather vane there is an iron cross with
leaves. On each end of the cross, the four
Latin letters, E, S, W, N, are to be seen. The
E points to the east or morning, the S to the
south or midday, the W to the west or evening,
and the N to the north or midnight. Above the
cross is a gold-plated rooster with a star
before it, an arrow behind it, and a crown
above it.

<u>17 April</u> - Yesterday a detachment of three
hundred men made an expedition against
Hackensack in Jersey. Seventy of the enemy
were brought back as prisoners. The Hessians
suffered six killed and thirteen wounded.[2]

18 to 24 April - In quarters at New York.

25 April - A provisions fleet, consisting of 95 sail, entered the local harbor this afternoon. It came from London.

26 and 27 April - In quarters at New York.

28 April - The von Voit Regiment conducted exercises, which went exceptionally well, for this year. General [James] Pattison, General Robertson, and the Brunswick General [Friedrich Adolf] von Riedesel, as well as a large number of officers, observed the exercises and maneuvers. Letters arrived from Europe.

29 and 30 April - In quarters at New York.

1 to 5 May - In quarters at New York.

6 May - The von Voit Regiment conducted firing exercises.

7 to 9 May - In quarters at New York.

10 May - The von Seybothen Regiment conducted exercises and maneuvers before the Generals von Knyphausen and Pattison.

11 and 12 May - In quarters at New York.

13 May - The 37th and 43rd English Regiments conducted maneuvers, with firing, this morning.

14 May - In quarters at New York.

15 May - The 44th English Regiment and the Hessian Lossberg Regiment were embarked and are to sail to Canada at once. The 54th Regiment replaced the 44th Regiment and went to Paulus Hook. The 38th Regiment [went to Jamaica on Long Island.][3]

16 to 19 May - In quarters at New York.

20 May - Private [Wilhelm] Braun, Jr., ran the gauntlet twelve times for theft and Private [Christian] Wetschell, eight times for drunkeness. Both are from Captain von Stain's Company.

The frigate Gaudalupe came from England and brought four prizes into the local harbor. Two were Spanish, one of which had 22 cannons, one was French, and one American. They were coming from the island of Martinique and all

48

were heavily laden with merchandise.

20 [sic] to 24 May - In quarters at New York.

25 May - Letters arrived from Europe. A court martial was held today for Medic [Friedrich] Drexel, of the Lieutenant Colonel's Company, who is under arrest.

26 May - In quarters at New York.

27 May - Medic Drexel's sentence was published today. For speaking in a disrespectful and argumentive manner, he was sentenced to one year in arrest and then to receive an honorable discharge.

28 May - In quarters at New York.

29 May - Yesterday evening a frigate entered the local harbor, bringing the news that Charleston had been surrendered by the Americans to the General-in-Chief Sir Henry Clinton, by accord. Six thousand Americans were made prisoners of war by this event, including six generals. The mentioned frigate, Iris, was not destined to enter here, but was meant to go to Halifax and England. However, because it had captured three American ships, one with twelve, one with fourteen, and one with twenty guns, it decided to enter here in order to bring in the prizes.

30 and 31 May - In quarters at New York.

1 June - In quarters at New York.

2 June - In quarters at New York.

3 June - In quarters at New York.

4 June - Today is the birthday of His Majesty, the King of Great Britain, and he is 42 years old. At Fort George a royal salute of 21 cannons was fired. All the armed ships fired a salute and following this there was a very loud hurrah shouted from every ship.

5 June - In quarters at New York.

6 June - An expedition was undertaken with a force of seven thousand men. They were carried to Staten Island in schooners and flatboats and halted there under the open sky.

7 June - The force broke camp at four
o'clock in the morning and was carried over to
New Jersey in flatboats. As soon as the
Jaegers, who constituted the advance guard,
arrived at Elizabethtown, continuous small arms
firing began. The army, which was under the
command of the Hessian Lieutenant General
[Wilhelm] von Knyphausen, marched forward
toward Connecticut Farms. During this
engagement 2nd Lieutenant [Friedrich] Ebenauer,
of the Jaeger Corps, was killed. During the
night the army retired to Elizabethtown and
spent the night under the open sky. The
English General Stirling was wounded in the
foot. Ensign [Bernhard Wilhelm] Wiederhold, of
the Hessian Leib Regiment, received two wounds.
    8 June - Early in the morning the 22nd
Regiment moved forward toward Elizabethtown, to
the right of a woods. The 17th Dragoon Regiment moved against the village of Elizabethtown. During the entire morning these two
regiments exchanged fire with the enemy.
Meanwhile one corporal and twelve privates of
the von Voit Regiment were sent forward as a
reinforcement, to occupy the road for the
Dragoons. This resulted in Private [Valentin]
Grau, of Stain's Company, being shot through
the shoulder. The 22nd Regiment and the
Dragoons had to retire back to our lines, so
the 1st Ansbach Regiment had to move forward
immediately, to attack the enemy. A battalion
fire was directed against the enemy, who did
not return the fire, but pulled back completely. During this action the enemy lost one
major, two subalterns, and seventy men. Only
five men of the von Voit Regiment were wounded,
namely: Grenadiers Bach, Goll, and Schmid, and
Privates Imhaeuser and Walter, of the Lieutenant Colonel's [Company]. Private Seffert,
of the Colonel's [Company] had a lock of hair
shot off and was also shot through his hat.
After half an hour the enemy again fired at our

pickets. The troops formed camp in a square before Elizabethtown and remained there. They were provided with huts made of boards and brush. Two deserters from the enemy infantry came in.

9 June - In camp at Elizabethtown. The firing by the enemy continued all morning against our outposts. However, when they saw that our outposts were being reinforced with jaegers, they pulled back and there was little firing this afternoon.

Private [Friedrich] Abt, of the von Seybothen Regiment, who had deserted on October 1, 1779, came back as a deserter from the enemy. He was a member of the Light Horse and had his horse and saddle and possessions with him.

10 June - The camp was changed this afternoon and moved nearer to Elizabethtown, and in a line. An enemy deserter from the Light Horse came in with his horse. He was previously in the Ansbach Jaeger Corps. His name was [Michael] Guenther.

The Jaeger Sergeant [Joseph] Bach was promoted to 2nd lieutenant in the Jaeger Corps.

11 June - The enemy withdrew almost all his troops from Elizabethtown and the sailors have taken a schooner from Elizabethtown. Work on the defenses on the water is continuing day and night.

12 June - An enemy deserter from the Light Horse came into our camp. Six citizens from Elizabethtown fired from a house and wounded a jaeger. Therefore, they were arrested and sent to New York. An engineer, surveying a field, near the church in Elizabethtown, was shot in the knee and had his foot amputated.

13 June - The Jaegers made a patrol beyond Elizabethtown and brought back the information that the enemy had withdrawn.

14 June - In camp at Elizabethtown.

15 June - The regiments moved out at two-thirty this morning to begin a march.

Nevertheless, we still remained in our old camp. Since we have been here, three defensive positions have been built to cover our retreat and a floating bridge, consisting of 29 one and two masted sloops, has been put together over the Kills River between Staten Island and Jersey.

16 June - The Jaegers wounded and captured a rifleman.

17 June - The bridge of ships is 270 paces in length. Colonel von Seybothen's Regiment entered camp here today. Since the von Voit Regiment left New York it has been in the brigade of the Hessian General [Karl Wilhelm] von Hachenberg. Now, however, the two Ansbach regiments are in the brigade of Colonel von Voit. Washington's army retreated during this night to Chatham.

18 June - In camp at Elizabethtown.

19 June - General-in-Chief Sir Henry Clinton entered camp yesterday and observed the army. The regiments paraded without weapons. Today there was firing against the outposts.

20 June - A detachment of fifty men moved through the woods on our left wing but found no trace of the enemy.

21 June - In camp at Elizabethtown. This morning the enemy fired on a whale boat lying in the Kills River. We fired three cannonballs at them and they ran away. Twenty-eight deserters from the enemy came in and four prisoners from the militia were brought in.

22 June - In camp at Elizabethtown. The Queen's Rangers, who had been at Charleston, entered the outposts here with the Jaeger Corps and the Donop Regiment. A patrol was made this evening by the Jaegers and the Queen's Rangers, during which a private of the Rangers was killed and one non-commissioned officer and one private of the mounted jaegers were wounded.

23 June - The army moved forward over Springfield. It consisted of the following

units: the Jaeger Corps, the 17th Dragoon Regiment, the blue and the green Hussars, the Guard Regiment, the English 22nd, 37th, 38th, and 57th Regiments, the 2nd Ansbach Regiment, and the Hessian Leib, Landgraf, and Bose Regiments.

The following officers were wounded: from the Jaeger Corps, Captain von Roeder, 1st Lieutenant von Diemar, Lieutenant Colonel [Ernst Karl] von Prueschenck, and Captain [Friedrich Heinrich] Lorey; of the 38th Regiment, Captain Norman. During this action Springfield was burned down. The dead and wounded amounted to about seventy men. The enemy, despite the heavy firing, stood his ground very well. During the evening the army retreated back to the line at Elizabethtown. The reserve corps consisted of the 43rd Regiment, the 1st Ansbach Regiment, and the Hessian Donop and Buenau Regiments. At ten o'clock at night the army received the order to vacate Jersey. This took place in the best order, across the floating bridge. The outer pickets made up the rear guard. During the retreat nothing was seen nor heard of the enemy. While marching out of Elizabethtown, Private [Wilhelm] Braun, Jr., of Stain's Company and Bauer, the servant of Staff Captain von Tritschler, deserted.

24 June – The regiment arrived on Staten Island at two o'clock in the morning. During the morning the English regiments were embarked on schooners again. Because there were not enough ships for the embarkation, the German regiments had to remain, without tents, on Staten Island.

25 June – This morning both Ansbach and Hessian regiments were embarked on schooners. At one o'clock in the afternoon we passed New York and, because of contrary winds, during the evening we anchored in the North River not far from Fort Knyphausen. The von Buenau Regiment

53

remained in its former camp on Staten Island.
The 43rd Regiment and the Donop Regiment are to
go into camp at New York.

26 June - We sailed at four o'clock in the
morning and during the evening ran in near
Philipsburg. The troops were immediately
landed and remained beyond Philipsburg, without
tents.

27 June - We entered camp in the
line about two and one-half miles from Philipsburg. Grenadier [Johann] Seifferlein deserted
from camp this evening.

28 to 30 June - In camp near Philipsburg.

1 July - In camp near Philipsburg. The
baggage, tents, and wives were brought to the
regiment.

2 to 4 July - In camp near Philipsburg.

5 July - In camp near Philipsburg. Staff
Servant [Johann Adam] Reuter and Private
[Johann] Stuelpner, of the Major's [Company],
deserted from camp, and Private Kraus, of the
Lieutenant Colonel's [Company], from his post
on picket.

6 July - Grenadier [Georg] Hohenberger deserted from camp.

7 July - Grenadier [Michael] Erhardt deserted from the field watch.

8 July - Grenadiers Braun and [Friedrich]
Gossler deserted from camp.

9 to 11 July - In camp near Philipsburg.

12 July - Pack Servant [Johann Heinrich]
Rhau, of the Colonel's Company, deserted from
camp today. He was captured by the Jaeger
picket and put in arrest at the fire watch.
The Ansbach Jaeger [Adam] Gardelow deserted
from the picket tonight.

13 to 16 July - In camp near Philipsburg.

17 July - A court martial was held today
concerning the desertion of Private Rhau. An
enemy deserter came into camp. A Hessian
grenadier planned to desert during the previous
night, but he was caught by the picket of the

von Seybothen Regiment and put in arrest.

18 July - Private [Martin] Zollfrank, of the Major's Company, deserted this evening while bathing.

19 July - The excess baggage was sent to New York.

20 July - In camp near Philipsburg.

21 July - At three-thirty in the morning the two Ansbach regiments marched to Harlem and entered camp there. At noon the enemy attacked the Refugees in Jersey, opposite Harlem, and burned two vessels. The Refugees defended their block house and during the enemy's retreat, captured two cannons.

22 and 23 July - In camp at Harlem.

24 July - The two Ansbach regiments marched to New York and entered the camp at the exercise ground on the East River.

25 July - In camp at New York.

26 July - In camp at New York. The deserter Private Rhau had his sentence published this morning. Because of his disloyal desertion he is to be hanged until dead. But this infamous death sentence was changed to death by a firing squad.[4]

At six o'clock this evening the Hessian Major General [Johann Christoph] von Huyn was buried in the garrison church according to his rank. The honors were performed by the Grenadiers of the 1st Ansbach Regiment and the Hessian Donop Regiment. With each salvo, three cannons were fired.

27 July - The deserter Private Rhau was executed at seven o'clock this morning, behind the front.

[There is no entry for 28 July 1780.]

29 July - In camp at New York.

30 July - Medic [Friedrich] Drexel, of the Lieutenant Colonel's Company, was released from jail and his arrest yesterday and rejoined the company.

31 July - A court martial was held at the

von Seybothen Regiment concerning the desertion of Private [Joseph] Glatz, of Captain von Eyb's Company. He was sentenced to be hanged, which was made known at once.

1 August - In camp at New York.

2 August - Private Glatz, of the von Seybothen Regiment, sentenced to be hanged, had the sentence changed to death by a firing squad. This was carried out at seven o'clock in the morning.

3 August - In camp at New York.

4 to 6 August - In camp at New York.

7 August - Private [Wilhelm] Braun, Jr., who deserted on June 23 of this year, wrote from Philadelphia that he had not deserted, but was captured. However, he was not taken on as a prisoner.[5]

8 to 11 August - In camp at New York.

12 August - Today was the Prince of Wales' birthday and all the ships displayed the appropriate honors. Houses at Brooklyn Ferry were illuminated and a fireworks display was presented.

13 August - Major General Pattison, the city commandant at New York, resigned his office due to poor health and this office was temporarily assigned to General Robertson by the General-in-Chief Sir Henry Clinton.

14 August - In camp at New York.

15 August - Today people were pressed onto the warships as sailors.[6] During the midday, from ten to one o'clock, a line was drawn across the city from the East to the North River.

16 August - In camp at New York.

17 and 18 August - In camp at New York.

19 August - Both Ansbach regiments marched out of camp at New York and entered camp at Harlem.

20 to 24 August - In camp at Harlem.

25 August - The enemy approached close to the North River, on the Jersey shore, today.

They burned some wood and fired a few small cannons.

26 August – Reportedly the enemy has five thousand men on the North River. Today they fired several times at a row galley.

27 to 31 August – In camp at Harlem.

1 to 20 September – In camp at Harlem.

21 September – Private [Erhard] Seidel, of the Lieutenant Colonel's Company, died at New York on the nineteenth of this month. The wife of Grenadier Wiedener died today in New York.

22 September – Because of the victory of General Lord Cornwallis over the army of the American General [Horatio] Gates, which was completely routed although three times as large, a feu de joie was fired by the garrison lying at New York.

23 September – In camp at Harlem.

24 September – This evening there was a strong thunderstorm, which struck Long Island. From our camp we saw the great flames of a fire.

25 September – In camp at Harlem. Privates [Heinrich] Hartung, of the Major's [Company], and [Andreas] Weiant and Fuchs, of Stain's [Company], were punished for marauding by running the gauntlet six times.

26 September – In camp at Harlem.

27 September – Today the 76th Regiment of Scots marched to Kingsbridge and the Guard Regiment will be embarked in their stead to go on an expedition to Virginia.

The American General [Benedict] Arnold with some twenty men arrived at the headquarters in New York as deserters.

28 September – As nothing came of the expedition noted yesterday. the English Guard Regiment returned to its former place.

29 September – In camp at Harlem.

30 September – In camp at Harlem.

1 October – In camp at Harlem.

2 October – Private [Johann] Klein, of the

Major's Company, while on a work detail at
Morrisania on September 29, tried to desert.
Therefore, he was punished today by running the
gauntlet ten times.

3 to 8 October - In camp at Harlem.

9 October - The unhappy fate which was
administered by the enemy to the English Major
[John] Andre, Adjutant General for His Excellence, the General-in-Chief Clinton, was made
known to the army today.

10 October - In camp at Harlem.

11 October - The expedition under the command of the English General [Alexander] Leslie
was embarked yesterday at Staten Island. It
consists of three thousand men and is to sail
to Virginia.

12 October - In camp at Harlem.

13 October - Mail arrived from Germany.
Regimental Quartermaster [Heinrich Hartmann]
Model and Quartermaster Sergeant Raedlein
received their recall.

14 October - In camp at Harlem.

15 October - A fleet from England, carrying the third Ansbach recruit transport,
arrived at the harbor of New York today.[8]

16 October - Colonel von Voit's wife arrived with the transport.

17 October - In camp at Harlem.

18 October - Recruits for both regiments
arrived in camp today and were divided among
the companies. Second Lieutenant [Ferdinand]
Foerster was assigned to the Colonel's Company;
Second Lieutenant [Johann] von Fabrice was
assigned to the Lieutenant Colonel's Company;
and Second Lieutenant [Heinrich] von Mattolay
was assigned to the von Seybothen Regiment.
The Regimental Surgeon [Johann Heinrich]
Schneller was also assigned to the von Seybothen Regiment.

19 October - The 2nd Ansbach Regiment entered the barracks at the brewery at New York
today.

20 October - In camp at Harlem.
21 October - In camp at Harlem.
22 October - In camp at Harlem.
23 October - In camp at Harlem.
24 October - In camp at Harlem.
25 October - As it was the coronation day of His Majesty, the King of Great Britain, the warships in the harbor at New York fired a salute from their cannons at one o'clock this afternoon.
26 October - In camp at Harlem.
27 October - In camp at Harlem.
28 October - The accord for the exchange of prisoners by England and America was agreed upon on the 25th of this month. This was published by the army today. Major General [William] Phillips commands a corps consisting of the English Grenadiers, the Light Infantry, and the 42nd Regiment of Scots.
29 and 30 October - In camp at Harlem.
31 October - In camp at Harlem. We had a thunderstorm today.
1 November - In camp at Harlem. A heavy snow fell today.
2 to 10 November - In camp at Harlem.
11 November - A provisions fleet from Cork, consisting of 61 sail, entered the harbor at New York today.
12 to 19 November - In camp at Harlem.
20 November - During the past night three buildings in the area of the Naval Stores watch in New York burned down.
21 November - In camp at Harlem.
22 November - The regiment entered winter quarters in New York and moved into the North Church. The Lieutenant Colonel's Company and the Artillery were quartered in a house near the North Church.
23 to 28 November - In quarters at New York.
29 November - A court martial was held today concerning Second Lieutenant [Georg] von

Hohendorf.[9]
    30 November - In quarters at New York.
    1 December - The findings of Second Lieutenant von Hohendorf's court martial were published. He is to be cashiered with loss of honor.
    2 December - Private [Paul] Straussberger, of the Major's Company, was drunk on the main watch. Therefore, he had to run the gauntlet eight times today. Commissary Meier is doing duty as regimental quartermaster and as soon as Regimental Quartermaster Model, who has been recalled, is gone, Meier will take his place.
    Quartermaster Sergeant Hermann, of the Colonel's Company, is doing duty in the pack house. Private [Johann Christoph] Ernst, of the Lieutenant Colonel's Company, has been promoted to quartermaster sergeant of the Grenadier Company and Private [Georg] Glaenzel, of the Colonel's Company, has been promoted to vice-corporal.
    3 December - In quarters at New York.
    4 December - An American frigate with 32 cannons, which was loaded with silk and wine from France and was sailing to Maryland, was captured by the English frigate Iris, Captain Dawson, in the Chesapeake Bay and brought into the local harbor today. The value of the merchandise is estimated at 50,000 pounds.
    5 December - A packet boat from England arrived, bringing letters from Europe.
    6 to 24 December - In quarters at New York.
    25 December - In quarters at New York.
    26 to 31 December - In quarters at New York.
    The regiment dressed in new uniforms today.

1781

1 January - In quarters at New York.

2 to 5 January - In quarters at New York.

6 January - Twenty-five hundred men of the Pennsylvania militia are reported to have quit Washington's army because they have not been paid for two years. They supposedly have spiked the cannons at Morristown and have set fire to the magazine there. They have fortified the hills near Amboy and ' have four cannons. Some troops from the Light Infantry and English Grenadiers have been sent in that direction, and it is believed the militiamen will come here.

7 January In quarters at New York.

8 and 9 January - In quarters at New York.

10 January - Private [Franz] Bischof, of the Colonel's Company, took two Spanish dollars from a local citizen and was punished today by running the gauntlet twelve times.

11 and 12 January - In quarters at New York.

13 January - The affair reported on the sixth of this month about the withdrawl of some American troops was confirmed. However, they received their pay in hard cash from General Washington and have returned to duty with their army.

14 to 16 January - In quarters at New York.

17 January - Private [Wilhelm] Braun, Jr., of Stain's Company, who deserted at Elizabethtown on 23 June of the past year, and Grenadier [Johann Wilhelm] Braun, Sr., who deserted at Philipsburg on 8 July of the past year, brothers, arrived here today as deserters from the Americans.

18 January - The English Commissary [William] Porter held muster today in the William Street.

19 to 23 January - In quarters at New

York.

<u>24 January</u> - The Ansbach invalids being returned to Germany were embarked this morning on the transport ship <u>Minerva</u>. Regimental Quartermaster Model has the command over them. The following non-commissioned officers of the von Voit Regiment went with them:
    1) Quartermaster Sergeant Raedlein, of the Grenadier Company.
    2) Corporal [Georg] Haehnlein, Sr. and
    3) Corporal Blank, of the Colonel's Company.
    4) Medic [Friedrich] Drexel, of the Lieutenant Colonel's Company.

<u>25 to 28 January</u> - In quarters at New York.

<u>29 January</u> - The fleet for England, consisting of two hundred sail with an escort of two frigates and a sloop-of-war, sailed out of the local harbor this afternoon. The Ansbach invalids were on board and the frigate <u>Clinton</u> is the commodore.

<u>30 January</u> - The fleet which sailed yesterday is lying at anchor at Staten Island.

<u>31 January</u> - In quarters at New York.

<u>1 February</u> - In quarters at New York.

<u>2 February</u> - The fleet for England, which sailed last Wednesday, sailed January 31 from Staten Island.

<u>3 February</u> - In quarters at New York.

<u>4 February</u> - The army was informed today that General Arnold had advanced on Richmond in Virginia and had captured the seat of government there. A magazine for munitions and armaments for the ships was captured by him, or in part destroyed, and very few troops were lost during the affair.

<u>5 to 14 February</u> - In quarters at New York.

<u>15 February</u> - A packet boat arrived with letters from Germany.

<u>16 to 23 February</u> - In quarters at New

York.
    <u>24 February</u> - In quarters at New York.
    <u>25 February</u> - In quarters at New York.
    <u>26 February</u> - Sentenced for marauding on Long Island - Jaeger Sergeant [Samuel] Schilling was demoted. Each of the last four, Field Jaegers Schmid, Pube, Meers, and Wienner, had to run the gauntlet ten times. This punishment was carried out at the von Voit Regiment.
    <u>27 and 28 February</u> - In quarters at New York.
    <u>1 March</u> - In quarters at New York.
    <u>2 March</u> - In quarters at New York.
    <u>3 March</u> - Private [Christoph] Uhlmann, of the von Voit Regiment, who was taken prisoner near Hackensack on 23 March 1780, died in captivity at Philadelphia.
    <u>4 March</u> - The English 76th Regiment and the Hessian Hereditary Prince Regiment were embarked today. The Hessian Knyphausen Regiment marched to Kingsbridge.
    <u>5 March</u> - The expedition which departed from here today, consisted of the two regiments mentioned yesterday and the Light Infantry, under the command of the English General Phillips, is now lying at anchor at Staten Island.
    <u>6 March</u> - On the third of this month an American colonel arrived here as a deserter.
    <u>7 March</u> - In quarters at New York.
    <u>8 to 18 March</u> - In quarters at New York.
    <u>19 March</u> - A court martial was held today concerning 1st Sergeant Hauff and Quartermaster Schoepler, of the Lieutenant Colonel's Company. Sentences of these two, who were under arrest, were published today. Sergeant Hauff, for improper language toward Quartermaster Sergeant Schoepler, was sentenced to six days on bread and water and to to be held in arrest at the regimental watch, locked up for four days and unlocked for two days.
    Quartermaster Sergeant Schoepler, on the

other hand, for neglect of duty, was sentenced
to two days of arrest at the regimental watch,
locked up, on bread and water.

20 March - At three o'clock this morning
Private [Gottlob] Schulz, of the Major's Company, deserted from the regimental watch.

21 March - Private Schulz, who deserted
yesterday, returned to the regiment again this
evening and was placed under arrest at the
regimental watch.

22 March - Drummer [Johann Burkhardt]
Koehler, who wounded a private of the [Hessian]
Prince Charles Regiment in a duel, was punished
by running the gauntlet twelve times, namely,
the one of the Colonel's Company. Private
Schneider, of Stain's Company, while on picket
duty on the ship Nicolaus and John, got drunk
and misbehaved on land. He was also punished
by running the gauntlet eight times. Yesterday
a military hearing was conducted concerning
Drummer [Johann Georg] Fleissinger, of the
Lieutenant Colonel's Company, and Corporal
Hoehl, of the Grenadier Company. These two
knew of the incident [the duel]. The latter
did nothing to prevent it and was therefore
demoted for an unspecified time. The first was
punished with 25 lashes on his rump.

23 to 25 March - In quarters at New York.

26 March - Private Schulz, who returned to
the regiment on the 21st of this month, was
punished by running the gauntlet eight times.
Private [Johann] Hopf, of the Major's Company,
was drunk at parade, and therefore punished by
running the gauntlet eight times.

27 to 29 March - In quarters at New York.

30 March - On the sixteenth of this month
a sea battle took place between Admiral
[Marriott] Arbuthnot and the French fleet, in
the region of Chesapeake Bay. The English
drove the French off. The latter sailed back
to Rhode Island, where three of their ships
entered without masts.

31 March — A boat with dispatches, which
had sailed from Rhode Island and been sent by
the French General [Dontien Vimeur, Comte de]
Rochambeau to General Washington, was captured
near Fishkill by a Refugee officer. An American picket, consisting of 21 men, was captured
by the Refugees near Elizabethtown and brought
here today.

1 April — In quarters at New York.

2 April — In quarters at New York.

3 April — Private [Georg] Seiffert, of the
Major's Company, was drunk at parade and
therefore punished by running the gauntlet
eight times.

4 April — In quarters at New York.

5 April — In quarters at New York.

6 April — Field Jaeger Hahn tried to drown
himself and therefore was punished by running
the gauntlet twelve times.

7 April — In quarters at New York.

8 April — In quarters at New York.

9 April — In quarters at New York.

10 April — In quarters at New York.

11 April — About twenty empty transport
ships arrived here from Virginia.

12 April — In quarters at New York.

13 April — Yesterday Admiral Arbuthnot arrived at Sandy Hook with his war fleet. Five
warships of this fleet, which were damaged in
the affair near the Chesapeake Bay on 16 March,
and must be repaired here, including the
admiral's ship, also entered the harbor and are
lying at anchor in the North River.

14 to 18 April — In quarters at New York.

19 April — In quarters at New York.

20 April — Yesterday the warship Roebuck
brought the best American frigate, named
Confederation, which was carrying a cargo of
uniforms, into the local harbor. These items
had an estimated value of 75,000 pounds.

21 April — In quarters at New York.

22 April — A provisions fleet from England

arrived in the local harbor.

23 and 24 April - In quarters at New York.

25 April - Private Brauning, of the Colonel's [Company], was punished for drunkeness by running the gauntlet ten times.

26 April - In quarters at New York.

27 April - Corporal [Friedrich] Prevost, of the Colonel's Company, died in the hospital at Vauxhall.

28 April - The arrival of His Majesty's Ship <u>Amphitrite</u>, with dispatches from Lieutenant General Lord Cornwallis, gives the General-in-Chief the opportunity to inform this part of the army of the victory of the troops under His Lordship's command on 15 March 1781, over the American army in North Carolina. The news of this victory, in his Lordship's own words, is as follows: The camp at Guilford, 17 April 1781 - General [Nathanael] Greene had been reinforced from Virginia with eighteen-month troops [Continentals] and all the militia from that province. He advanced with his army of about six thousand men and four 6-pound cannons as far as this place. I attacked him on 15 March and after a very furious battle, I routed his army and captured his cannons. The great exhaustion of the troops, the number of wounded, and the shortage of provisions prevented our pursuit until after the life saving work on the afternoon of the action.

A feu de joie was therefore fired by the local garrison at eight o'clock this evening.

29 April - In quarters at New York.

30 April - Both the von Voit and the von Seybothen Regiments were embarked. The 43rd Regiment at Staten Island was also embarked. We remained lying at anchor at New York during the day.

1 May - We sailed this morning and then anchored near Staten Island.

2 to 5 May - At anchor at Staten Island.

6 May - At anchor at Staten Island. The

man-of-war <u>Roebuck</u>, Captain Douglas, brought an American frigate, <u>Protector</u>, into the local harbor today. It was loaded with flour and was bound for the French army at Rhode Island from Chester. The commodore of our fleet is the frigate <u>Charon</u>. The transport ships for the two Ansbach regiments are called:

<u>Alicia</u> - the Colonel
<u>Providence</u> - the Lieutenant Colonel and Major
<u>Ocean</u> - Captain von Stain, of the von Voit Regiment
<u>Alexander</u> - the Colonel
<u>Wisk</u> - the Major
<u>Caldonia</u> - Captain von Eyb, of the von Seybothen Regiment.

<u>7 May</u> - At anchor at Staten Island. There was a storm all day and all night.

<u>8 May</u> - At anchor at Staten Island.

<u>9 May</u> - At nine-thirty this morning both Admirals Arbuthnot and [Thomas] Graves, the war fleet, and the transport ships sailed from Staten Island and anchored at one o'clock in the afternoon at Sandy Hook.

<u>10 May</u> - We sailed at ten o'clock in the morning and the commodore and the transport ships, consisting of 23 sail, dropped anchor at eleven o'clock near Sandy Hook. This evening a merchant ship entered here from London, having crossed in eight weeks.

<u>11 May</u> - Lying at anchor at Sandy Hook. The warships, which had lain at anchor near the Flagstaff, sailed this morning and at eleven o'clock anchored not far from the lighthouse. This fleet consists of the following warships:

1) <u>Adamant</u> with 50 cannons
2) <u>Roebuck</u> with 44 cannons
3) <u>Royal Oak</u> with 74 cannons and Admiral Arbuthnot
4) <u>Medea</u>, frigate, with 28 cannons
5) <u>Bedford</u> with 74 cannons and the commodore

6) <u>Europe</u> with 64 cannons
7) <u>Prudent</u> with 64 cannons
8) <u>Assurance</u> with 44 cannons
9) <u>Chatham</u> with 50 cannons[2]
10) <u>Robust</u> with 74 cannons
11) <u>America</u> with 64 cannons
12) <u>London</u> with   98 cannons and Admiral Graves.

The last named ship ran upon a sandbar not far from the Flagstaff. Therefore, sailors from every ship were sent to help.

<u>12 May</u> - The transport fleet sailed at eight-thirty in the morning. When it was twelve miles beyond the lighthouse, it turned around and the fleet then anchored behind the war fleet at Sandy Hook. The war fleet remained lying at anchor. During the past night the <u>London's</u> repairs were completed and it also lay at anchor here.

<u>13 May</u> - Both fleets set sail at nine o'-clock in the morning and we entered the ocean together. At noon we met a merchant ship named <u>Nancy</u>. It came from London and had been underway for two months. An enemy ship had been seen during the evening and the frigate <u>Medea</u> went in search of it.

<u>14 May</u> - The wind swung to the west today and was contrary for us. About eleven o'clock, at midday, the marines and sailors on the warships conducted firing exercises with muskets. On our right we still saw the land of Jersey where the Americans still have the small seaport of Egg. At three o'clock in the afternoon the naval fleet left us, turning back toward the north. Three ships of the naval force, namely <u>Assurance</u>, <u>Charon</u>, and <u>Roebuck</u> remained with the transport fleet, with the <u>Charon</u> still the commodore.

<u>15 May</u> - During the past night we lost sight of land and sailed during the day with fairly good wind.

<u>16 May</u> - We sailed with fairly good wind.

17 May – At four o'clock in the morning
bottom was sounded at 23 fathoms. Yesterday
afternoon at four o'clock the Charon had chased
two enemy ships near the Delaware Bay and this
evening they were brought back to the fleet as
prizes. There was a strong thunderstorm at ten
o'clock in the evening. The wind today was
weak and contrary, but during the night a good
wind arose.

18 May – There was a calm this morning.
During the afternoon a good wind sprang up and
continued until midnight. At six and eight
o'clock the sea was eleven fathoms deep.

19 May – The wind continued favorable but
during the morning such a heavy fog set in that
not a single ship of the fleet could be seen.
The ships had to signal one another with musket
shots and drum rolls and because it was feared
we would get too close to the land, the ships
again turned back toward the north. At two
o'clock in the afternoon the sea was already
seventeen and one-half fathoms deep again. At
four o'clock the fog lifted and the fleet
changed course again.

20 May – At seven o'clock in the morning
the Virginia coast was seen and toward noon we
passed Cape Henry and entered Chesapeake Bay.
Hampton lies to our right. It should be noted
here that a fathom is six feet and a league is
three English miles, or one [German] hour.
This evening we anchored in Chesapeake Bay
eight English miles from Portsmouth, namely in
Hampton Roads, where two frigates, the Thames
with 32 cannons and the Gaudalupe with 28
cannons, already lay at anchor. At seven
o'clock in the evening the transport ships
sailed into the James River, where they
anchored at nine-thirty in the evening.

21 May – The anchor was raised at seven
o'clock in the morning and the ships sailed up
the James River. Note. The ship Providence
struck a sandbar near Hampton and therefore

fired two cannon shots as an emergency signal. At two o'clock in the afternoon we anchored in shallow water at Black Walnut Point. We sailed again at four o'clock and anchored at five-thirty. To the right of this place lay the District of Williamsburg and to the left Hog Island. At seven o'clock in the evening we sailed again and anchored at eight-thirty at Talbot's Point.

22 May - We set sail at seven o'clock in the morning and passed Old Jamestown on our right and New Jamestown on our left. Cape Henry lies half way between Sandy Hook and Richmond. On our right lies Santee Point. At noon we anchored at Branthom. It is ninety miles to Richmond from here. We received information that the English General Phillips died of a fever at Petersburg. Nine transport ships lie at anchor on which is to be found the baggage for the regiments of Arnold's Corps.

23 May - At anchor. The Providence, which had grounded on a sandbar yesterday, arrived here today.

Apollo, Belona, and Charming Nancy are transport ships for the 43rd Regiment. Nicolaus and Jane are ships for the convalescents. Providence Increase is the victual's ship.

24 May - At anchor at Branthom Point. We hear that Lord Cornwallis is returning with the army from Petersburg. This morning General Leslie arrived here at the fleet. The James River has already changed to sweet or fresh water at this place. The land in Virginia is completely flat and covered with unusual and beautiful woods. Most of the houses are of brick and built like the most beautiful castles in the air. All foodstuffs are cheap. No stones are to be found in this land.

25 May - The ships were ordered to sail back. At twelve o'clock the fleet departed and anchored in the region of the District of Williamsburg at seven o'clock in the evening.

26 May - We sailed at seven o'clock in the morning and anchored at four o'clock in the afternoon at Willoughby Bay. We sailed again at five o'clock. The ships Ocean and Wisk ran aground on the sandbar but were refloated after a few minutes. We anchored a mile from Portsmouth.

27 May - We sailed at eight o'clock in the morning and entered the harbor at Portsmouth at eleven-thirty and anchored. Opposite Portsmouth lies the beautiful city of Norfolk which the English General [John Murray, Earl of] Dunmore, while on an expedition from Boston, had burned down five years ago. The Elizabeth River flows between Norfolk and Portsmouth.

28 May - We landed at four o'clock in the morning, paraded through Portsmouth, and entered camp, outside the line. General Leslie commands the troops. The 17th Regiment is quartered in Portsmouth, where the Hessian Hereditary Prince Regiment lies in garrison.

29 May - In camp at Portsmouth. Corporal [Conrad] Erlbacher, of the von Seybothen Regiment, deserted from the picket this afternoon.

30 May - In camp at Portsmouth. The transport ships sailed back to New York this afternoon, escorted by the frigate Charon. Private Schneider, minor, tried to desert from his post with the picket during the night, but was caught by a patrol.

31 May - In camp at Portsmouth. Yesterday morning the 17th Regiment moved ten miles from here. General Arnold arrived here in Portsmouth and is to return to New York. General Lord Cornwallis has left Petersburg and moved toward Richmond.

1 June - In camp at Portsmouth.

2 June - In camp at Portsmouth. The previously noted, on 30 May, Schneider, minor, of Captain von Stain's Company, told a fellow of the von Seybothen Regiment, that he planned to desert from the most dangerous outpost.

Therefore he was punished by running the gauntlet eighteen times.

3 June - In camp at Portsmouth.

4 June - In camp at Portsmouth. Today is
the birthday of His Majesty, King George III.
A 21-gun salute was fired at the Artillery Post
and all the ships in the local harbor fired
their cannons.

5 June - In camp at Portsmouth.

6 June - In camp at Portsmouth. General
Lord Cornwallis sent fifty prisoners of war to
Portsmouth to be guarded.

7 to 9 June - In camp at Portsmouth.

10 June - In camp at Portsmouth.

11 to 17 June - In camp at Portsmouth.

18 June - In camp at Portsmouth. Five
thousand English troops arrived from England.
Of these, two thousand go to Charleston and
fifteen hundred remain with Lord Cornwallis at
Williamsburg. Fifteen hundred men have gone to
New York.

19 June - In camp at Portsmouth. Private
[Johann Adam] Egler, of the Lieutenant Colonel's Company, had the little finger of his
right hand cut off by Private Mueller, III,
while on a patrol. The remainder of the finger
was amputated at the hospital in Norfolk today.

20 June - In camp at Portsmouth.

21 June - Seven American prisoners were
brought here this morning by the Refugees.
They had been captured thirty miles from here
at Fort Great Bridge.

22 to 27 June - In camp at Portsmouth.

28 June - The Hereditary Prince Regiment
embarked yesterday evening at five o'clock in
the new flatboats. It was ordered to join the
army of Lord Cornwallis at Williamsburg. En
route it received the order to return here and
to reenter its former quarters.

29 June - In camp at Portsmouth.

30 June - In camp at Portsmouth.

1 July - The 17th Regiment marched into

the city this morning and entered quarters in the church. This evening a detachment, under the command of General Leslie, left here in flatboats. It consisted of the following: the 17th, 76th, and 80th English Regiments and the Hereditary Prince Regiment. The strength of this detachment is nine hundred men. These troops had gone about two miles up the James River when they received the order from General Lord Cornwallis to return to Portsmouth.

2 July - In camp at Portsmouth.

3 July - In camp at Portsmouth. The 17th Regiment entered camp here, near Fort Arnold, today.

4 to 6 July - In camp at Portsmouth.

7 July - In camp at Portsmouth. A bear, which had been shot ten miles from here, was brought to the Portsmouth market to be sold. One pound cost four coppers.

8 and 9 July - In camp at Portsmouth.

10 July - A fleet of sixteen empty transport ships arrived here in the harbor this afternoon from New York.

11 July - In camp at Portsmouth.

12 and 13 July - In camp at Portsmouth.

14 July - The Hereditary Prince Regiment marched into camp. During the afternoon this regiment marched back to Portsmouth. The 43rd and 76th Regiments, the Queen's Rangers, and both Ansbach regiments received the order to embark.

15 July - At six o'clock in the evening the two Ansbach regiments embarked on the following ships:

Shipwright - Colonel von Voit

Providence - Lieutenant Colonel von Reitzenstein and Major von Seitz

Harmony - Captain von Eyb

Houston - Colonel von Seybothen

Present Succession - Major von Beust.

The Queen's Rangers and the 43rd and 47th Regiments arrived here at Portsmouth this morning. The Light Infantry is one and one-half miles from Portsmouth. The Hereditary Prince Regiment moved into camp twelve miles from Portsmouth. Four hundred Negroes with 347 women and 223 children were brought here to Portsmouth today. They are from North and South Carolina and Virginia.[9]

16 July - Lying at anchor at Portsmouth. The following regiments were embarked today: the Light Infantry, the Queen's Rangers, and the 43rd and 76th Regiments.

17 July - At two-thirty in the afternoon we sailed from the city of Portsmouth and shortly thereafter anchored.

18 July - We sailed at seven o'clock in the morning and then during the morning anchored at Hampton Roads.

19 July - Lying at anchor at Hampton Roads. At six o'clock this evening there was a severe thunderstorm.

20 to 23 July - At anchor at Hampton Roads.

24 July - At anchor at Hampton Roads. This morning General Lord Cornwallis arrived at the fleet at eight o'clock and looked the region over in comfort. He remained aboard the frigate Richmond until seven o'clock in the evening and then returned to Portsmouth. When he arrived, the frigate Richmond, as commodore, fired a 15-gun salute. The sailors on all the warships climbed the masts and extended honors to him.

25 July - At anchor at Hampton Roads. General Lord Cornwallis came out to the fleet again this morning.

26 July - At anchor at Hampton Roads. Yesterday General Leslie sailed for Charleston on a frigate and will assume command there.

27 July - At anchor at Hampton Roads.

28 July - At anchor at Hampton Roads.

29 July - At nine-thirty this morning the fleet set sail and because the wind was con-

74

trary, it anchored at a quarter to eleven, opposite Hampton. We sailed again at a quarter to eight in the evening but anchored again. General Lord Cornwallis went aboard the frigate Richmond at eight o'clock this morning.

30 July - At five o'clock in the morning the fleet sailed and the anchor was dropped at noon near Cape Henry.

31 July - We sailed at five o'clock in the morning and anchored in Chesapeake Bay at eight o'clock in the morning. We sailed again at three o'clock and anchored in Chesapeake Bay at eight o'clock in the evening.

1 August - At six o'clock in the morning the transport ships, which had not anchored near enough to the warships, set sail and then anchored again at eight o'clock in the morning. On the 29th of the previous month the 80th Regiment came out of Portsmouth, joined the fleet in Hampton Roads, and came here with us in flatboats. We sailed at three o'clock in the afternoon on 1 August and anchored in the York River at eight o'clock in the evening.

2 August - We sailed at seven o'clock in the morning and at nine o'clock anchored at Yorktown. Yesterday evening the 80th Regiment landed at Gloucester, which lies on the right side of the York River.

The remaining regiments debarked today in the following order:

The Jaeger Detachment and the Queen's Rangers to Gloucester.

The 43rd and 76th Regiments, the Light Infantry, and the 1st and 2nd Ansbach Regiments to York.

The headquarters was established at York and the line was formed outside this place.

3 August - In camp at York. The baggage was unloaded and both Ansbach regiments received their tents.

4 August - In camp at York. The transport ships returned to Portsmouth in order to pick

75

up the remaining troops. Private [Wilhelm] Braun, Jr., and [Michael] Vogel, of Captain von Stain's Company, deserted from camp this morning.

5 August - In camp at York.

6 August - In camp at York. It was made known in orders today that 2nd Lieutenant Foerster and Private [Eli] Oettinger, of the Colonel's Company, had died in the hospital at Norfolk.

Promotions in the Colonel's Company

First Sergeant [Georg] Beyer to 2nd lieutenant.

Second Sergeant Albrecht to 1st sergeant.

Corporal [Johann Leonhard] Fickel to 2nd sergeant.

Vice-Corporal Schuster to corporal.

7 August - Privates [Leonhard] Busch and [Johann Michael] Oed, of the Lieutenant Colonel's Company, deserted from camp yesterday. The Hereditary Prince Regiment arrived in the local harbor from Portsmouth in flatboats and landed at Gloucester.

8 August - In camp at York. Nine ships arrived here this afternoon from Portsmouth, bringing troops and baggage.

9 August - In camp at York. There were two very strong thunderstorms today. During the morning two lightning bolts hit. A ranger was hit and killed at his post at the windmill and five sailors in the frigate Spitfire were struck and injured. During the afternoon a private and the wife of a sergeant of the 43rd Regiment were struck dead.

10 August - In camp at York.

11 August - In camp at York.

12 August - In camp at York.

13 and 14 August - In camp at York.

15 August - In camp at York. An express ship arrived from New York today.

16 August - In camp at York. Private [Simon] Hopfer, of the Major's Company, deserted

from the cattle watch.

<u>17 and 18 August</u> - In camp at York.

<u>19 August</u> - In camp at York. A fleet arrived here yesterday evening from Portsmouth.

<u>20 and 21 August</u> - In camp at York.

<u>22 August</u> - This morning a fleet with the remaining troops from Portsmouth arrived here in the local harbor. The [Hessian] Bose Regiment was landed this afternoon and moved into camp on the left wing.

<u>23 and 24 August</u> - In camp at York.

<u>25 August</u> - The frigate <u>Richmond</u> and three other ships sailed for New York this morning.

<u>26 August</u> - A lightning bolt struck a tree not far from the field watch in the Light Infantry camp.

<u>27 August</u> - In camp at York.

<u>28 August</u> - Yesterday evening Pack Servant Birngruber, of the Artillery, and Pack Servant [Johann Konrad] Baumann, of Captain von Stain's Company, deserted from camp, each with two horses.

<u>29 August</u> - In camp at York. The camp was moved at ten o'clock this morning. Both Ansbach regiments moved to where the Light Infantry had been and that unit moved further forward.

<u>30 August</u> - In camp at York. A French naval fleet appeared before the harbor. Therefore, during the night a battery was established at the waterside and fortification of the rest of the line was continued vigorously.

<u>31 August</u> - In camp at York.

<u>1 September</u> - In camp at York.

<u>2 September</u> - It is reported that six thousand French landed yesterday at Hampton Roads. Four French warships came to anchor this afternoon at the mouth of the local harbor. The cannons of the warship <u>Charon</u>, which lies at anchor here in the harbor, were unloaded and placed in the battery at the

waterside.   Efforts to   complete the   defenses
are continuing day and night.
   3 September - In camp at York.
   4 September - Second Lieutenant Schuchard,
of Colonel von Seybothen's Regiment, died of a
high fever at one-thirty this afternoon at York
and was buried this evening without ceremony.
The 80th   Regiment was brought   over from
Gloucester and entered camp here.
   5 September - The entire army changed camp
and Colonel von Voit's Regiment was placed in
the first line. Private [Johann] Blind, of the
Lieutenant Colonel's [Company], deserted from
the cattle guard.
   Three French ships joined those warships
lying at anchor at the mouth of the harbor.
   6 September - Five French ships sailed a-
way this afternoon and only two now remain
lying at anchor.
   7 September - The French warships still
lying at anchor sailed away at nine o'clock
this morning.
   8 to 11 September - In camp at York.
   12 September - Two small express boats arrived from New York. This afternoon the French
war fleet passed by on the York River and
sailed out into Chesapeake Bay because Admiral
Graves supposedly has arrived with twenty
warships.
   13 September - Two French warships made a
patrol as far as the mouth of the harbor, but
then sailed back into Chesapeake Bay.
   14 September - This morning an enemy patrol, consisting of fifty cavalry, clashed with
Colonel [Banastre] Tarleton's outposts and they
exchanged fire. During the afternoon three
French warships sailed into the mouth of the
harbor and dropped anchor. Two other ships
were seen in the bay. The English guard ship
had to pull further back into the harbor.
   15 September - The three French warships
mentioned yesterday are still at anchor in the

78

harbor.

16 September - All of our transport ships
were pulled back in a line very close to the
city. The powder magazine was established in
the ground outside the city.

17 September - One of the three French
ships moved farther out in the bay and dropped
anchor there.

18 September - In camp at York.

19 September - The French fleet sailed
past the mouth of the harbor and took on either
troops or provisions at Baltimore.

20 September - A French warship arrived
today and anchored at the usual place.

21 September - All houses at York which
stand outside the lines will be torn down. The
fortifications continue to be strengthened.

22 September - During the night a fireship
was sent out of the harbor against the four
French warships lying at anchor. Two of these
warships were set afire at one o'clock in the
night. The other two still lie at anchor but
have moved further out in the bay. It is
believed they ran aground as they are lying
very near land. During the night numerous
cannon shots were heard from one o'clock until
it was day. Some may have been emergency
shots, but some may have been cannons on the
burning ships, which were loaded [and due to
the heat exploded].

Private May, of the Major's Company, deserted from camp at five o'clock this morning.

Note well! - The above incident is re-
peated. Four fireships were sent out and
because they were ignited too soon, the French
ships cut their anchor ropes and two sailed
away. The other two ran aground but were
refloated and once again are lying at anchor at
the previous location.

23 September - The two French ships which
lay at anchor have withdrawn so far that
nothing but the tips of their masts can be

seen.

<u>24 September</u> - In camp at York. Three French warships have anchored at the mouth of the harbor.

<u>25 September</u> - The three French warships are still lying at anchor.

<u>26 and 27 September</u> - In camp at York.

<u>28 September</u> - The enemy took post today a mile from our camp and the outposts have exchanged fire continuously. Two 4-pound cannonballs landed near the non-commissioned officers picket this evening. Some transport ships were sunk in the harbor. The Hereditary Prince Regiment was brought across from Gloucester and entered the second line on the left wing. The baggage and tents were sent to the city.

<u>29 September</u> - At daybreak the firing against the outposts resumed. The enemy troops have massed primarily against our left wing and attacked our pickets, but our cannons have stoutly resisted them. The following men of the Ansbach picket have been killed or wounded:

Private [Egide] Zeilmann, of Colonel von Seybothen's Regiment, killed and three privates of the regiment wounded.

Grenadier Roetter and Private Gruber, of the von Voit Regiment, wounded.

<u>30 September</u> - During the night, at two o'clock, our army pulled the line back toward the city of York. During this retreat Grenadier [Georg Jakob] Mueller and Private [Leonhard] Hartlein, Jr., of Captain von Stain's Company, deserted. The first from the picket; the latter remained in the camp. Three men also deserted from the von Seybothen Regiment. As soon as we had retreated, the enemy entered our [former] positions and attacked the right wing. However, our cannonfire, which was well directed, drove the enemy back in less than half an hour.

The 80th Regiment was transferred over to

Gloucester.

<u>1 October</u> - The enemy laid out two defensive positions. Therefore, the workers were heavily fired upon from our line, both day and night.
Yesterday a brigadier general[4] and today a French hussar were captured and brought in.

<u>2 October</u> - In camp in the line at York. Because of the enemy workers, today our cannons fired upon them more heavily than yesterday. Because of a shortage of forage, most of the horses' throats were cut.[5] An express entered here at nine o'clock tonight from New York. The French ships fired heavily on this ship. It brought the news that a war fleet of thirty sail and five thousand English troops was being sent here.

<u>3 October</u> - The cannonfire from our lines against the enemy workers was not as heavy as yesterday and the day before.

<u>4 October</u> - Today there was little cannonfire from our lines. At nine-thirty at night the enemy attacked a Light Infantry work detail on the left wing. At Gloucester, at the same time, there was an enemy attack. The attack lasted less than half an hour. The remainder of the night we fired cannons continuously at the enemy workers.

<u>5 October</u> - The cannonfire from our lines was not heavy today. The picket on the left wing was constantly under attack by the enemy, all night long, and our cannonfire into the enemy camp continued without let up.

<u>6 October</u> - At eight o'clock in the evening the right wing, and in particular the redoubt beyond our line, in which the 23rd Regiment stood, was attacked by the enemy. A rocket rose from the redoubt at once, as a signal to our line, whereupon the cannonfire from all our positions in the line began and continued throughout the night. Within a few minutes the enemy had to withdraw. Fifteen

transport ships which were in the harbor were
sunk quite close to the city.

7 October - The cannonfire from our lines
today was not as heavy as yesterday. The enemy
constructed redoubts and trenches opposite our
lines. Grenadier [Lorenz] Jacobi deserted from
his post with the picket.

8 October - At five o'clock in the morning
an enemy patrol engaged several posts on our
left wing, causing them to fire at one
another. At Gloucester during this night we
made a small attack against the enemy pickets.

9 October - At three o'clock in the afternoon the enemy opened fire with the cannons in
his newly constructed fort opposite our right
wing. There was heavy fire against the frigate
Gaudalupe and the ship had to retreat into the
harbor. The English Quartermaster General Par-
kins and Lieutenant Robinson,⁶ of the 76th Regiment, were both killed [by enemy fire] while
eating. Grenadier [Johann Georg] Dorsch and
two privates of the von Seybothen Regiment
deserted from their posts with the picket.

10 October - At two o'clock in the morning
the enemy, from the defensive positions
opposite our left wing, began to fire bombs and
cannonballs into our camp, causing serious
damage. During the morning five men of Colonel
von Seybothen's Regiment were wounded, including Privates [Johann Wilhelm] Seewald and
Durer, fatally wounded. The latter had a foot
amputated.

Major Gordon arrived as an express from
New York and brought the news that the English
fleet was near Chesapeake Bay.

Private Boser, of the Colonel's [Company],
deserted from the picket. Seewald died this
afternoon of his wound.

The enemy fired bombs at the frigate Charon, which caused it and a transport to be
destroyed by fire.

11 October - At two o'clock this morning

the Ansbach picket was attacked and had to
retreat. Two transport ships in the harbor
were set afire by enemy bombs this morning.

Sergeant [Michael] Hoffmann, of Captain
von Stain's Company, and Grenadier Roser, were
wounded. The first by a cannonball; the latter
by shrapnel from a bomb.

Privates [Johann Georg] Bessenecker, of
the Colonel's [Company], and [Nikolaus] Schubert, of the Lieutenant Colonel's [Company],
died in the hospital.

Private Ferch, of the Major's [Company],
was wounded by a piece of shrapnel from a bomb,
and Private Kaempf, of Colonel von Seybothen's
Regiment, was wounded by wood splinters which
had been hit by a bomb.

Private Tuerk, of Captain von Stain's Company, and a private of the von Seybothen Regiment, were killed on patrol, and two privates
of Colonel von Voit's Regiment were wounded.

During the night the following deserted
from the picket:

Privates [Johann Michael] Ostertag[7] and
Stockmohr, of the Lieutenant Colonel's [Com-
pany],

Escherich and Roessler, Sr., of Captain
von Stain's [Company], and

Private [Ignatius] Laeus, of the von Seybothen Regiment.

This night the enemy attacked the defensive positions manned by the 23rd Regiment, but
was again driven back by our cannonfire.

The Light Infantry picket was attacked
twice.

12 October - Private Lauterbach, while on
work detail, had his heel shot off.

Yesterday the enemy fired a heavy cannonade and many bombs fell on us. Wounded were:

1) Grenadier Wolf,

2) Private Schuler, of the Lieutenant
Colonel's [Company],

3) Private [Andreas] Cantusch, of von

Stain's Company.
    Drummer Schindelbauer, of the von Sey-
bothen Regiment, deserted while on patrol.
    13 October - The Light Infantry picket was
attacked this morning.
    Wounded in the tents in the trenches were:
        1) Private [Konrad] Koerner and
        2) Private [Kaspar] Appold, of the Colo-
nel's [Company], by a bomb which landed in a
tent. The first lost a foot; the latter was
wounded in the knee.
        3) Fuchs, of Stain's [Company], wounded
in the breast by shrapnel from a bomb.
    Private Wagner, of the Lieutenant Colo-
nel's Company, was killed by a bomb which hit
his tent.
    The enemy's cannonade was heavy and before
the many bombs, which constantly came in, a
person is no longer safe in camp. Grenadier
Stuezel, of Colonel von Seybothen's Regiment,
had his foot shot off by a bomb.
    Corporal [Christian] Schuster, of Colonel
von Voit's Regiment, while with the picket on
patrol, had his right arm shot off. Private
[Konrad] Koerner, of the Colonel's [Company],
had his foot amputated.
    The following deserted from the lieuten-
ant's picket:
        1) Grenadier Ratler
        2) Private [Johann Simon] Rueckert,[8] of
the Lieutenant Colonel's [Company]
        3) Private [Michael] Vogel, of the Ma-
jor's [Company], and
        4) Two privates of the von Seybothen Reg-
iment.
    Private [Johann] Fricker, of the Major's
[Company] deserted from the non-commissioned
officer's picket.
    The servants of both Captains von Eyb and
von Metzsch were wounded while trying to dig up
a bomb.[9]
    Private Riess, of the Grenadier Company,

was wounded by a bomb.

A regimental cannon was blown up by a bomb.

Captain [Hermann Christian] Roll, of the [Hessian] Bose Regiment, was killed while on picket.

At eight o'clock at night the enemy attacked our right wing but was driven back. Immediately after this attack, both our [outer] defensive positions on the left wing were attacked and conquered by the enemy.[10] The larger position had one hundred men under the command of Lieutenant Colonel McPherson and the smaller one was commanded by Major Kempel.

Corporal Boser, of the Lieutenant Colonel's [Company], was killed by a bomb while on work detail.

First Lieutenant von Reitzenstein was wounded on the shin bone by shrapnel from a bomb.

[There is no entry dated 14 October 1781.]

15 October - The following deserted from picket:

Grenadier [Michael] Marquart,[11]

Private [Johann] Meier, II, of the Major's [Company], and

two privates from the von Seybothen Regiment.

The hospital was transferred across to Gloucester.

A bomb hit the regimental bake oven, wounding Corporal [Christoph] Schilling and Private [Wilhelm] Auernheimer, of Stain's Company.

Throughout the night there was little cannonfire from the enemy and only four bombs fell into our camp.

16 October - The English Grenadiers and Light Infantry made a sortie during the night and spiked eleven enemy cannons. One captain and three grenadiers of the French army were made prisoners. According to [their] reports a

war fleet of 33 sail has arrived in Chesapeake Bay near our fleet. The French army has about fifteen thousand men here. Since yesterday four French ships are lying at the local harbor entrance.

Today the enemy opened new batteries opposite our left wing and cannonaded us in a frightful manner.

This afternoon a non-commissioned officer of the Hereditary Prince Regiment was wounded when both his feet were shot off.

A sailor had a hand and a foot shot off.

An English engineer was shot through the body by a cannonball.

The wife of an English cannoneer was shot through the body, also.

At four-thirty in the afternoon the wife of Lieutenant Rummel died in the Ansbach hospital.

The Light Infantry was transferred across to Gloucester.

17 October - The enemy fired an astonishing cannonade this morning. A flag of truce went to the enemy camp this morning. The Light Infantry was returned here from Gloucester at midday. A detail of Ansbachers took duty at the Hornwork, under the command of Lieutenant Colonel von Reitzenstein, during the absence of the Light Infantry. Private [Johann Simon] Kern, Sr., of the Colonel's Company, while carrying food out to his comrades, was killed by a cannonball. Shortly thereafter a member of the Light Infantry had his head shot off.

Private [Georg] Schmelzer, of the Major's Company, deserted from a patrol.

The enemy sent over a flag of truce. During the afternoon we sent one to the enemy which resulted in a ceasefire after five o'-clock in the afternoon.

At eight o'clock in the evening a powder magazine blew up due to the carelessness of an

artilleryman, who took in a light. Twelve
people were killed by this accident, including
Private [Jakob] Gunckel, of the Major's Company, who was present as he had just gone on
watch at this time and was killed by the blast.
    18 October - Private [Christoph] Meissner,
of the Colonel's [Company], died yesterday in
the hospital at Gloucester.
    Private Rosenbauer was promoted to vice-
corporal on the sixteenth of this month and
Vice-Corporal Gackstetter was promoted to
corporal in the Lieutenant Colonel's Company.
Grenadier [Johann Michael] Eberlein died at
Gloucester. Corporal [Johann Heinrich] Popp,
of Colonel von Seybothen's Regiment, was promoted to 2nd lieutenant.
    19 October - In camp at York. Two French
warships entered the harbor and took over the
English fleet.
                _ _ _ _ _ _ _

Order from General Lord Cornwallis
Headquarters, October 19, 1781
    Lord Cornwallis can not adequately express
the appreciation he owes the officers and men
of this army for their good conduct at every
opportunity since he has had the honor to
command them, but especially for their
extraordinary courage and determination in
defending this position. He sincerely regrets
that their exertions were unable to withstand
the superior artillery which opposed them and
that the blood of such brave people was shed in
vain. Lord Cornwallis had done everything in
his power to get the provision enabling the
army to be returned to Europe. Since this
could not be ratified, he had tried to obtain
the best treatment for the troops as long as
they would be in captivity. Above all, he
wanted to insure that they were always provided
with the necessities until their freedom was
again obtained. The tents and remaining supplies are not to be wasted.

- - - - - - -

At three o'clock in the afternoon the
entire army marched out, with music playing,
after the defensive positions on the left wing
were occupied by the French and American
troops. From the enemy trenches on, the French
stood on the right and the American army stood
on the left, both of which paraded in the most
splendid and best order. We marched through
both armies and where they ended, we marched in
two lines and at four-forty-five lay down our
weapons. Afterward we returned through both
armies, which had their weapons by their feet,
and into our camp in the city.

20 October – An American commissary conducted a muster of the regiments this morning.

Those of our soldiers who had served with
the French or American armies were released
yesterday. Those of Colonel von Voit's Regiment were Grenadier Braun and Private Katzenwinkel, of Captain von Stain's [Company].
Corporal Schuster, of the Colonel's Company,
died of his wounds in the hospital at Gloucester. The corps which General Lord Cornwallis had commanded consisted of five thousand
men. On the other hand, the Americans and
French armies amounted to forty thousand men.

21 October – The prisoners were escorted
out of York in the afternoon by an American
escort.[12] Halfway to Williamsburg the night camp
was made in an open field.

22 October – The following officers of
Colonel von Voit's Regiment marched into captivity with the regiment. The others went on
parole to Long Island, 32 miles from New York.
    From Colonel von Voit's Regiment
    1)   Captain von Ellrodt
    2)   Captain von Stain
    3)   Captain von Koenitz
    4)   1st Lieutenant von Marschall
    5)   1st Lieutenant von Trechsel
    6)   2nd Lieutenant Prechtel

7) 2nd Lieutenant Drexel
8) 2nd Lieutenant Baumann
9) 2nd Lieutenant von Fabrice
10) 2nd Lieutenant Halbmeier
11) Artillery Lieutenant Hofmann
12) Regimental Surgeon Rapp
13) Chaplain Wagner
From Colonel von Seybothen's Regiment
1) Major von Beust
2) Captain von Quesnoy
3) Staff Captain von Metzsch
4) 1st Lieutenant von Kruse
5) 1st Lieutenant von Reitzenstein
6) 2nd Lieutenant Weinhart
7) 2nd Lieutenant von Cyriacy
8) 2nd Lieutenant Graebner
9) 2nd Lieutenant Lindemeier

- - - - - - -

[At this point in the German manuscript Prechtel entered the articles of capitulation. As the articles are available in English in a number of publications, they have not been included with this translation.]

- - - - - - -

List of the Dead, Wounded, and Missing
of the British Army
From September 28 to October 19, 1781[13]

In all 2 captains, 4 lieutenants, 13 sergeants, 4 drummers, and 133 privates killed.

Five lieutenants, 1 ensign, 24 sergeants, 11 drummers, and 285 privates wounded.

One major, 2 captains, 1 subaltern, 5 sergeants, and 63 privates missing.

Total 552

Report

Those soldiers of the 1st Regiment of His Serene Highness of Brandenburg-Onolz and Kulmbach who have died in the hospital in New York [in 1777].

From Captain von Ellrodt's [Grenadier] Company

1. 2nd Lieutenant Kublan, July 15, 1777
2. Grenadier [Johann] Deuer, August 1, 1777
3. Grenadier [Johann Nikolaus] Geitz, Sr., August 8
4. Sergeant [Heinrich] Schreiner, August 22
5. Grenadier [Balthasar] Balz, August 27
6. Grenadier [Jakob] Frohmueller, August 28
7. Grenadier [Johann Simon] Beck, August 30
8. Grenadier [Christian Felix] Heumann, September 3
9. Corporal [Ernst Abraham] Wirth, September 17
10. Grenadier [Leonhard] Maltz, September 17
11. Grenadier [Johann Michael] Kriegbaum, October 10
12. Captain [Ludwig Heinrich Vollrath] von Erckert, October 11
13. Grenadier [Johann Michael] Lutz, November 6
14. Grenadier [Nikolaus] Doerrer, December 8

From Colonel von Voit's Company

15. Musketeer [Georg] Wender, June 24
16. Musketeer [Johann] Broegel, July 8
17. Musketeer [Georg] Mader, July 8
18. Musketeer [Johann] Foertsch, July 29
19. Musketeer [Johann Leonhard] Wuestendoerfer, August 4
20. Musketeer Feeh, August 5
21. Musketeer [Johann Leonhard] Seiss, August 8

22. Musketeer [Johann] Schorr, August 17
23. Musketeer [Johann Michael] Rinnecker, September 5
24. Musketeer [Johann] Foerster, October 28

[From Major Christoph Ludwig Baron von Reitzenstein's Company]

25. Musketeer [Heinrich Wilhelm] Zinn, July 11
26. Musketeer [Gottlieb] Stoll, July 24
27. Musketeer Christian Hoffmann, July 26
28. Musketeer Foerster, August 11
29. Musketeer [Jakob] Zeller, August 20
30. Musketeer [Peter Paul] Schmidt, August 20
31. Musketeer Wintermann, October 13

[From Captain von Waldenfels' Company]

32. Musketeer Kaufmann, July 12
33. Musketeer [Wolfgang] Seehausen, July 29
34. Musketeer [Wendel] Hammerter, September 3
35. Musketeer [Johann] Wiebemann, September 5
36. Musketeer [Peter] Stintz, September 7
37. Musketeer [Georg] Eyrisch, September 7
38. Musketeer [Andreas] Brey, September 8
39. Musketeer Kirsch, September 26
40. Musketeer [Georg] Ermert, September 3
41. Corporal [Leonhard] Vetter, September 20
42. Musketeer [Christoph] Reuther, October 3
43. Corporal [Johann] Lehr, July 23
44. Musketeer [Johann Christoph] Flechtner, August 26
45. Musketeer [Michael] Stummer, August 31

From Captain von Stain's Company

46. Musketeer [Johann] Reiss. September 4
47. Musketeer [Johann Christoph] Fischer,

September 4
      48.   Musketeer [Johann Peter] Hipsch, Oc-
tober 13
      49.   Musketeer Bauer II, January 23, 1778
            From the Artillery
      50.   Cannoneer [Johann] Zink, September 7
      51.   Cannoneer Waeger, October 3
            From the Lower Staff
      52.   Regimental   Quartermaster   [Johann
Christoph] Fuchs, September 27
      All 52 of these men died and were buried
in New York from June 24, 1777, to December 8,
1777, unwounded, except that enemy balls
fatally wounded both Captain von Erckert and
Grenadier Kriegbaum at Fort Montgomery. Bauer
II, of Stain's Company, died on January 23,
1778.
            - - - - - - -
      Those who died here and there [in 1777 and
                        1778]
      1.   Grenadier [Johann Georg] Hochwein, Ap-
ril 17, at sea
      2.   Grenadier [Johann] Meyer, August 8, in
the camp at Harlem
      3.   Cannoneer [Michael] Zeder, and
      4.   Grenadier [Matthias] Lorenz, [both on
August 21], drowned while bathing
      5.   Grenadier [Johann Nikolaus] Geitz,
Sr., at Martin's Wharf, 1777
      6.   Musketeer [Philipp Matthias] Sitzmann,
aboard ship near Staten Island
      7.   Grenadier [Johann] Koerner, on the
voyage from New York to Philadelphia
      8.   Musketeer [Johann Adam] Fuekentscher,
of the Colonel's Company
      9.   Musketeer [Leonhard] Rothgangel, of
the Major's Company
      10. Musketeer Weiant, of the Major's Com-
pany
      11.   Musketeer Hohberger, of the Major's
Company
      12.   Cannoneer [Georg] Kern, Rhode Island

during August 29, 1778 battle
   13. Grenadier [Johann Georg] Elmajer,
killed by a cannonball
   14. Musketeer [Johann] Lenkum, killed by
a musketball
   15. Grenadier [Johann Michael] Frueh, fatally wounded by a cannonball, died September 3
at Newport.
   Died in the hospital at Newport
   16. Corporal Schultheiss, February 2,
1779, he had previously had both legs amputated
   17. Grenadier [Jakob] Kaufmann, February
2, 1779, and
   18. Musketeer [Andreas] Herterich, February 8, 1779, both were from the first recruit
shipment
   19. Grenadier [Johann Georg] Schultheiss,
February 16, 1779
   20. Musketeer [Peter] Meier, of Major
Seitz' Company, April 4, 1779
   21. Musketeer [Johann Christian] Auernheimer, of Stain's Company, April 8, of the
first recruit shipment suddenly taken sick
after eating a poison root which one of his
comrades had gathered and cooked, thinking it
was something else, but which kills many.
Within an hour, from being healthy, he was
dead. His comrades, however, by induced vomiting, were kept alive.
   Rhode Island, in the city of Newport
   22. Musketeer [Friedrich] Klein, of the
Major's Company, May 8, 1779
   23. Musketeer [Georg Michael] Vogel, of
the Colonel's Company, May 1
   24. Musketeer Lehr, from Stain's Company,
in New York, July 23, 1777
   25. Medic [Friedrich] Gollwitz, on September 9, when he suddenly died of an
apoplectic stroke. At eight o'clock in the
morning he had shaved and he had eaten at noon
with his cook. He then lay down and slept
well, but did not awaken again. As soon as the

troops in the quarters were aware of this, he
was dead. He was buried at three o'clock on
the eleventh.

Desertions
From the Grenadier Company

1. Uebelacker
2. [Friedrich] Stoll
3. [Christoph] Bernhart
4. [Johann Georg] Rummel
5. [Simon] Gruber

From Colonel von Voit's Company

1. Corporal Klein
2. Private Dreschel
3. Private [Johann Ludwig] Dietlein
4. Private [Johann Balthasar] Schoenell
5. Private [Michael] Lorenz
6. Private [Georg] Ermert
7. Private [Heinrich] Bonn

From [Lieutenant] Colonel von Reitzenstein's Company

1. Private [Johann] Luck
2. Private [Matthias] Rhau
3. Private Telorac
4. Private [Jakob] Dill

From Major von Seitz' Company

1. Carpenter [Johann Michael] Eckert
2. Private Thormann
3. Private [Johann] Brummer
4. Private Schard
5. Private [Gottlob] Friedrich
6. Private [Heinrich] Blecker
7. Private Zipfel, Jr.
8. Private Zipfel, Sr.
9. Private [Lorenz] Baumann
10. Private [Johann] Stadler

From Captain von Stain's Company

1. Private Katzenwinkel
2. Private Braun
3. Private [Johann] Erlwein
4. Private Kassel
5. Private [Johann Georg] Ulzhoeffer
6. Private [Peter] Hunger

7.   Private Schaeffer, of the first recruit shipment but brought back to the regiment
and punished by having to run the gauntlet
twelve times a day for two days in a row.

THE PRECHTEL DIARY

1777-1783

by Johann Ernst Prechtel

From the Bavarian State Archives
Munich, Germany

THE PRECHTEL DIARY

1777-1783

March 1777 '

After Colonel von Voit's Bayreuth Regiment was ordered to Ansbach, and on
The 5th - assembled there, then on
The 6th - the baggage from both the Infantry Regiments von Eyb and von Voit, and the Jaeger Company von Cramon, was sent from Ansbach.
The officers of both regiments and the Field Jaeger Company, who marched out with us, are:²

I - Colonel von Eyb's Regiment

Colonel [Friedrich Ludwig Albrecht] von Eyb
Major [Christoph Ludwig] Baron von Reitzenstein
Grenadier Captain [Ludwig Heinrich Vollrath] von Erckert
Captain [Christian Philipp] von Ellrodt
Captain von Stain, or Stein
Staff Captain [Christoph Friedrich Joseph] von Waldenfels
1st Lieutenant [Friedrich Wilhelm] von Roeder
1st Lieutenant [Christoph] von Metzsch
1st Lieutenant [Ernst Ludwig] von Tritschler von Faulkenstein
1st Lieutenant [August Christian Friedrich] von Koenitz, Adjutant
1st Lieutenant Wilhelm Friedrich Ernst], Baron von Reitzenstein
1st Lieutenant [Friedrich] von Schoenfeld
1st Lieutenant [Moritz Wilhelm] von der Heyde
2nd Lieutenant [Karl Friedrich] von Adels-

heim
        2nd Lieutenant   [Johann Friedrich] Sichart
von Sichartshof
        2nd Lieutenant   [Friedrich] von Soden
        2nd Lieutenant   [Karl Friedrich Eugen] von
Woellwarth
        2nd Lieutenant   [Friedrich] von Keller
        2nd Lieutenant   [Wilhelm] Marschall   von
Bieberstein
        2nd Lieutenant   [Ernst Ludwig] Trechsel von
Teufstetten
        2nd Lieutenant   [Johann Wilhelm]   von Mar-
defeld
        2nd Lieutenant von Diemar, Sr.
        2nd Lieutenant Kublan

Lower Staff

        Artillery Lieutenant   [Nikolaus Friedrich]
Hofmann
        Lieutenant and Auditor [Konrad] Rummel
        Doctor [Johann David]   Schoepf, Field Phy-
sician
        Regimental   Quartermaster   [Johann Chris-
tian] Fuchs
        Regimental Surgeon [Friedrich] Rapp
        Field Chaplain [Johann Christoph] Wagner

II - Colonel von Voit's Regiment

        Colonel   [August Valentin]   von   Voit von
Salzburg
        Major   [Johann   Heinrich Christian Franz]
von Seybothen
        Captain [Friedrich Ernst Carl] von Beust
        Grenadier Captain [Philipp Friedrich] von
Seitz
        Captain [Friedrich Ludwig] von Eyb
        Staff Captain [Andreas Friedrich] von Rey-
her
        1st Lieutenant [Christian   Theodor Sigis-
mund] von Molitor

1st Lieutenant [Georg Heinrich] von Quesnoy

1st Lieutenant von Witzleben

1st Lieutenant [Friedrich] von Kruse

1st Lieutenant [Christoph] Seidel, Adjutant

1st Lieutenant [Philipp Otto Heinrich] von Beust

1st Lieutenant [Friedrich] von Adelsheim

2nd Lieutenant [Ludwig] Baron von Reitzenstein

2nd Lieutenant [Maximilian] von Streit

2nd Lieutenant [Karl Alexander] von Weitershausen

2nd Lieutenant von Diemar, Jr.

2nd Lieutenant [Georg Gustav Lebrecht] von Tunderfeld

2nd Lieutenant [Andreas Karl] von Altenstein

2nd Lieutenant [Philipp Christian] Wagner

2nd Lieutenant [Johann Sebastian] von Molitor

2nd Lieutenant [Adolf Daniel] von Strahlendorf

2nd Lieutenant [Heinrich] Weinhart

Lower Staff

Lieutenant and Auditor [Johann Friedrich von] Herrnbauer

Regimental Quartermaster [Johann Georg] Daig

Regimental Surgeon [Christian] Pflug

Catholic Regimental Chaplain Peter Pierot

Field Jaeger Company

Captain [Christoph] von Cramon

1st Lieutenant [Heinrich Carl Philipp] von Feilitzsch

2nd Lieutenant [Friedrich] Ebenauer

2nd Lieutenant [Karl] von Forstner

Each grenadier company had one hundred men
and each musket company, 123 men. The field
jaeger companies consisted of one hundred men,
also.[3]
    The 7th - Both regiments, as well as the
Field Jaeger Company, marched from Ansbach and
entered their quarters:
    1)   The Eyb Regiment at Marktbergel
    2)   The Voit Regiment at Burgbernheim
    3)   The Field Jaegers were sent to Otten-
hofen.
    The 8th - The troops were put into night
quarters at Uffenheim.
    The 9th - The march continued to Ochsen-
furt and the regiments were loaded aboard ship
during the evening.
    The 10th - Because the ships were rather
crowded and therefore more had to be brought
from the ships' [supplier] from Wuerzburg, they
remained lying at anchor on the Main River.[4]
    The 11th - The Prince arrived at his
regiments at Ochsenfurt this morning and himself made the journey to Dordrecht in the staff
ship.
    We departed Ochsenfurt this morning at
nine o'clock.
        Inhabited Places on the Main River
    On the left: Gossmannsdorf, Winterhausen,
Hazfeld, Festung Marienburg, Kloster Himmels
Pfortia, Kloster Ink, Zell, Marienhoechheim,
Erlabrunn, Zellingen, Himmelstadt, Laudenbach,
Muehlbach, Karlburg, Harrburg
    On the right: Klein Ochsenfurt, Sommers-
hausen, Bibelstadt, Randersacker, Wuerzburg,
Veitshoechheim, Thuengersheim, Retzbach, Karl-
stadt, Wernfeld - Anchored here at night.
    The 12th - Underway at two-thirty in the
morning.
    On the left: Steinbach, Sendelbach,
Pflochsbach, Erlach, Zimmern, Hattenfeld, Leng-
furt, Homburg, Arfeld, Eichel, Wertheim, Gruen-

enwoert, Mondfeld, Freudenberg, [Klein] Heu-
bach, Laudenbach, Rennfeld, Woerth, Obernburg,
Gross Wallstadt
     On the right: Gemuenden, Langenprozellen,
Sackenbach, Lohr, Rodenbach, Neustadt, Rot-
henfels, Hafenlohr, Loeffelstein, Trannfeld,
Kreuzwertheim, Hasloch, Faulbach, Stadtpro-
zellen, Dorfprozellen, Fechenbach, Geichsen-
hausen, Engelsburg, Grossheubach, Klingenberg,
Erlenbach, Elsenfeld, Klein Wallstadt -
Anchored here at night.
     The 13th - Underway at six o'clock in the
morning.
     On the left: Niederberg, Leider,
Stockstadt, Dittingen, Kleinen Welzheim, Sel-
ingenstadt, Klein Krotzenburg, Hastadt, Au,
Kleinen Steinheim, Grossen Steinheim
     On the right: Obernau, Aschaffenburg, Ox-
fort, Klein Ostheim, Mainflingen, Grossen
Welzheim, Gross Kortzenburg, Hanau, Keestadt,
Philippruf - Anchored here.
     The 14th - The regiments received other
ships near Hanau and during the morning
transferred to them. Because of contrary winds
the ships had to remain at anchor.
     Note - The Pilot Bechtel from Hanau guided
the ships to Dordrecht.
     From the Colonel's Company of the Eyb Reg-
iment, deserters at Hanau were: Corporal Klein
and Private Drexel.
     The 15th - Underway early, at daybreak.
     On the left: Dietesheim, Muehlheim,
Rumpelheim, Bergel, Offenbach, Sachsenhausen,
Niederrad, Kelsterbach, Raunheim, Ruesselsheim,
Weisenau - The Rhine flows past Mainz where the
Main river enters. We anchored below Mainz.
     On the right: Doernigheim, Bergen, Fech-
enheim, Frankfurt, Griesheim, Schwanheim, Nied,
Hoechst, Sindlingen, Hattersheim, Floersheim,
Kostheim, Rotheim.
     The 16th - Underway at seven o'clock in
the morning.

Inhabited Places on the Rhine River

On the left: Mombach, St. Rochusberg, Bingen - the Nahe River enters the Rhine here, Mouse Tower and nearby Bingen Gap, Klemenskapelle, Dreieckshausen, Heimbach, Bacharach, Ober Wesel, Hessian Rheinfels - the Cat, St. Goar, Konstein, Boppard, Spay, Nieder Spay, Kappeln

On the right: Bieberich, Walluf, Ochfeld, Hattenheim, Oestrich, Winkel, Mittelheim - to the right side of Kloster Johannisberg, Geisenheim, Ruedesheim, Lorch, Lorchhausen, The Pfalz, Kaub - castle above, St. Quer - outside, above the Mouse, Assmannshausen, Wellmich, Hezenach, Pflaz/Valsing, Osterspai, Braubach - castle above, Lahnstein, Niederlahnstein - Here the Lahn River enters the Rhine. Pfaffendorf - Anchored here in the evening.

The 17th - Underway at daybreak.

On the left: Koblenz - the Mosel joins the Rhine River here, Kesselheim, Zollengers, Bendorf - to the right of County Sayn - Carpenter Ecker deserted here. Urmitz - We anchored here from twelve o'clock noon until two o'clock in the afternoon because of contrary winds. Weissenthurm - We anchored here opposite an island at four-forty-five because of contrary winds.

On the right: Koblenz - in a valley with a ferry - The large fortress Ehrenbreitstein, above, fired a 24-cannon salute as we passed. Pastianni, Engers

The 18th - Underway at five-thirty in the morning.

On the left: Andernach, Rhein Brohl, Bad Breisig, Remagen, Kloster Apronobis-Berg, Muehheim, Bonn, Hersel, Rheindorf, Niederhersel, Wesel, Wiess, Suerth, Roenkirchen, Cologne - Anchored here in the evening.

On the right: Neuwied - from which a 24-cannon salute as we passed, Leutesdorf, Hammerstein, Linz, Linzhausen, Erpel, Unkel,

Bad Honnef, Ober Winter, Unter Winter, Dol-
lendorf, Adorf, Zuendorf
    The 19th - Sailed at daybreak.
    On the left: Stiel, Langen, Worringen,
Dormagen, Zons, Stuerzelberg, Machesschoen,
Grimlingshausen, Nichts Eine Vestung, Heerds,
Uerdingen, Batberg, Essenburg, Homberg, Imhal -
Because a severe thunder storm arose, we
anchored.
    On the right: Porz, Muehlheim, Stammheim,
Fluehdorf, Wuestdorf, Rheindorf, Westdorf,
Hitdorf, Baumberg, Himmelgriss, Betlehem,
Osterstein, Duesseldorf - A 20-gun salute was
fired three times as we passed. Kaiserwerth,
Wittlaer, Eng, Angeroth, Wanum, Muehlheim, Ruhr
- The Ruhr River enters the Rhine and a strait
has been built for the Dutch ships.
    The 20th - Because of weak and contrary
winds, the entire day was spent lying at anchor
near Imhal.
    The 21st - Underway at six-thirty in the
morning.
    On the left: Ball, Orsoy, Blauhaus
    On the right: Diebek, Lentershaus, Wied-
schlagen, Betlehem, Inruhalem, Bek, Hamm -
Because of contrary winds we anchored at nine
o'clock in the morning. At ten o'clock, on
orders of the Prince, the regiments were landed
and the first prayer hour was held with the
Prince present.
    Underway again at five o'clock in the eve-
ning.
    On the left: Rumberg, Trompet, Buerk
    On the right: Wesel - a Prussian garrison
- The Lippe River enters the Rhine River here.
In the evening a strong storm arose. Therefore
we had to anchor.
    The 22nd - Underway at five-thirty in the
morning.
    On the left: Sanda - Because a strong
storm struck again, we anchored at eight o'-
clock in the morning.

On the right: Sander, Bislich
The 23rd - Underway at five o'clock in the morning.
On the left: Kalken, Grali, Bauern-schanz, Kalkar, Krind
On the right: Rees, Endenbusch, Turenk -
Because of strong storm winds, we anchored at eight-thirty.
As the weather improved, underway at two-thirty in the afternoon.
On the left: Klackerberg, Cleve, Goecken - Anchored here at five-thirty.
On the right: Emmerich, Ober Eltern, Nieder Eltern
The 24th - Underway early.
On the left: Goeckertheim, Hoelehausen, Nijmegen - a Holland city, where we anchored at nine o'clock in the morning
On the right: Baendern - where the Rhine flows toward Amsterdam - The river is called the Waal here.
The 25th - The troops were put ashore during the morning. The regiments were formed and marched to the parade ground in Nijmegen, where a muster was held and an oath was sworn to His Majesty, King George the Third, of England.
After this procedure, Colonel [Charles] Rainsford, the English envoy, took over the regiments.
Nijmegen is a rather well-developed place, complete with a garrison and the many clock styles are of special interest.
Underway from Nijmegen at one o'clock in the afternoon. During the departure a Dutch single-masted, wooden ship ran against our number four, which was punctured, but at once repaired.
Inhabited Places on the Waal
On the left: Tiel - a small barracks where we anchored at evening.
The 26th - Underway at daybreak.

On the left: Fort Andreas, Sommel - a
Dutch city - The Waal flows into the Meuse
River here.

Inhabited Places on the Meuse
On the left: Wammeln, Lobenstein, Herr-
werden, Dordrecht - We anchored in the harbor
in the evening.

On the right: Gorken, Hattingsfeld - Here
the ebb and flood tides are met. Poppenruth

Dordrecht is an important Dutch seaport,
which is built entirely on piles in the water.
Through all the streets of the city are canals
so that ships can pass through all the
streets. In this harbor English transport
ships are already to be seen.

The 27th - In the morning the English
sailors approached our ships and took us to the
English transport fleet lying about five miles
below Dordrecht.

During the afternoon the troops were embarked on the transports lying at anchor there.

The following transport ships have taken
on the troops:

The von Eyb Regiment
1)   Stag - was the staff ship on which
were Colonel von Eyb, Major von Reitzenstein,
and Grenadier Captain von Erckert

2)   Semetry - Captain von Ellrodt

3)   Myrtle - Captain von Stain

4)   Friendship - Staff Captain von Waldenfels

The von Voit Regiment
1)   Durand - was the staff ship on which
were Colonel von Voit, Major von Seybothen, and
Grenadier Captain von Seitz

2)   Hopewell - Captain von Beust

3)   Diana - Captain von Eyb

4)   Little Providence[5] - 1st Lieutenant von
Beust

Artillery and Hospital Ship for both Regiments
1)   Nancy - Artillery Lieutenant Hofmann

Jaeger Ship

1) _Juno_ – Captain von Cramon
The Hanauers are also embarked here and have received the ship _Great Providence_.

- - - - - -

Most of the transport ships had three masts and the ships' companies thereon consisted of:
 1 Ship's Captain, who however, is not a naval officer
 1 Helmsman, or Mate
 1 Assistant Helmsman
 1 Steward, who issues the provisions and keeps the ship's accounts
 1 Ship's Carpenter
 1 Ship's Cook, and
 20 Sailors
 26 Men total crew
Monthly pay, in pounds sterling, of the ship's crew, in addition to the ship's food twice daily and a berth:
 Ship's Captain – 10 pounds
 Helmsman – 5
 Assistant Helmsman – 3.5
 Steward – 3.5
 Ship's Carpenter – 4
 Ship's Cook – 3.5
 Sailor – 3
 The 28th – The ships' crews were busy taking on fresh water and putting everything in the best condition for sailing.

Ship's Provisions

Six men received On Sunday – four pounds of pork and one quart of peas.
 On Monday – one-half pound of salted butter, one-half pound of rice, and one quart of greens.
 On Tuesday – four pounds of salted beef, two pounds of flour, and one pound of wine.
 On Wednesday – one and one-half pounds of salted butter, one and one-half pounds of rice, one quart of peas, and one quart of greens.

On Thursday - as on Sunday.

On Friday - as on Wednesday.

On Saturday - as on Tuesday, plus one quart of vinegar.

Daily, two gallons of English beer, and when the beer aboard ship was gone, one quart of rum was substituted. Also daily, six men received four pounds of bread, in place of which we constantly received zwieback.

Each provision is paid for at five coppers or six and one-quarter groschen.

Note - On land four men daily received as many provisions as six men received daily aboard ship.

The wives received a half portion and the children a quarter portion, without receiving any rum.

The 29th - His Highness, the Margrave, today began his return trip to Ansbach.

This morning at seven o'clock the transport fleet went under sail, but because of stormy winds anchored at a Dutch harbor opposite Hellevoetslius.

The 30th - Because of continued storms we remained at anchor.

The 31st - Went under sail. Most of our people were attacked by seasickness, but most had recovered within 48 hours.

The water on which we sailed is called the Channel.

April 1777

The 1st - On the left we sailed past Calais, an important French city with a good harbor, and on the right Dover, a small English city with an excellent harbor, which is protected by a strong castle on a hill. The English weapons are made here.

In the evening we also saw the chalk cliffs of England and on

The 2nd - anchored in the harbor at Portsmouth.

Portsmouth is a very famous seaport and to be found there are:

1) A university at which the necessary skills are taught those who go to sea.

2) The incomparably great dockyard where most English warships are built. These are built in an inclosure, which has a gate built leading to the water. When the ships are finished building, they are not knocked from the piling like other ships, but the gates are opened and the water rushes into the inclosure so that the warship can enter the harbor. In short everything possible pertaining to ship construction can be seen here.

<u>From the 3rd to 7th</u> - Lying at anchor at Portsmouth because the warship <u>Somerset</u>, which will escort us to America, still is not completely ready to sail.

<u>The 8th</u> - The fleet, which consists of the warship <u>Somerset</u>, eleven transports for the troops, and four provisions ships, got underway. We soon lost sight of land and entered onto the open sea. On this day our troops again succumbed to seasickness, which, however, again had subsided within five days.

<u>Note</u> - The warship <u>Somerset</u> has 64 cannon, 200 marines, and 300 sailors on board, and later, in the year 1781, became stranded near Boston.[6]

<u>The 9th</u> - Sailing on the Atlantic Ocean. On the ocean one can see about forty English miles.

<u>The 10th</u> - Sailing, but during the night, a very strong storm arose.

<u>The 11th</u> - The storm continued rather angrily and the fleet had to sail widely separated.

<u>The 12th</u> - The ships drew together and from

<u>The 13th to 16th</u> - sailed with a good wind.

The 17th - Sailed with contrary winds.
All sorts of sea spiders were to be seen. They
appeared quite pretty in the water because of
their many colors. However, out of the water
they did not look so good.
    The 18th and 19th - Sailed in a strong
storm. During the storm the soldiers all had
to remain in the holds and the entrances to the
deck, each time, were covered with oilcloth so
that the waves could not beat into the ship.
    The 20th - Sailed with contrary winds.
    The 21st - Sailed with contrary and very
stormy wind.
    The 22nd and 23rd - Sailed with contrary
winds.
    The 24th to 26th - Sailed with good winds.
    The 27th - Calm or still seas.
    On the ocean, by such weather, every day
at twelve o'clock noon, on all ships, the
ship's captain and both helmsmen take a sun
reading with the quadrant. As soon as the sun
aligns with the sea, it is twelve o'clock. The
sea officers and ships' captains, from these
transport ships thereafter make their
calculations and know at which degree they are
with their ships.
    Every four hours the sailors and sea of-
ficers are relieved from work.
    At eight o'clock in the morning, at twelve
o'clock noon, and at four o'clock in the
afternoon the bells on the ship are rung. A
person can not hear as many bells, even in the
largest city, as can be heard in a large fleet.
    The 28th and 29th - Sailed with a good
wind.
    The 30th - Sailed with a contrary wind.

May 1777

    The 1st - Sailed with a good wind.
    The 2nd - Sailed with a fair wind. During
the afternoon we saw the Portuguese island of

St. Michael, from which we were forty English
miles distant. This island disappeared again
during the evening and faded into the threaten-
ing stormy weather.

The 3rd - Sailed with fair winds.

The 4th - Sailed with contrary winds.

The 5th and 6th - Sailed with good winds.

The 7th - Sailed with contrary winds.

The 8th - We had no wind and a calm sea.

The 9th - Sailed with a good wind.

The 10th - Sailed with a contrary wind.

The 11th - Sailed with a very good wind.

The 12th to 14th - Sailed with a good
wind.

The 15th - Sailed with a contrary wind.

The 16th and 17th - Sailed with a good
wind.

The 18th - Sailed with a good wind.

Officer's servant Peter, servant to Lieutenant von Diemar, Sr., lowered himself into
the sea from the ship on a rope from the ship
Myrtle at five o'clock in the evening. He was
seen swimming in the water, because the waves
did not immediately pull him under. A quarter
of an hour later he was brought back to the
ship dead, in a boat which had been sent after
him. He was buried in the ocean with a bag of
sand hung on him.

The 19th - Sailed with a good wind.

The 20th - Sailed 116 English miles in 24
hours, with a good wind.

The 21st - Sailed 121 miles with a good
wind.

The 22nd - Sailed 60 miles with a good
wind.

The 23rd - Sailed 86 miles with a good
wind.

The 24th to 26th - Sailed with contrary
winds.

The 27th - Sailed with a good wind.

During the evening, at seven o'clock, a
strong storm arose. Before this storm struck

the large fish, which are called porpoise, appeared in unbelievably large numbers. These fish are usually the sign of a storm.

The 28th - Sailed with stormy but still good winds.

The 29th - Again with stormy but very good wind, we sailed 177 miles.

When the ship sails at night on the ocean, the wake of sea water appears like real fire.

The 30th and 31st - Sailed with contrary winds.

June 1777

The 1st - Sailed with a good wind.

The water in the Atlantic Ocean appears almost dark blue.

The 2nd - Sailed with good but very weak wind.

This morning, after finding bottom at forty fathoms, toward nine o'clock land could be seen. Thank God!

The land when seen from the sea appeared like a distant black cloud.

As soon as the ships see land, they immediately raise their flags.

Note - 1) No flag is raised at sea because this means a ship has been seen in the distance.

2) When ships lie at anchor in the harbor, no flag is raised except on Sundays or when a warship enters or leaves the harbor.

3) As soon as enemy ships appear, the ships' flags are at once raised.

The fleet had to halt this evening because it was only thirty miles from Sandy Hook and could no longer enter the harbor at New York.

The 3rd - At four o'clock this morning we sailed past Sandy Hook and Staten Island, in the Jerseys, on our left, and Long Island on our right.

At five o'clock in the evening we anchored

in the seaport of New York close to Fort
George.
Sandy Hook is the place where the lighthouse or lighttower is built. This tower is
wide below but very narrow at the top. Every
night a fire is burned in the tower as a light
for the ships. Furthermore, the light can be
seen more than twenty miles across the water.
All American harbors are equipped with
similar lighttowers.
What our arrival in America seems to mean,
is this: That we went aboard ship in Germany
shortly after wintertime and came to America
during the most beautiful summertime, when
everything was in the most prosperous condition; came to this land and here have seen a
true paradise.
The 4th - At anchor at New York. Today
the birthday of His Royal Highness, George the
Third of Great Britain, was celebrated. The
cannons on the warships lying at anchor at New
York fired a salute at eleven o'clock at
midday, and at night, the entire city and
surrounding region was illuminated.
New York lies on the foremost part of York
Island. On the right flows the East River and
on the left the North River. Here are to be
found:
1) Fort George, built with clean cut
stone facing and equipped with a double row of
cannons which can fire over the entire harbor.
Near this point, on the left, are the quarters
of the commanding general on the street called
White Hall.
2) The beautiful courthouse in which,
during the war period, the government offices
are to be found.
3) Eleven churches are also to be seen:
A) The English Evangelical St.
George Chapel with a very beautifully constructed tower which underneath is four-sided,
with nine large gold-plated globes standing

over it and above is eight-sided.

B)   The English Reformed Church of St. Paul on the Common Place.

C)   The North   Church built   in the William Street, which belongs to the English Reformed religion.

D)   The German Evangelical Church.

E & F)   Among those on the William Street, including the   Schwam Church which during the war has been made into the garrison church. Of the two above, one is by custom, the other but from time to time, used as regimental quarters.

G)   The Low German, or Dutch Church.

H)   The Herrnhuter Church.

I)   The church on the Common Place, in which an English hospital has been estab-lished.

J)   Two churches near the courthouse, which have been converted to English storehouses.

4)   In the holy ground, the university in which the English main hospital is to be found.

5)   The Army House on the Common Place.

6)   The Vauxhall on the North River which is now the Ansbach regiments' hospital.

7) The sugar houses at various places in which sugar is refined.

8)   The flea market in the middle of the city.

9)   The large tea water fountain in the Chatham Street, which is horse-powered. Before all the houses of the city this sweet water is conducted daily and a pail or a "kettle-full" sells at two coppers of two and one-half groschen.

10)   The suburb which is called the Bow-ery, in which only Germans are to be found.

11)   The great parade ground, which is more than two and one-half miles in circumference and on the Bowery, is commonly called the Farmers' Gardens.

12) The shipyard lying on the East River,
which is rather well-equipped for shipbuilding.
13) The Fort Bunker Hill, located on a
height on the Bowery.
Additionally, New York is built on a regu-
lar plan and primarily with houses made of
brick. When the Americans first fled, 1,500
houses with five churches, including the
largest church at that time, the Holy Trinity,
along the North River, were laid in ashes,
which, however, in this city, is almost unno-
ticed.
Except for the bells in St. George Chapel
and two bells on the courthouse, the fleeing
Americans have taken all the bells away to be
cast into cannons.
The inhabitants of this city are a mixture
of English and German, and many Negroes, who
are slaves.
Females throughout America are greatly in-
fluenced by French fashions.
The soil of the island is exceptionally
good and all possible fruits and vegetables
grow well here in the city.
It is also noteworthy that no American
city is provided with city gates.
Concerning York Island, on the East River,
Corlaers Hook, Martin's Wharf, and Turtle Bay,
three small villages, are to be seen and on the
tip of the island, Kingsbridge. At Blooming-
dale, which is a certain district of the land,
lies Harlem, which consisted of three houses
which nevertheless have all been burned down.
On the right bank of the North River lies
Fort Knyphausen, which was formerly called
Washington. It was conquered by the Hessian
Lieutenant General [Wilhelm] von Knyphausen and
named after him.
The very extensive plantations which are
to be found on this island and the beautiful
woods cannot be imagined.
The 5th - Our troops received orders that

115

they were to debark at Staten Island. The transport ships therefore traveled three hours back [down the bay]. Also we were landed during the afternoon on this island near Cole's Ferry and entered our first camp close to the ferry.

Anyone who has been on a ship for a long time, and comes on land, can believe nothing other than that the land quivers.

Staten Island is not one of the best islands, nor provided with extensive woods. However, many plantations are encountered, here and there.[7]

Because of the troops, which from time to time, have found themselves on this island, truly everything has been cut down, and since our arrival there has been very little foodstuff available.

Note - The English troops had arrived in America already in the year 1775, and initially were landed at Boston.

The Hessian troops, which consist of 12,000 men, sailed to America in two divisions and landed on the water side of Long Island in September 1776. The enemy, following this arrival, was immediately driven across the East River to York Island and then settled at Fort Washington.

The Americans then had a great fear of the Hessian troops.

The year 1776. On 24 December, on Christmas Eve,[8] a detachment, including the Hessian von Knyphausen Regiment, under the command of Colonel [Johann] Rall, was attacked at Trenton in Jersey and made prisoners of war.

The 6th and 7th - In camp at Cole's Ferry.

The 8th - During the night an alarm was sounded at the picket. Immediately the half regiment von Eyb, under the command of Major von Reitzenstein, moved out of the advanced camp of the main defenses. Because none of the enemy could be found, this force returned to camp.

The 9th - The entire von Eyb Regiment was detached and again posted before these forward lying defenses. Throughout this entire night there was one of the strongest thunderstorms, during which the regiment had to remain under arms, until daybreak.

The 10th - The regiment marched back into the previously occupied camp.

The 11th - The troops received the order to fall out and to march through the whole of Staten Island. They were then carried across the Kills River to Jersey and arrived in camp at Amboy, under the command of the Hessian Lieutenant General [Leopold] von Heister.

The 12th - The main army, under the command of the English Commanding General Sir William Howe, already during the morning, advanced over Brunswick, or in German, Braunschweig. Our Field Jaeger Company joined with several regiments already camped there.

Here, near Amboy, I remained, as did the Ansbach Regiments and the Waldeck Regiment, which consisted of five companies. It came to America in the year 1776 and spent the entire previous winter lying in winter quarters in the barracks just outside Amboy. The main army, on the other hand, lay in winter quarters in the region of Brunswick, but have been disturbed by enemy attacks.

Because of our eventual retreat and transfer back across the Kills River, two English frigates are lying at anchor on the water side of the city. On the land side two large redoubts have been thrown up. Between the redoubts, which were provided with some iron cannons, the Ansbach regiments were posted.

Amboy, a small but beautiful little city in a pleasant region where all the land is flat, had a well-built, quite new church with a beautiful door. The church, lying outside the

city, was built completely of wood. During our
arrival, because of a shortage of wood, it was
immediately broken up.
      In this small city there was not the least
foodstuff more to be had, because all the
American men and women   have fled further
inland, leaving the now empty houses behind.
      The 16th - In camp near Amboy.
      As the enemy fired on our pickets this
afternoon, the regiments went under arms.   A
relief command was sent forward, from which
only Grenadier [Karl] Frank, of the von Eyb
Regiment, was wounded in the knee.
      From the 17th to 21st - In camp near Am-
boy.
      The 22nd - In camp near Amboy.
      As Lieutenant General von Heister returned
to Europe, these regiments came under the
command of the English Major General [John]
Vaughan.
      The 23rd - In camp near Amboy.
      As the Commanding General Howe came here
today, both Ansbach regiments passed in review.
      The 24th - In camp near Amboy.
      The main army broke camp today at Bruns-
wick and moved forward to Princeton.
      From the 25th to 27th - In camp near Am-
boy.
      The 28th - Because the main army, under
the command of General Howe, near Princeton,
could not accomplish its purpose, it marched
back today and was then carried over to Staten
Island.
      The 29th - The two defensive positions be-
tween which the Ansbachers were posted, were
destroyed and the troops remaining here, at the
same time, were carried over to Staten Island
and entered camp about two and one-half miles
from the Kills River.
      The 30th - Remained in this camp.

July 1777

The 1st - Broke camp and marched into camp at Cole's Ferry.

The 2nd - In camp at Cole's Ferry.

1st Lieutenant von Molitor was promoted to staff captain replacing Staff Captain von Reyher who returned home from Hanau because of illness.

From the 3rd to 7th - In camp at Cole's Ferry.

The 8th - The entire army was embarked at Cole's Ferry.

From the 9th to 12th - Lying at anchor near Cole's Ferry with a fleet of at least 300 sail.

The 13th - The 1st Ansbach Regiment received the order to be shipped to New York and is to enter camp at Harlem on York Island.

The transport ships on which the von Eyb Regiment were embarked went under sail, but because contrary winds struck the fleet, the anchors were dropped again.

The 14th - Went under sail at five o'clock in the afternoon, and then anchored in the seaport at New York.

The fleet with the main army, under the command of the Commanding General Howe, sailed toward the Chesapeake from Staten Island this morning.

Second Lieutenant Kublan died of a high fever at New York and was buried at the Schwam Church.

The 15th - At anchor near New York.

More than three hundred men of the 2nd Regiment have gradually been struck down with high fever and almost one-half of them have died from it.

A fire broke out on the von Eyb Regiment's staff ship Durand when a ship's carpenter upset a frying pan. However, it was quickly extinguished.

From the 16th to 21st - Lying at anchor at New York.

The 22nd - During the morning the von Eyb Regiment landed at New York, paraded through the city with music playing and flags flying, and entered the camp at Harlem, eight miles from New York, under the command of the English General [Henry] Clinton.

From the 23rd to 31st - In camp at New York.

August 1777

From the 1st to 3rd - In camp at Harlem.

The 4th - Today General Clinton reviewed the regiment and it paraded before him.

The Regiment von Voit had not embarked at Staten Island but had remained there in camp.

From the 5th to 10th - In camp at Harlem.

The 11th - In camp at Harlem.

From four o'clock in the afternoon until ten o'clock at night, a very strong storm struck with hail the size of the largest fist, which knocked down many trees in the woods.

The Quartermaster Sergeant Guard Ulm, of Major von Reitzenstein's Company, died in camp today of a high fever.

From the 12th to 20th - In camp at Harlem.

The 21st - In camp at Harlem.

This evening Gunner [Michael] Zeder and Grenadier [Matthias] Lorenz, the later who wanted to come to the help of the first, drowned in the North River while bathing.

The 22nd - In camp at Harlem.

Because of the frequent attacks against Staten Island, the von Eyb Regiment Grenadier Company was sent over as a reinforcement.

The 23rd - In camp at Harlem.

Because the rebels who attacked Staten Island had been defeated and driven back into Jersey, the Grenadier Company was withdrawn and returned to the regiment.

From the 24th to 30th - In camp at Harlem.

September 1777

From the 1st to 5th - In camp at Harlem.
The 6th - In camp at Harlem.
General Clinton had the von Eyb Regiment Grenadier Company placed close to his headquarters, which was located at the Morris house.
From the 7th to 24th - In camp at Harlem.
The 25th - In camp at Harlem.
Today the von Eyb Regiment conducted shooting exercises.
The 26th and 27th - In camp at Harlem.
The 28th - In camp at Harlem.
First Sergeants [Georg Friedrich] Guttenberg, of the Grenadiers, and [Johann Ernst] Prechtel,[9] of Major von Reitzenstein's Company, were both promoted to 2nd lieutenant; the first to Captain von Ellrodt's Company, the latter to Captain von Stain's Company.
The 29th and 30th - In camp at Harlem.

October 1777

From the 1st to 11th - In camp at Harlem.
The 12th - In camp at Harlem.
Grenadier Captain von Erckert, of the von Eyb Regiment, who was wounded at the storming of Fort Montgomery, and who died of his wounds at New York, was buried today at the Schwam Church. The funeral command was provided by the Hessian Hereditary Prince Regiment which lies in garrison here in New York.
Grenadier [Johann Michael] Kriegbaum was also killed in the attack on Fort Montgomery.
Second Lieutenant von Reitzenstein, of the von Voit Regiment, was promoted to 1st lieutenant.
The 13th - The 2nd Ansbach Regiment today was ordered to Albany to relieve the English General [John] Burgoyne. The von Eyb Regiment

was also ordered aboard two transport ships, near John's house on the North River and the von Voit Regiment was embarked at Staten Island. The ships immediately went under sail and by evening anchored in the vicinity of Fort Knyphausen.

The 14th - At two o'clock in the afternoon they sailed and then anchored during the evening in the North River.

The 15th - Under sail at six o'clock in the morning and the anchor was dropped off York Island in the evening.

The 16th - The troops were landed on York Island and the regiments camped at Planx Point,[10] without tents. The Grenadiers were reunited with the von Eyb Regiment again.

News was received that the entire army of General Burgoyne, consisting of four thousand men, including most of the Brunswickers under the command of General [Friedrich von] Riedesel, was captured by the rebels.

The 17th and 18th - In camp at Planx Point.

On 14 July, this year, the Ansbach Regiment received a German named Mosengail,[11] who was promoted to captain in a provincial regiment in the year 1779, but who remained by the Ansbach Regiments.

The 19th - The troops were again embarked on the above mentioned transport ships. The defenses built on York Island were demolished and at one o'clock in the afternoon the ships sailed down the stream and anchored at evening in the North River.

The 20th - Underway at seven o'clock in the morning and anchored in the North River.

The 21st - Sailed during the morning and anchored near Kingsbridge.

The 22nd - Sailed at two o'clock in the morning and anchored at New York.

The 23rd and 24th - Lying at anchor at New York.

The 25th — The regiments received the order to proceed to the main army at Philadelphia and therefore, during the afternoon, changed ships.

The von Eyb Regiment went aboard the transport ships:

    1) John — the staff ship, on which was Major Reitzenstein

    2) Hopewell, and

    3) Hanyriette

Today the troops remained at anchor.

Because of illness, Colonel von Eyb did not go aboard ship, but had to remain in New York and, in the meantime, Major von Reitzenstein commanded the regiment.

All the warships lying at anchor fired a salute as it was the celebration of the coronation of His Majesty, King George III.

It has been learned that the Commanding General Howe, with the main army, has fought a battle at Brandywine in Pennsylvania with the rebel army commanded by Lieutenant General Washington, in which the rebels put up a very strong resistance.

During the battle 2nd Lieutenant von Forstner, of the Field Jaeger Company, was fatally wounded, and after being taken to Wilmington, died of his wounds.

    1. First Sergeant [Johann] Stiegler

    2. Corporal [Johann Andreas] Haehnlein, and

seven privates were killed.

The 26th — Sailed and then anchored at Staten Island.

From the 27th to 29th — Because of storms, still at anchor at Staten Island.

The 30th and 31st — At anchor at Staten Island.

November 1777

The 1st — At anchor at Staten Island.

The 2nd — Grenadier [Philipp Matthias] Sitzmann, of Captain von Stain's Company, died aboard the ship John and was buried on land on Staten Island.

The 3rd and 4th — At anchor at Staten Island.

The 5th — The troops, which are in the fleet consisting of forty sail, departed from Staten Island, commanded by the English General [Thomas] Wilson, and consist of the two Ansbach regiments in Colonel von Voit's brigade.

During the morning the fleet went under way and already during the afternoon arrived at the open sea, having lost sight of land in very stormy weather.

The 6th — At four o'clock at night a storm with contrary winds struck and an English transport ship collided with the ship John, carrying [elements of] the von Eyb Regiment. The bowsprit broke, which caused much damage and need for repairs.

The 7th — Under sail and already during the evening we saw land and a very large whale.

The 8th — We passed the lighttower on the left of the Delaware Bay and during the evening anchored opposite the village of Porthen [Port Penn ?].

The Delaware River is thirty English miles wide at its mouth.

The 9th — Because of contrary winds we did not sail until two o'clock in the afternoon. During the evening we anchored at New Castle.

Because this region is occupied only by rebels, no one was allowed ashore.

The 10th — Underway at six-thirty in the morning. On the left we passed both villages Wilmington and Marcus Hook. During the evening we entered the harbor at Chester and anchored.

It was necessary to take provisions from here to the main army at Philadelphia on flatboats, a distance of five miles, and these flatboats had to sneak past the rebel ships lying at anchor near Fort Redbank.

The 11th and 12th - At anchor at Chester.

The English warships heavily cannonaded Fort Billingsport, which lay before us, on the Delaware River, in Jersey.

The 13th - At anchor at Chester.

The 14th - At anchor at Chester.

The firing by the English warships against Billingsport was continuous.

The 15th - At anchor at Chester.

The terrible bombardment by the English warships continued without let-up.

The 16th - The enemy evacuated both Fort Billingsport and Mud Bank on the left of the Delaware River in Pennsylvania, setting fire to the latter and retreated to Fort Redbank in Jersey.

The 17th - Underway and then anchored at Fort Billingsport.

The 18th - The troops were landed near Billingsport and entered camp, without tents, close to this fort.

Billingsport, one of America's best designed forts, on the Delaware River, in Jersey, has accommodations for ten thousand men.

The 19th - In camp at Billingsport.

Today the troops were placed under the command of the English General [Charles, Earl] Cornwallis who came here from the main army at Philadelphia.

The Hessian Colonel [Karl Emil] von Donop attacked Fort Redbank where the Hessian Grenadiers suffered greatly and Colonel von Donop was himself fatally wounded.[2] The enemy brought him into the fort where he died and was buried by the enemy with a nine-cannon salute.

The 20th - In camp at Billingsport.

During the night the enemy evacuated Fort Redbank, leaving a great many provisions behind, which were divided among the troops.

The 21st - We marched from Billingsport into camp at Woodbury.

The 22nd and 23rd - In camp at Woodbury.
The 24th - Camp was moved very close to
the [Big] Timber Creek.
This evening the Hessian jaegers attached
to our camp, who occupied the outer post on the
land side, in a woods, were attacked by the
enemy.
The Hessian Staff Riding Master Heppe, of
the mounted jaegers, was fatally wounded and
died the next day.
During this attack several jaeger privates
were likewise killed.
After the chain across the Delaware River
between Fort Redbank and Mud Island, as well as
the chevaux de frise(*) had been cleared, today
the English fleet which had been lying at
anchor at Billingsport sailed into the harbor
at Philadelphia.
(*) Chevaux de frise are large casings
filled with stone which are placed in the
water, close to one another, in which large
iron spikes are set. When a ship runs against
such, it is seriously damaged and quickly
sinks.
The 27th - The army at Gloucester was set
across the Delaware from Jersey to Pennsylvania. The last regiments were attacked by the
enemy and were carried across under a steady
fire from four frigates lying at anchor. The
march was immediately made to Philadelphia.
The troops joined the main army in camp near
the Spring Gardens. The two Ansbach regiments
paraded through the entire city, along Seventh
Street, and entered the barracks there, in
which ten thousand men can be quartered.
Philadelphia lies in Pennsylvania on the
Delaware River. It is an entirely newly built
and very large city, about two and one-half
miles long and two and one-half miles wide.
According to the basic plan there are 23
principal streets in the city which stretch
from the Delaware across the Schuylkill, a

small river busy with many small ships. All the streets are regularly laid out and the houses are at least four or five stories high, of various colors, and built of brick.

On all sides of the houses there are footpaths about six feet wide and paved with bricks, and washed and painted with a fresh red color. Above these walkways, the roofs of the houses are extended so that everyone can go through all the streets of the city with dry feet.

Along the entire Market Street, which extends from the Delaware to the Schuylkill, a covered market house has been built in which all buyers can obtain all the goods for sale and remain completely dry. While the English army has been here, a portion of the market house has been converted to horse stalls for the cavalry. There are seven churches here:

1) An English Church in the Second Street.

2) The English Reformed Church which was occupied by an English hospital.

3) The new German Reformed Church in which a Hessian hospital was to be found.

4) The new German Evangelical Church in which there is an English hospital.

5) The German Evangelical Church of St. Margaret was the garrison church.

6) The University Church, beside the university, completely closed.

7) The Catholic Church.

These do not include the many Quaker Meeting and other Prayerhouses.

In all of Philadelphia there is only a single bell on the English Church to be seen. The others, as in New York, had been taken away by the enemy.

The court or Congress House stands in the middle of the city.

The new jail or prison is an excellent new

building with beautiful towers in which the American prisoners are held.

The seaport is very beautiful. However, no large warships can enter, only frigates, because the water is not deep enough. Also, the Delaware here is already sweet water.

Twelve defensive positions, numbered one through twelve, have been built on the land side of Philadelphia.

The beautiful houses outside the city in the so-called Spring Gardens have mostly been torn down by the army and in part, laid in ashes.

Half of the village of Kensington, about a mile from Philadelphia, due to a shortage of wood, has been completely torn down.

Firewood for the army must be brought in from outside the defensive lines, about three or four miles distant, and two to three thousand men must be sent as a covering force, as frequent attacks occur.

All the inhabitants of the city, since the arrival of the English army here, have left. They consist of English and German people among which are many merchants and all possible artesians and professionals.

Pastor [John Peter Gabriel] von Muhlenberg,[13] of the Evangelical Church, has joined the American troops and received the rank of general.

Pennsylvania is one of the most beautiful and fertile provinces in North America. In the province are many beautiful cities, villages, and plantations, and most of the inhabitants are Germans.

The 28th - In the barracks at Philadelphia.

Note - The officers are not quartered in the barracks, but in the city.

1) Captain von Ellrodt received the Grenadier Company of the von Eyb Regiment.

2) Staff Captain von Waldenfels, of the

von Eyb Regiment, received Captain von Ellrodt's Company of this regiment.

3) Staff Captain von Molitor, of the von
Voit Regiment, was transferred to the von Eyb
Regiment.

4) 1st Lieutenant von Quesnoy, of the von
Voit Regiment, was promoted to staff captain of
that regiment.

5) 2nd Lieutenant von Streit, of the von
Voit Regiment, was promoted to 1st lieutenant
of that regiment.

6) 2nd Lieutenant von Sichart,

7) 2nd Lieutenant von Woellwarth, and

8) 2nd Lieutenant von Keller, of the von
Eyb Regiment, were promoted to 1st lieutenant.
The first two were transferred to the von Voit
Regiment.

The 29th and 30th - In the barracks at
Philadelphia.

December 1777

From the 1st to 4th - In the barracks at
Philadelphia.

The 5th - The Commanding General Howe
moved forward with the main army and both Ansbach regiments moved into the army camp at
Spring Gardens near Philadelphia.

The 6th and 7th - In camp near Philadelphia.

The 8th - As the main army returned at
eight o'clock in the evening, the two Ansbach
regiments vacated the camp at once and returned
to the barracks at Philadelphia.

From the 9th to 12th - In the barracks at
Philadelphia.

The 13th - The main army entered winter
quarters in Philadelphia.

The Ansbach regiments were quartered with
the von Eyb Regiment in Water Street; the von
Voit Regiment in Front Street.

The 14th and 15th - In quarters in Philadelphia.

The 16th - In quarters at Philadelphia.
The von Eyb Regiment was mustered today in Front Street.

From the 17th to 21st - In quarters at Philadelphia.

The 22nd - Because of foraging, the main army marched across the Schuylkill River and camped, without tents, near Darby.

From the 23rd to 27th - In camp at Darby.

The 28th - Because the foraging ended today, the army broke camp and marched back to Philadelphia, where the regiments again entered the previous winter quarters.

While the English troops were on the foraging command at Darby, Private Thormann, of Captain von Waldenfels' Company of the von Eyb Regiment, deserted.

From the 29th to 31st - In quarters at Philadelphia.

January 1778

The 1st - In quarters at Philadelphia.

This morning the alarm place was designated as the Schuylkill River, in battle formation, so the main army marched to that place and in the evening returned again to Philadelphia.

From the 2nd to 11th - In quarters at Philadelphia.

The 12th - In quarters at Philadelphia.

An English private soldier who robbed an officer and was again caught by the officer whom he had attacked, was hung this morning outside the city, in the region of the poor-house.

Note - At an English execution, the reserve pickets from all regiments of the army are formed in a circle.

From the 13th to 17th - In quarters at Philadelphia.

The 18th - In quarters at Philadelphia.

Today the birthday of Queen Sophia Charlotte, of Great Britain, was celebrated. The cannons on the warships that are here fired a salute at one o'clock in the afternoon.

From the 19th to 31st - In quarters at Philadelphia.

February 1778

From the 1st to 14th - In quarters at Philadelphia.

The 15th - In quarters at Philadelphia.

At three o'clock this morning the watch at the defensive positions across the Schuylkill, under the command of the following officers: Grenadier Captain von Ellrodt, 1st Lieutenant von Keller, of the von Eyb Regiment, and 1st Lieutenant von Reitzenstein, of the von Voit Regiment, was attacked by the enemy. The fighting lasted three-quarters of an hour. The watch, which consisted primarily of Ansbachers, held the positions so bravely, that the enemy had to retreat.

From the 16th to 18th - In quarters at Philadelphia.

The 19th - In quarters at Philadelphia.

At ten-thirty at night Grenadier [Friedrich] Stoll, of the von Eyb Regiment, deserted from defensive watch number one at the double post.

From the 20th to 28th - In quarters at Philadelphia.

March 1778

From the 1st to 4th - In quarters at Philadelphia.

The 5th - In quarters at Philadelphia.

Private [Johann Ludwig] Dietlein, of the Colonel's Company of the von Eyb Regiment, deserted today in the city.

From the 6th to 8th - In quarters at Philadelphia.

The 9th - In quarters at Philadelphia.

At twelve-thirty tonight Privates [Johann] Brummer and [Johann] Schard, of Captain von Waldenfels' Company of the von Eyb Regiment, deserted from the defensive watch number one at the double post.

The 10th - In quarters at Philadelphia.

Private [Heinrich] Katzenwinkel, of Captain von Stain's Company of the von Eyb Regiment, deserted from the quarters today.

From the 11th to 18th - In quarters at Philadelphia.

The 19th -In quarters at Philadelphia.

Private [Johann Adam] Hohberger, of Captain von Stain's Company of the von Eyb Regiment, died in the hospital of consumption.

From the 20th to 22nd - In quarters at Philadelphia.

The 23rd - In quarters at Philadelphia

Two English soldiers who had gone over to
the enemy, and again fled, were caught outside
the city.
From the 24th to 27th - In quarters at
Philadelphia.
The 28th - In quarters at Philadelphia.
Colonel von Eyb arrived here from New York
with the convalescents and baggage of the Ans-
bach regiments.
From the 29th to 31st - In quarters at
Philadelphia.

April 1778

From the   1st to   15th - In quarters at
Philadelphia.
The 16th - In quarters at Philadelphia.
                   Recalled
1) Colonel von Eyb
2) 1st Lieutenant   Sichart,   of the von
Voit Regiment, as captain
                   Promotions
1) Colonel von Voit received the von Eyb
Regiment.
2)   Major von Seybothen was promoted to
colonel and received the von Voit Regiment.
3)   Staff Captain von Molitor, of the von
Voit Regiment, received a company in the von
Seybothen Regiment.
4)   1st Lieutenant von Roeder, of the von
Voit Regiment, was promoted to staff captain of
that regiment.
5)   Captain von Beust, of the Seybothen
Regiment, was   promoted to major   in that
regiment.
6)   1st Lieutenant von Metzsch was trans-
ferred from Captain von Waldenfels' Company to
Major von Reitzenstein's Company of the von
Voit Regiment.
From the 17th to 21st - In quarters at
Philadelphia.
The 22nd - In quarters at Philadelphia.

A newly built row galley was launched into the Delaware River this morning from the piling on which it had been built.

The General-in-Chief Howe was present. The number of onlookers and those gathered to watch is indescribable.

From the 23rd to 30th – In quarters at Philadelphia.

May 1778

The 1st – In quarters at Philadelphia.
Today a spy was caught outside the city.
The 2nd and 3rd – In quarters at Philadelphia.

The 4th – In quarters at Philadelphia.
Today General-in-Chief Howe watched the Hessian troops pass in review.

From the 5th to 10th – In quarters at Philadelphia.

The 11th – In quarters at Philadelphia.
Colonel von Eyb and Captain von Sichart began their return to Europe.

From the 12th to 15th – In quarters at Philadelphia.

The 16th – In quarters at Philadelphia.
An English deserter who fled from the city was caught.

The 17th – In quarters at Philadelphia.
The 18th – In quarters at Philadelphia.
Today the English staff officers held an entertainment for the General-in-Chief, Sir William Howe. The entire retinue came together at Redoubt Number One at three o'clock in the afternoon. They embarked in flatboats and passed down the Delaware River with musical accompanyment. When the retinue passed the fleet of warships and transports lying at anchor in the harbor, all of which had their flags flying, a strong salute was fired from all the cannons. In a garden outside Philadelphia a banquet and ball was held, and at night a mag-

nificent fireworks display was presented.

The 19th - In quarters in Philadelphia.

The 20th - In quarters at Philadelphia.

After the enemy had shown himself, in rather large numbers, for a number of days at Germantown, seven miles from here, today the entire army, under the command of the Commander-in-Chief Sir William Howe, marched out five miles above Germantown to attack the enemy.

Before the army arrived, the enemy retreated in the greatest haste, and our troops therefore returned again to their quarters in Philadelphia.

Germantown, in Pennsylvania, is a well built, small German city, two and one-half miles long and provided with a city hall and a church. It has, however, only a single street.

From the 21st to 28th - In quarters at Philadelphia.

The 29th - In quarters at Philadelphia.

Privates [Gottlob] Friederici and [Heinrich] Blecker, both of Captain Waldenfels' Company, and Private [Johann] Luck, of Major von Reitzenstein's Company, deserted today. The first from the quarters and the latter two from the post at Redoubt Number One.

The 30th and 31st - In quarters at Philadelphia.

June 1778

The 1st - In quarters at Philadelphia.

Take Note! - While the former von Eyb Regiment was camped at Harlem, and the former von Voit Regiment on Staten Island, the following officers died of putrid fever in New York, and were buried in the Schwam Church there.

From the von Eyb Regiment

1) 2nd Lieutenant von Adelsheim
2) 2nd Lieutenant von Sodon, and
3) Regimental Quartermaster Fuchs

From the von Voit Regiment

1) 1st Lieutenant von Witzleben and
2) Catholic Chaplain, Father Pieret

The latter was buried outside the city of New York.

Both Privates Zipfel, of Captain von Waldenfels' Company of the von Voit Regiment, deserted at Philadelphia.

The 2nd and 3rd — In quarters at Philadelphia.

The 4th — In quarters at Philadelphia.

Today the birthday of His Majesty, King George III, of Great Britain, was celebrated. The frigate Vigilant fired a salute from all its cannon at one o'clock in the afternoon.

The 5th and 6th — In quarters at Philadelphia.

The 7th — In quarters at Philadelphia.

General Lord Cornwallis and the English [Peace] Commissioners arrived from England, in order to undertake negotiations with the Congress.

The 8th — In quarters at Philadelphia.

The 9th — At two o'clock in the morning both Ansbach regiments were embarked on horse ships. The fleet went under sail at daybreak and passed Gloucester, Fort Redbank, and Fort Billingsport on the left, and Fort Mud Island on the right.

As the tide arrived at nine o'clock in the morning, we anchored near Fort Billingsport.

Underway at two o'clock in the afternoon and we passed Chester and Wilmington on the right. During the evening we anchored here, where the warships lay at anchor.

The 10th — Underway at two o'clock in the morning, and at eight o'clock in the morning arrived near the large fleet at Reedy Island, where the fleet was anchored.

The 11th — The Ansbach regiments were embarked on large transport ships which remained lying at anchor at Reedy Island.

136

The 12th - Lying at anchor at Reedy Island.

The 13th - Underway at ten o'clock in the morning and as a contrary wind arose, we anchored in the Delaware.

The 14th - Underway at three o'clock in the afternoon and during the evening we anchored in the Delaware.

The 15th - Underway at three o'clock in the morning. At twelve o'clock noon a calm settled in and because the ships could not anchor, they were driven against one another in a surprising manner, which often can cause damage.

At two o'clock the calm ended and although the wind was contrary, we entered the ocean and the land was lost from view.

Most of our troops again became seasick.

The 16th - We sailed with a good wind.

The 17th - Sailing and during the morning, at eleven o'clock, we saw land. During the evening a strong thunderstorm arose which strong storm was frightening, but the fleet fortunately reached Sandy Hook where it anchored in the bay.

The 18th - Underway in the morning, but as a calm was encountered at eleven o'clock, we anchored.

At one o'clock in the afternoon a good wind arose with which we immediately went underway and during the evening the fleet entered the seaport of New York.

The 19th - Lying at anchor at New York.

The 20th - This morning two sailors were hanged for espionage aboard a frigate lying at anchor in this harbor.

The warship on which the execution was to take place raised a yellow flag first thing in the morning.

From every warship lying at anchor in the harbor, a boat with a sea officer and about thirty sailors was sent to the ship which had raised the yellow flag. This flag continues to fly until the execution has been carried out.

Further, a signal is given with a cannon shot, whereupon the criminals are suddenly hanged on the mainyard of the forward mast.

We went under sail at twelve o'clock noon and passed Martin's Wharf and Turtle Bay on the left, on the East River, and on the right, Brooklyn, a small city lying on Long Island, where there are always many seamen living.

The transports lay at anchor at Blackwell's Ferry and the regiments were landed on Long Island and entered their camp near Blackwell's house. At that time, the command was held by the English General Tryon.

During the debarkation Private [Johann Ullrich] Teufel, of Captain von Molitor's Company of the von Seybothen Regiment, fell into the water, when he was about to enter a boat from the ship, and was not seen again.

The 21st - In camp near Blackwell's house.

Long Island, a very pleasant island two hundred miles long and thirty miles wide. This island is exceptionally fertile and is generally called the vegetable garden of New York. Although English troops were everywhere, at no time was there a shortage of any produce.

Very many small cities, villages, and plantations have been built there.

The inhabitants, surprisingly, consisting mostly of English and Dutch, during the present war have declared for the King.

The 22nd - In camp near Blackwell's house.

On this island the heat is exceptionally great, so that during the daytime, it can not be avoided.

Mosquitoes, or the American mosquitoes, are here in the greatest numbers. They bite very hard and every bite quickly grows as large as a hazelnut and no one can get rest from them during the night.

From the 23rd to 25th - In camp near

Blackwell's house.
    The 26th - In camp near Blackwell's house.
    The Grenadier Teufel, who drowned on the
20th of this month, was washed up on land today, from the water, and buried in the earth,
on Long Island.
    From the 27th to 30th - In camp near
Blackwell's house.

July 1778

    From the 1st to 4th - In camp near Black-
well's house.
    The 5th - In camp near Blackwell's house.
    Today Artillery Lieutenant Hofmann put on
a fireworks display in camp.
    The 6th - Both Ansbach regiments broke
camp at Blackwell's house this morning at three
o'clock. They were carried across the East
River and entered the camp on York Island, near
Morris' fifth house.
    At five-thirty this evening the order came
that the regiments should return to Long Island
and enter their previous camp near Blackwell's
house.
    This was carried out this evening.
    The 7th - In camp near Blackwell's house.
    The 8th - In camp near Blackwell's house.
    After the Commanding General Sir William
Howe was relieved and had gone back to England,
General Sir Henry Clinton received command of
the entire army.
    The army under the command of General-in-
Chief Sir Henry Clinton left Philadelphia and
moved, on land, across Jersey to New York.
    The 9th -
        Recalled and En Route to Europe
    1) Jaeger Captain von Cramon
    2) 1st Lieutenant von Woellwarth, of the
von Seybothen Regiment
    3) 2nd Lieutenant von Mardefeld, of the
von Voit Regiment

Promotions

1) Captain von Waldenfels received the Jaeger Company.

2) Staff Captain von Quesnoy, of the von Seybothen Regiment, received the von Waldenfels Company of the von Voit Regiment.

3) 1st Lieutenant von Metzsch, of the von Voit Regiment, was promoted to staff captain of the von Seybothen Regiment.

4) 1st Lieutenant Tritschler was transferred from Captain Stain's Company to Major von Reitzenstein's Company of the von Voit Regiment.

5) 2nd Lieutenant von Marschall was promoted to 1st lieutenant and remained in Captain von Stain's Company of the von Voit Regiment.

6) 2nd Lieutenant von Weitershausen, of the von Seybothen Regiment, was promoted to 1st lieutenant in that regiment.

Both Ansbach regiments were embarked on the transport ships still lying at anchor in the East River at Blackwell's Ferry, and today remained lying at anchor.

The 10th - At three o'clock in the afternoon the fleet went under sail and during the evening anchored in the East River.

The 11th - Underway at eight o'clock in the morning and dropped anchor at five o'clock in the evening.

The 12th - Under sail at six o'clock in the morning and the anchor was not dropped during the entire night.

The 13th - Because the wind became contrary, we anchored in the East River.

Under sail at two o'clock in the afternoon, but as the wind continued poor, we anchored again in the East River.

As soon as the anchor had been dropped, at five o'clock in the evening, the fleet, and especially the transport ship John and Betty, on which was Grenadier Captain von Seitz, of the von Seybothen Regiment, was attacked by two

140

enemy row galleys. The frigate escorting the
fleet and several transport ships immediately
fired on them.
      The enemy row galleys retired toward land
without having gained any advantage.
      The 14th - We sailed at six o'clock in the
morning but because of contrary winds, anchored
at eight o'clock in the morning.
      The water here is called the [Long Island]
Sound.
      Sailed at two o'clock in the afternoon,
but anchored during the evening in the Sound.
      The sea is already very close here and
therefore no anchors will hold and it is very
dangerous for ships approaching near one
another.
      The 15th - Underway at four o'clock in the
morning and on our right passed the small
island of Block Island, where we then entered
upon the ocean. At nine o'clock in the evening
the fleet entered the seaport at Newport, on
Rhode Island.
      The 16th - At one o'clock in the afternoon
we debarked at Newport. The regiments entered
camp about one-half mile from the Pitch.'
      Newport is a splendid city in whose harbor
all the largest warships can enter and remain
during the winter.
      There are four English churches in the
city, of which, however, during the war, only
one was usable because all the others are used
by the troops and as hospitals.
      Above the city, on the land side, there is
a Quaker Meetinghouse built entirely of wood,
in which both Ansbach Regiments, as long as
they remained in the city, had their religious
services.
      The courthouse, built of bricks, stands on
the market place.
      Not far from the courthouse, on the market
place, was the main watch.
      Below on the water, the picturesquely laid

141

out Thames Street, about one-half mile long, is
to be seen.
    Rhode Island is ten miles long and four
miles wide and except for the city of Newport,
nothing but individual plantations and a small
city, Middletown, is built on this island.
    The land is very fertile and much wheat,
barley, and Turkish corn is grown.
    Also, hay grows here in abundance. During
the war much hay was taken on ships to the
English army at Philadelphia.
    Every plantation had an especially beauti-
ful fruit garden. The fruit trees, however,
have all been cut down and the wood used to
construct defenses.
    On this island are to be found only Eng-
lish people and there is not a single German to
be met.
    When the Ansbach regiments arrived here on
Rhode Island, the following regiments were on
the island, under the command of the English
General [Robert] Pigot, namely:
        1)   The English Light Infantry
        2)   The 22nd
        3)   The 38th, and
        4)   The 43rd English Regiments
        5)   The Brown and
        6)   Fanning Provincial Corps
        7)   The Landgraf
        8)   The Ditfurth
        9)   The Huyn, and
        10)   The Buenau Hessian Regiments, and
        11)   The 54th English Regiment.
    On the water side of Newport are the fol-
lowing defenses:
        1)   The fort on Brenton's Point, which is
continuously manned with one captain, one
lieutenant, and one hundred men.
        2)   Fort Goat Island, in the middle of the
Newport harbor, on which the Stone Battery is
manned by one lieutenant and thirty men.
        3)   The North Battery, which also has one

lieutenant and thirty men.

From the 17th to 19th - In camp on the Pitch.

The 20th - Today the two Ansbach regiments were transferred to Conanicut Island and entered camp under the command of Colonel von Voit.

The strait here is about four miles wide.

Conanicut is a rather small island on which there are only a few plantations. It is productive, especially for growing hay and is also called the Hay Island.

From the 21st to 28th - In camp on Conanicut.

The 29th - This morning in the region of the lighthouse we saw a French war fleet which anchored not far from the lighthouse at eleven o'clock at midday.

We received the order from headquarters at Newport, at the same time, for the regiments to leave the camp and to return to Newport. The regiments entered the camp close to the city of Newport.

During the afternoon, as no enemy was to be found on Conanicut, the baggage and tents were retrieved.

Private Braun, Sr., of Captain von Stain's Company of the von Voit Regiment, took the opportunity, while on the baggage command, to desert.

The 30th - In camp at Newport.

The French war fleet consisting of about eighteen sail, spread out to the left and right of the Newport harbor and fired a cannonade against the outer defenses on Conanicut Island.

The 31st - In camp at Newport.

August 1778

The 1st and 2nd - In camp at Newport.

The 3rd - In camp at Newport

Six transport ships were sunk in the Newport harbor today so that the French war fleet could not sail into the harbor.

The 4th - In camp at Newport.

Colonel von Voit's Regiment was sent on patrol this evening to Fogland Ferry. Three French frigates lay at anchor a rifle shot away, opposite it.

The 5th - In camp at Newport.

At daybreak the regiment again marched away from the defensive position.

Two more ships were sunk in the harbor and some walls outside the city were destroyed.

The 6th and 7th - In camp at Newport.

The 8th - In camp at Newport.

Many houses behind our front were burned down today by the English.

As the French war fleet had a good wind, this evening it sailed into the harbor with ten ships and anchored. Our three defensive positions on the water side, Brenton's Point, the Stone Battery, and the North Battery, gave a good account of themselves.

The French ships fired a frightful cannonade against the defenses. It lasted two hours but no one was wounded.

During the night the English set fire to a frigate in the harbor and four houses behind our front.

The 9th - Today the army formed two lines and the von Voit Regiment was placed in the front line not far from Newport.

An English fleet consisting of about 26 ships appeared near Block Island and because of the war fleet lying at anchor in the harbor, returned to New York.

During the night our picket was constantly attacked by the enemy.

Private [Johann Georg] Lochmueller, of Captain von Stain's Company of the von Voit Regiment, was wounded on the right foot by a musket ball.

The 10th - In camp at Newport.

At nine o'clock this morning the French

war fleet prepared to sail and with a very strong cannonade, which lasted one and one-half hours, sailed out of the harbor.

The French war fleet therefore left the harbor because they thought that the fleet, which had been seen near Block Island yesterday, was a new English war fleet. However, it had been a provisions and convalescent fleet from New York.

While the cannonade continued, both lines at the front were under arms.

The 11th - This evening the camp was changed. The right wing was moved to where the left one had been.

First Lieutenant von Reitzenstein's picket caught and brought in three French officers.

The 12th - In camp at Newport.

During this night we had a strong rain and wind storm so that almost all the tents were torn. The officers, as a result, had to take quarters in the surrounding houses until the tents could be repaired.

The 13th - In camp at Newport.
Deserters from the Camp
1) Grenadier [Christoph] Bernhart
2) Grenadier [Johann Georg] Rummel
3) Private [Michael] Lorenz, of the Colonel's Company
4) Private [Lorenz] Baumann and
5) Private [Johann] Stadler, of Captain von Quesnoy's Company of the von Voit Regiment.

The 14th - In camp at Newport.

The enemy army, under command of the American General [John] Sullivan, daily drew nearer to our army.

The 15th - In camp at Newport.

Today the enemy set up camp about one mile from us and we could see it on a height lying opposite our front.

The 16th - In camp at Newport.

The 17th - In camp at Newport.

This morning the army moved forward and

remained under arms for two and one-half hours.

Private [Johann] Erlwein, of Captain von Stain's Company of the von Voit Regiment, deserted from his post at the picket this morning.

The 18th - In camp at Newport.

Deserters from the von Voit Regiment

1)   Private [Simon] Gruber, of the Grenadiers

2)   Private [Matthias] Rhau

3)   Private [Johann Jakob] Dill, and

4)   Private [Johann Michael] Telorac, of Major von Reitzenstein's Company, and

5)   Private [Peter] Hunger, of Captain von Stain's Company.

The von Voit Regiment, as well as the entire army, moved out at three o'clock in the morning and remained under arms, before the front, until after reveille.

Our defenses cannonaded the enemy camp throughout the day.

On this island of Rhode Island, during the summer, every day, at about three o'clock in the afternoon, a strong fog sets in, so that it is impossible to see more than four or five paces, and this lasts until sunrise the next day. This fog comes from the sea and is very unhealthy for the people.

The 19th - In camp at Newport.

Deserters from the von Voit Regiment

Privates Ulzhoeffer and Kassel, of Captain von Stain's Company, both of whom deserted from picket duty.

During the entire day our defenses cannonaded the newly constructed enemy forts.

Today the enemy fired his cannons, 18-pounders, at our defenses and our camp for the first time.

A soldier in the English camp had his foot shot off.

A ball went through the tent of an English private and killed and wounded eight musketeers at one time.

Therefore, no one was safe in our camp and during the evening it was moved behind the great defensive position of Tominy Hill.

At three o'clock in the morning the army was again under arms before the front.

The 20th - In camp at Tominy Hill.

The cannonade from our and the enemy forts lasted all day, without let-up.

At three o'clock in the morning, as is customary, the army was placed under arms before the front.

The French war fleet, now consisting of thirteen sail, arrived before the entrance to this seaport this evening and dropped anchor.

The 21st - In camp at Tominy Hill.

The French war fleet, before daybreak, cut their anchor ropes and sailed into the ocean.

The army, during the early morning hours, again moved forward, under arms.

The cannonade from both armies continued very strong today.

At ten o'clock at night the army, because of incoming musket fire, immediately moved forward.

The 22nd - In camp at Tominy Hill.

The cannonade on this day, especially from the enemy, was not as strong. However, from the English side, bombs were thrown at the enemy workers.

The 23rd - In camp at Tominy Hill.

At daybreak today an English regiment sent a patrol to the enemy camp. One man from the enemy was killed and two were brought back as prisoners.

As usual the army moved out early this morning. Throughout the day there was an exceptionally heavy cannonade.

During the night, from our and the enemy forts, there was a rather heavy bombardment.

A private from the English troops, on command at the defenses, was shot dead.

The 24th – In camp at Tominy Hill.

The army moved out early in the morning, as usual, and the cannonade on this day was not as heavy.

The 25th – In camp at Tominy Hill.

The army as usual moved out early and the cannonade today was somewhat lighter.

The 26th – In camp at Tominy Hill.

The army, as usual, moved out early.

Both Privates [Johann Balthasar] Schoenel and [Georg] Ermert, of the Colonel's Company, deserted tonight from picket duty while on patrol.

Today the cannonade was very light. At night, however, one of our redoubts threw many bombs at the enemy workers.

The 27th – In camp at Tominy Hill.

At one 'clock tonight, 2nd Lieutenant Prechtel,[2] of the von Voit Regiment, at the forward post with 23 men, was attacked by the enemy, who had a strength of about two hundred men.

Private Riess, of Captain von Stain's Company of the von Voit Regiment, was wounded during this incident.

Early in the morning the army moved out, as usual.

Three English frigates arrived in the local harbor this afternoon from New York.

After tattoo the army, in battle order, moved ahead of the line. Today there was not much cannonfire.

The 28th – In camp at Tominy Hill.

At daybreak the army marched back into camp. There was little cannon fire.

During the night one battalion of each regiment entered the lines.

At eleven o'clock at night 2nd Lieutenant Cyriacy was attacked three times at the outpost.

One man at this post was killed and two men were wounded in the feet while on patrol.

The 29th - In camp at Tominy Hill.

The battalions which were in the line this morning marched back into camp.

As the enemy General Sullivan vacated his camp during the night, our army of 4,000 men immediately marched forward, in order to fall on the enemy's rear.

Near Windmill Hill a battle took place. This lasted from seven o'clock in the morning until four o'clock in the afternoon.

Further, the regiments withstood the cannonade from the enemy's defenses the entire day and spent the night on Fort Windmill Hill.

Deaths in the von Voit Regiment

Grenadiers [Johann Georg] Ettmeier and [Johann Michael] Frueh were killed by cannonballs and Private [Johann] Leikam, of Captain von Stain's Company, was killed by a musketball.

Deaths in the von Seybothen Regiment

Three privates were killed by a cannon ball.

Deaths in the Hessian von Huyn Regiment

Captain [Georg Friedrich] Schaller was killed by a cannonball.

Wounded of both Ansbach Regiments

Twelve men, including Sergeant [Paul] Schmid, of Captain von Stain's Company of the von Voit Regiment who was wounded in the arm.

Two Hessian captains were severely wounded, one of whom was Captain [August Christian] Noltenius, of the Buenau Regiment.

The enemy army, consisting of 20,000 men, retreated behind the large defensive positions of Windmill Hill and the Artillery Post.

The 30th - Our army withstood the enemy's cannonade which was like yesterday's, but no one was wounded.

The 31st - During the past night the rebels shipped their troops across to New England at Bristol Ferry, and all their troops are posted there. Therefore, early this morning

both evacuated forts, Windmill Hill and the Artillery Post, were occupied by fifty men of the
Ansbach and Hessian troops. This occupation,
however, was replaced by the Hessian Landgraf
and Ditfurth Regiments, during the morning.

The Ansbach regiments entered camp at the
defensive position of Windmill Hill.

General Pigot departed for England and
therefore the command over the local troops was
assumed by the English General Prescott.

September 1778

The 1st - In camp at Windmill Hill, in
tents.

General-in-Chief Sir Henry Clinton arrived
in the harbor at Newport with a fleet of
seventy sail, as a relief force. Because the
enemy had already left Rhode Island, General-
in-Chief Clinton and the fleet sailed back to
New York.

The 2nd and 3rd - In camp at Windmill
Hill.

The 4th - In camp at Windmill Hill, oc-
cupying the defenses in front of Windmill Hill.

This evening the enemy cannonaded our camp
from the water.

The 5th - In camp at Windmill Hill.

On the end of this island, toward New England, there are two defensive positions which
had previously been built by the English and
Hessians, namely, Fort Bristol Ferry and the
Buenau Redoubt, both of which we have strongly
occupied.

From the 6th to 29th - In camp at Windmill
Hill.

The 30th - In camp at Windmill Hill.

Riding Master von Dieskau, of the Ansbach
Guards, arrived in our camp today with the
first recruit transport which he escorted to
America.

October 1778

The 1st and 2nd - In camp at Windmill Hill.

The 3rd - In camp at Windmill Hill.

Promotions

Corporals [Christian Gottfried] Baumann and [Johann Christoph] Doehlemann, of the Grenadier Company, and 1st Sergeant [Johann Gottfried] Minameier, of Major von Reitzenstein's Company of the von Voit Regiment, were promoted to 2nd lieutenant in that regiment.

The 4th - In camp at Windmill Hill.

The 5th - In camp at Windmill Hill.

First Sergeant [Johann Christian] Drexel, of Captain von Quesnoy's Company of the von Voit Regiment, was promoted to 2nd lieutenant in that regiment.

The 6th and 7th - In camp at Windmill Hill.

The 8th - In camp at Windmill Hill.

At noon today about thirty men from the rebels landed on this island in order to obtain hay and dry wood. Therefore, a captain, a subaltern, and fifty privates were immediately sent from the camp and the rebels were chased away without contact. Nevertheless, twelve cannonballs were fired at our people from two positions which the rebels had built in New England.

The 9th - In camp at Windmill Hill.

The 10th - In camp at Windmill Hill.

The Ansbach recruits arrived at Newport.

The 11th - In camp at Windmill Hill.

The 12th - In camp at Windmill Hill.

During the night the recruit transport arrived here in camp.

The 13th - In camp at Windmill Hill.

The 14th - In camp at Windmill Hill.

Corporal Schmid, of Captain von Quesnoy's Company of the von Voit Regiment, was promoted to 3rd sergeant.

The recruits were apportioned among the companies.

The 15th to 17th - In camp at Windmill Hill.

The 18th - In camp at Windmill Hill.

Field Chaplain [Georg Christoph Elias] Erb, of the von Seybothen Regiment, gave his first sermon.

The following officers arrived in America with the first recruit shipment:

1) 2nd Lieutenant [Ferdinand] Feder
2) 2nd Lieutenant [Friedrich Sigmund] Nagler

The first was assigned to the von Voit Regiment and the latter to the von Seybothen Regiment.

From the 19th to 25th - In camp at Windmill Hill.

The 26th - In camp at Windmill Hill.

A muster was held today.

From the 27th to 31st - In camp at Windmill Hill.

November 1778

From the 1st to 4th - In camp at Windmill Hill.

The 5th - In camp at Windmill Hill.

Today the von Seybothen Regiment marched away from here and into the camp at Turkey Hill.

From the 6th to 25th - In camp at Windmill Hill.

The 26th - We broke camp at Windmill Hill and marched into winter quarters at Newport, where the von Voit Regiment was quartered in Thames Street.

The 27th - In quarters at Newport.

The 28th - In quarters at Newport.

The von Seybothen Regiment entered winter quarters and received quarters in the district of the North Battery.

152

The 29th and 30th - In quarters at Newport.

December 1778

From the 1st to 9th - In quarters at New-
port.
The 10th - In quarters at Newport.
During the night there was such a terrible
windstorm that the houses, which here are all
made of wood, swayed like ships.
From the 11th to 13th - In quarters at
Newport.
The 14th - In quarters at Newport.
The eleven English men-of-war, which until
now had spent the winter in this port, sailed
for the West Indies today, under the command of
Admiral [John] Byron.
From the 15th to 25th - In quarters at
Newport.
The 26th - In quarters at Newport.
Today there was such a wind and snow that
the people in the street of the city could
hardly breathe. The snow reached the windows
of the second story.
From the 27th to 31st - In quarters at
Newport.

January 1779

From the   1st to 10th - In   quarters at Newport.

The 11th - In quarters at Newport.

A wood fleet consisting of   fourteen sail arrived here   from Long Island.   Each ship was loaded with 46 cord (*) of wood.

The recruits who had   remained in New York arrived with this fleet as convalescents.

(*) A   cord of wood is four   feet high and eight   feet wide, [and four   feet thick;   128 cubic feet].

From the 12th to 16th - In   quarters at Newport.

The 17th - In quarters at Newport.

Commencing   today, the   regiments, because of a shortage of provisions, received bread made from oats, peas, and Turkish cornmeal.

The 18th - In quarters at Newport.

Because it was the   birthday of Queen Sophia Charlotte of Great Britain, at one o'clock this afternoon two frigates lying at anchor in the   local harbor   fired a   salute with their cannon.

The   19th and 20th - In quarters at Newport.

The 21st - In quarters at Newport.

Vice-Corporal Schultheiss, of the Grenadier Company of the von Voit Regiment, had a foot amputated because of gangrene.

Six provisions ships   arrived in the local harbor from New York under escort of a frigate.

The 22nd - In quarters at Newport.

Vice-Corporal Schultheiss today   had his other foot amputated.

The 23rd - In quarters at Newport.

The 24th - In quarters at Newport.

From today onward the army again received wheat bread in which Turkish cornmeal was mixed.

The 25th - In quarters at Newport.

<u>The 26th</u> - In quarters at Newport.
Major General [Carl Ernst Johann] von
Bose, of the Hessian Landgraf Regiment, and the
English Light Infantry went aboard ship today.
<u>From the 27th to 29th</u> - In quarters at
Newport.
<u>The 30th</u> - In quarters at Newport.
At seven o'clock this morning the fleet
with the troops which boarded ship on the 26th
of this month, sailed from here for New York.
This evening a frigate from New York en-
tered the local harbor.
The 31st - In quarters at Newport.

February 1779

<u>The 1st</u> - In quarters at Newport.
<u>The 2nd</u> - In quarters at Newport.
Today Vice-Corporal Schultheiss, whose
feet had been amputated on January 21 and 22,
died.
<u>From the 3rd to 6th</u> - In quarters at
Newport.
<u>The 7th</u> - In quarters at Newport.
Grenadier [Jakob] Kaufmann, of the von
Voit Regiment, died in the hospital of a high
fever.
<u>The 8th</u> - In quarters at Newport.
Private [Andreas] Herterich, of Captain
von Stain's Company of the von Voit Regiment,
died from vomiting.
Mail from Europe arrived here on a ship
from New York.
<u>From the 9th to 16th</u> - In quarters at New-
port.
<u>The 17th</u> - In quarters at Newport.
Grenadier [Johann Georg] Schultheiss died
in the hospital of consumption.
<u>From the 18th to 23rd</u> - In quarters at
Newport.
<u>The 24th</u> - In quarters at Newport.
The wood fleet from Long Island and a pro-

visions fleet from New York entered the harbor this evening.

From the 25th to 28th - In quarters at Newport.

March 1779

From the 1st to 9th - In quarters at Newport.

The 10th - In quarters at Newport.

The Medic [Johann Wolfgang] Greiner, of the von Seybothen Regiment, died in the hospital of consumption.

From the 11th to 20th - In quarters at Newport.

The 21st - In quarters at Newport.

The Jaeger Sergeant [Jakob Ernst] Kling was promoted to 2nd lieutenant of the Jaeger Company.

Two new forts were laid out on Conanicut Island, namely, Fort Brown, close to the channel, and Fort Green, in the middle of the island. The first is occupied by Brown's Provincial Corps, because it was built by that corps. The latter, however, is occupied by one captain, one subaltern, and sixty privates, who are relieved every eighth day from Newport.

The 22nd - In quarters at Newport.

The 23rd - In quarters at Newport.

Admiral [James] Gambier arrived with a man-of-war from New York and then sailed back there with a fleet from this harbor.

From the 24th to 27th - In quarters at Newport.

The 28th - In quarters at Newport.

A wood fleet of eighteen sail entered the harbor.

From the 29th to 31st - In quarters at Newport.

April 1779

From the   1st to 3rd - In quarters   at Newport.

The 4th - In quarters at Newport.

An empty transport fleet sailed from here for New York under escort of a frigate. The English   invalids,   who are being   sent to England, departed with the fleet.

From the 5th to 7th - In quarters at Newport.

The 8th - In quarters at Newport.

Thirteen men, of Captain von Stain's Company of the von Voit Regiment, cooked and ate root cicada, or schirling.   Immediately after eating them, all became deathly sick.   They were given milk and liquids to drink to cause vomiting, after which twelve of the men,

1) Medic Roessler
2) Corporal [Georg] Fuerst
3) Drummer [Georg Nikolaus] Reichart
4) Private [Thomas] Salamon
5) Private [Johann Stephan] Goert
6) Private [Georg Friedrich] Seehart
7) Private Schneider
8) Private [Heinrich] Scherz
9) Private Hoepf
10) Private [Bartholomai] Hiller
11) Private [Christian] Wetschell, and
12) Private Bauer

recovered. Private [Johann Christian] Auernheimer, who could not be made to vomit, died after three-quarters of an hour.

The Refugees brought three prizes, which had a value of 20,000 pounds sterling, into the local harbor.

From the 9th to 16th - In quarters at Newport.

The 17th - In quarters at Newport.

An enemy two-masted privateer was captured and brought into the local harbor. It had come from the West Indies and was bound for New

England.

From the 18th to 25th - In quarters at Newport.

The 26th - In quarters at Newport.

A transport fleet, which consisted of a frigate and eleven other ships, arrived from New York. It brought the new uniforms for the von Seybothen Regiment.

From the 27th to 30th - In quarters at Newport.

May 1779

From the 1st to 8th - In quarters at Newport.

The 9th - In quarters at Newport.

Private Klein, of Captain von Quesnoy's Company of the von Voit Regiment, died in the hospital of consumption.

From the 10th to 13th - In quarters at Newport.

The 14th - In quarters at Newport.

Private [Georg Michael] Vogel, a minor, died in the hospital of dysentery.

The 15th and 16th - In quarters at Newport.

The 17th - In quarters at Newport.

A wood fleet escorted by a frigate arrived in the harbor.

The 18th - In quarters at Newport.

The 19th - In quarters at Newport.

The warship Renown,[1] which had lain at anchor, and the frigate, which arrived here on the seventeenth of the month, sailed out this morning.

The 20th - In quarters at Newport.

The 21st - In quarters at Newport.

The Refugees made an expedition against Bristol during which they captured an enemy picket of twenty men and also seized very many cattle and sheep.

Because cattle are very scarce on this is-

land, none are slaughtered except those brought
in by the Refugees.

From the 22nd to 24th - In quarters at
Newport.

The 25th - In quarters at Newport.
The English 43rd Regiment entered cantonment quarters at Middletown.

The 26th and 27th - In quarters at Newport.

The 28th - In quarters at Newport.
Colonel Fanning's Regiment of provincial
troops entered cantonment quarters on Conanicut
Island.

The 29th - In quarters at Newport.
At twelve-thirty tonight, due to drunkeness and negligence, the transport ship Christiana, which lay at anchor in the harbor, caught
fire and burned completely.

The 30th and 31st - In quarters at Newport.

June 1779

The 1st - In quarters at Newport.
The warship Renown entered the harbor this
afternoon and brought in an enemy ship with
three masts and ten cannons which it had
captured.

The 3rd - In quarters at Newport.
Private [Christian] Schaeffer, of Captain
von Stain's Company of the von Voit Regiment,
while in arrest, deserted from quarters.

The 4th - In quarters at Newport.
Because it was the birthday of His Majesty, George III, King of England, at twelve
o'clock noon a 21-gun salute was fired at the
North Battery. The warship Renown and the
other armed ships in the harbor also fired
their cannons.

The 5th - In quarters at Newport.
The 6th - In quarters at Newport.
During the past night the warship Renown,

159

with the Refugees, left the harbor.

At noon the Refugees brought eight men, whom they had captured, and forty head of cattle into Newport.

The 7th and 8th - In quarters at Newport.

The 9th - In quarters at Newport.

The Refugees returned from their expedition. They had seized 150 head of cattle and 300 sheep, but nineteen men were wounded.

At ten o'clock at night the warship Renown entered the harbor.

The 10th - In quarters at Newport.

This morning three regiments were marched into camp.

1) The 38th English Regiment to Fogland Ferry

2) The English 54th Regiment, and

3) The Hessian Landgraf Regiment to Windmill Hill.

A provisions fleet escorted by a frigate entered the local harbor from New York.

The 11th - In quarters at Newport.

This morning the English 22nd Regiment and the Hessian Ditfurth Regiment marched into camp.

Promotions

1) Major von Reitzenstein, of the von Voit Regiment, was promoted to lieutenant colonel of that regiment.

2) Grenadier Captain von Seitz, of the von Seybothen Regiment, was promoted to major of the von Voit Regiment and received Captain von Quesnoy's Company.

3) Captain von Molitor, of the von Seybothen Regiment, received the Grenadier Company of that regiment.

4) Captain von Quesnoy, of the von Voit Regiment, received the von Molitor Company of the von Seybothen Regiment.

5) Quartermaster Sergeant Meier, of the von Voit Regiment, became the commissary.

The 12th - In quarters at Newport.

Promotions

First Lieutenant von Tritschler promoted to staff captain of the Lieutenant Colonel's Company of the von Voit Regiment.

The 13th and 14th - In quarters at Newport.

The 15th - In quarters at Newport.

The English 54th Regiment and the Hessian Landgraf Regiment were embarked.

The von Seybothen Regiment marched into camp beyond the line.

The von Voit Regiment, because it has not yet been issued new tents, must remain in quarters until further orders are issued.

The 17th - In quarters at Newport.

The two regiments which embarked yesterday, sailed today, escorted by the frigate which arrived here on the tenth. As soon as they reached the ocean, a contrary wind arose, so they reentered the harbor at noon.

Colonel Fanning's Regiment of provincial troops embarked today.

From the 18th to 22nd - In quarters at Newport.

The 23rd - In quarters at Newport.

Major [Karl Gottlieb] von Arnberg, of the Hessian Landgraf Regiment, fell out of a chaise about six weeks ago, whereby he splintered his foot. Gangrene set in and he died.

The 24th - In quarters at Newport.

Major von Arnberg, who died yesterday, was buried today in the churchyard of the English Church. A detachment of 150 men of the Hessian Huyn Regiment fired three volleys.

The 25th - In quarters at Newport.

The fleet with the embarked regiments, which had lain here for eight days because of contrary winds, sailed this morning for New York.

The 26th - In quarters at Newport.

The enemy this evening drove the local fishing boats back into the harbor.

The 27th - In quarters at Newport.
During the past night the enemy landed at Brenton's Point and wanted to seize livestock.
From the 28th to 30th - In quarters at Newport.

July 1779

From the 1st to 6th - In quarters at Newport.
The 7th - In quarters at Newport.
At three o'clock this morning the warship Renown sailed from here for New London to participate in the expedition.
The von Seybothen Regiment received orders to change its camp and moved to the vicinity of Fort Tominy Hill.
From the 8th to 22nd - In quarters at Newport.
The 23rd - In quarters at Newport.
This afternoon a wood and provisions fleet of about forty sail entered the local harbor from New York.
The 24th - In quarters at Newport.
The warship Renown, which sailed to New London on the seventh of this month, again entered the harbor here during the afternoon.
From the 25th to 27th - In quarters at Newport.
The 28th - In quarters at Newport.
The frigate Thames entered the local harbor from New London.
The 29th - In quarters at Newport.
The 30th - In quarters at Newport.
The deserter, Private Schaeffer, who deserted on 3 June, was arrested on the 26th of this month, in Holms' house on this island, and brought to the regiment at Newport. This morning, at a courtmartial his sentence was pronounced. Schaeffer, because of his disloyal desertion and his intention to go over to the enemy, was to be executed by hanging. After

half an hour, he was informed that instead of paying with his life, he must run a gauntlet of two hundred men, 36 times in two days.
The 31st – In quarters at Newport.

August 1779

From the 1st to 17th – In quarters at Newport.
The 18th – In quarters at Newport.
A Negro, Karl, out of meanness, cut off the ears of a provisions horse. Therefore, he was punished with 250 lashes, at the main watch.
From the 19th to 30th – In quarters at Newport.
The 31st – In quarters at Newport.
This afternoon a wood fleet, escorted by the frigate Restoration,[2] which belongs to the English Commissary Lehnert, entered the harbor.

September 1779

From the 1st to 5th – In quarters at Newport.
The 6th – In quarters at Newport.
The warship Rainbow, in German, Regenbogen, which had been cruising on the Delaware River, entered the harbor here.
The 7th – In quarters at Newport.
The 8th – In quarters at Newport.
The frigate Restoration and fifteen small armed ships sailed out of the harbor this morning.
The 9th – In quarters at Newport.
An empty fleet, escorted by the frigate Delaware, sailed from here for New York.
The 10th – In quarters at Newport.
The 11th – In quarters at Newport.
Medic [Friedrich] Gollwitz, of Major von Stain's Company of the von Voit Regiment, died in his quarters of an apoplectic stroke.

From the 12th to 28th - In quarters at Newport.

The 29th - In quarters at Newport.

The frigate <u>Hunter</u> entered the local harbor this afternoon from New York. It brought the news that seventeen French warships had arrived at Sandy Hook, and then again sailed into the ocean.

The 30th - In quarters at Newport.

October 1779

The 1st - In quarters at Newport.

The frigate <u>Hunter</u> sailed from here for New York before daybreak.

The 2nd - In quarters at Newport.

The 3rd - In quarters at Newport.

The Hessian Buenau Regiment marched out of camp at Turkey Hill and entered camp close to the city of Newport.

The 4th - In quarters at Newport.

Deserters

Private [Friedrich] Abt and Quartermaster Guard Kreyer, of Captain von Eyb's Company of the von Seybothen Regiment, deserted during transfer to Conanicut.

From the 5th to 10th - In quarters at Newport.

The 11th - In quarters at Newport.

Fifty-four ships, escorted by three frigates, entered the local harbor. They are all empty transport ships on which the local army is to embark.

Today the embarkation of the artillery was begun, during which an English artillery soldier was crushed by an howitzer.

The 12th - In quarters at Newport.

The embarkation of the artillery and provisions was well under way.

Mister Lehnert entered the harbor here with his frigate <u>Restoration</u> and other armed vessels.

The 13th - In quarters at Newport.
The regimental baggage was loaded.
The 14th - In quarters at Newport.
The warship <u>Rainbow</u> and a sloop-of-war,
with eighteen cannons, sailed out of the harbor
this evening, in order to capture the enemy
ships which were seen today on the ocean.
The 15th - In quarters at Newport.
The Ansbach regiments received the follow-
ing transport ships for embarkation:
The von Voit Regiment

1) <u>Mertschery</u>
2) <u>Shipwright</u>
The von Seybothen Regiment

1) <u>Silver Eel</u>
2) <u>Nestor</u>
The 16th and 17th - In quarters at New-
port.
The 18th - In quarters at Newport.
The North Battery was demolished.
The 19th - In quarters at Newport.
The defenses on Goat Island were demol-
ished and the woodwork of the North Battery was
set on fire.
The 20th - In quarters at Newport.
At the North Battery more fortifications
were destroyed and munitions set on fire.
The sick were taken aboard the transport
ships.
The cattle belonging to the army were
slaughtered and fresh provisions were delivered
to the army.
The captured enemy ships, previously dis-
armed, which are here in the harbor, were made
completely unusable.
The 21st - In quarters at Newport.
The regimental horses were embarked and
the fort at Brenton's Point, demolished.
The 22nd - In quarters at Newport.
The English Artillery troops and the American prisoners of war were embarked.
Many useless ships, including the frigate

<u>Flora</u>, were set on fire this evening.

All the transport ships left the city and anchored close to the warships on the sea.

Some provisions, which could not be loaded aboard ship, were thrown in the water.

The 23rd - In quarters at Newport.

Following the attack at Windmill Hill, the troops here had laid out three exceptionally fine defensive positions ahead of the lines, namely:

1) Fort Clinton
2) Fort Prescott, and
3) The Star Fort,

which prior to our retreat were completely destroyed.

The 24th - In quarters at Newport.

The 25th - The army at Rhode Island broke camp and retired to Brenton's Point, where the regiments were embarked in the following order:

1) The Hessian von Buenau Regiment
2) The von Voit Regiment, and
3) The von Seybothen Regiment of Ansbach
4) The von Huyn Regiment, and
5) The von Ditfurth Regiment of Hessians
6) The 43rd Regiment
7) The 38th Regiment, and
8) The 22nd Regiment of Englanders
9) The Hessian Jaegers and English Light Horse, and
10) Brown's Corps of provincial troops, which had been on Conanicut Island.

After the embarkation, the fort at Brenton's Point was set on fire.

During the entire retreat, nothing was seen nor heard of the enemy.

After all the troops were on board, the fleet, consisting of 130 sail, went underway at seven o'clock in the evening. The frigate <u>Blonde</u> carried the Commodore.

We sailed the entire night with a very favorable wind and at twelve o'clock at night, the fleet had already entered the Sound at

Block Island.

The 26th - We sailed all day with good wind and at twelve o'clock at night, near Huntington, a small city lying on Long Island, we anchored.

The 27th - We sailed at seven o'clock in the morning and during the morning passed the numerous rocks in the water, the dangerous Hell's Gate, or in German, Hoellen Thuer. At one o'clock in the afternoon the fleet entered the seaport at New York.

From Newport to New York it is 175 miles and we sailed this in 36 hours.

At Hell's Gate the transport ship carrying General Prescott's baggage ran onto a sandbank. The transport ship Mertschery, which sailed behind the ship, and had to follow the same path, raised all sails and sailed past this ship. In this manner no one was hurt and the ship was moved off the sandbank so that it could not sink, and the baggage was still saved.

From the 28th to 30th - At anchor at New York.

The 31st - At anchor at New York.

The von Seybothen Regiment was landed and entered the camp at the Farmers' Gardens at New York.

November 1779

The 1st - Lying at anchor at New York.
The 2nd - Lying at anchor at New York.

Corporal [Carl] Graebner, of the von Seybothen Regiment, was promoted to 2nd lieutenant of that regiment.

The 3rd - The von Voit Regiment landed and entered quarters at New York.

Promotions

The Jaeger Corps was divided into two companies, following which:

1) Captain Lieutenant von Roeder received

a company.

2) First Lieutenant von der Heydte and

3) Second Lieutenant von Diemar, Sr., were promoted to 1st lieutenants in the Jaeger Companies.

4) Staff Captain von Tritschler went to the Colonel's Company.

5) First Lieutenant and Adjutant von Koenitz was promoted to staff captain of Lieutenant Colonel von Reitzenstein's Company.

6) Second Lieutenant von Trechsel was promoted to 1st lieutenant of the Colonel's Company.

7) Second Lieutenant Feder became adjutant.

8) First Sergeant Halbmeyer was promoted to 2nd lieutenant and

9) Corporal Beyer, of the Colonel's Company, became 1st sergeant.

Three 2nd lieutenants came here about two and one-half months ago with the recruits.

1) von Hohendorf was assigned to the von Voit Regiment.

2) Schuchard and

3) Hirsch both went to the von Seybothen Regiment.

<u>Recalled</u>

1) First Lieutenant von Feilitzsch, of the Jaeger Corps, and

2) Second Lieutenant von Strahlendorf, of the von Seybothen Regiment.

<u>The 4th</u> - In quarters at New York.

The recruits of the second transport, which 2nd Lieutenant von Hohendorf brought here, were divided among the companies.

<u>From the 5th to 7th</u> - In quarters at New York.

<u>The 8th</u> - In quarters at New York.

On the South Wharf watch tonight a sailor was stabbed to death.

<u>The 9th</u> - In quarters at New York.

Private [Johann Christoph] Mercklein, of

Colonel von Voit's Company, was promoted to medic.

From the 10th to 18th - In quarters at New York.

The 19th - In quarters at New York.

Because of the conquest of the city of Savannah in Georgia, a feu de joie was fired. The regiments at the headquarters at New York, are the following:

The 42nd Scottish Regiment
The two Ansbach regiments, and
Four Hessian Grenadier Battalions.

At five o'clock in the evening these marched to the great parade ground, outside the city, on the North River. When it was completely dark, a 21-gun salute was fired from Fort George. Following this, a rotational firing [of small arms] was carried out from the right to the left wing. From the troops on command at Paulus Hook, the same type of firing was carried out. When the three volleys were finished, the regiments gave a very loud shout of hurrah. Those persons favoring the Crown, illuminated their houses. The Commanding General-in-Chief Clinton, with his entire suite, was present.

The 20th - In quarters at New York.

The 21st - In quarters at New York.

Recruit Seidel, of Colonel von Voit's Company, died in the hospital of bilious fever.

The 22nd - In quarters at New York.

The von Seybothen Regiment moved into winter quarters in the brewery on the North River.

From the 23rd to 30th - In quarters at New York.

December 1779

From the 1st to 5th - In quarters at New York.

The 6th - In quarters at New York.

This morning the von Voit Regiment was

mustered.
    From the 7th to 12th - In quarters at New
York.
    The 13th - In quarters at New York.
    Promotions in the von Voit Regiment
           In the Colonel's Company
    1)   Corporal [Andreas] Albrecht was pro-
moted to 2nd sergeant.
    2)   Vice-Corporal   [Johann   Christoph]
Schirmer to corporal.
Lieutenant Colonel von Reitzenstein's Company
    3)   Vice-Corporal Schoepler was promoted
to quartermaster sergeant.
    4)   Private [Johann David] Prechtel to
corporal.
    5)   Private Gackstetter to vice-corporal.
           Major von Seitz' Company
    6)   Second Sergeant [Ludwig Theodor] Hil-
pert was promoted to 1st sergeant.
    7)   Third Sergeant Schmid to 2nd sergeant.
    8)   Corporal [Johann] Blauhoeffer to 3rd
sergeant.
    9)   Vice-Corporal Decker to corporal.
    10)   Private [Johann Sebastian] Blank to
corporal.
    11)   Private [Johann]   Preiss to vice-
corporal.
           Captain von Stain's Company
    12)   Second Sergeant [Michael] Hofmann to
1st sergeant.
    13)   Corporal [Johann] Flohr to 2nd ser-
geant.
    14)   Vice-Corporal [Johann Georg Michael]
Winkler to corporal.
    15)   Private Kretsch to vice-corporal.
    Private [Heinrich] Bauschinger, of Lieu-
tenant Colonel von Reitzenstein's Company, was
made a cannoneer.
    Quartermaster Sergeant [Johann Georg]
Beck, of the Jaeger Corps, was recalled and his
place was taken by Quartermaster Sergeant
[Leonhard] Hausselt, of Captain von Stain's

Company.
　　Corporal [Johann Georg Friedrich] Schmalz,
of Colonel von Voit's Company, was promoted to
quartermaster sergeant in Captain von Stain's
Company.
　　The 14th - In quarters at New York.
　　Promotions in Colonel von Voit's Company
　　1) Vice-Corporal Haehnlein was promoted
to corporal.
　　2) Private Haehnlein was promoted to
vice-corporal.
　　The 15th - In quarters at New York.
　　The invalids, who are to return to Europe,
were embarked.
　　Non-commissioned Officers of the von Voit
Regiment
and Invalids Returned to Europe
　　1) Second Sergeant [Johann Heinrich] Wiederhold, of the Colonel's Company
　　2) Quartermaster Sergeant [Johann Fried-
rich] Dorn and
　　3) Corporal [Johann Adam] Weiss, of the
Lieutenant Colonel's Company
　　4) First Sergeant [Johann] Raab and
　　5) Corporal [Leonhard] Schneider, of the
Major's Company, and
　　6) First Sergeant [Paul] Schmid, of Cap-
tain von Stain's Company.
　　First Lieutenant von Feilitzsch, of the
Jaeger Corps, and Second Lieutenant von
Strahlendorf, of the von Seybothen Regiment
began their trip to Europe today.[3]
　　From the 16th to 18th - In quarters at New
York.
　　The 19th - In quarters at New York.
　　The four Hessian Grenadier Battalions, the
English 64th Regiment, and a detachment from
the Jaeger Corps embarked.
　　The 20th - In quarters at New York.
　　The 21st - In quarters at New York.
　　The troops embarked on the nineteenth of
this month sailed from here this morning for

Charleston.

The 22nd - In quarters at New York.

The 23rd - In quarters at New York.

A transport ship, on which were fifty jaegers of the troops which left the harbor on the 21st of this month, and was lying at anchor at Sandy Hook, had the anchor rope broken by an ice flow. Therefore, it was driven through the entire harbor by the very strong storm and onto land near Brooklyn. This ship was stove in and taking water. The jaegers were saved and were landed at New York.

The 24th - In quarters at New York.

Private Baender, of Colonel von Voit's Company, on the forward post of the Naval Stores watch, had challenged, in English and German, a boatload of sailors that was approaching him, four or five times. It was transferring baggage from the ship involved in yesterday's accident. As no one answered, he fired and killed a sailor.

From the 25th to 31st - In quarters at New York.

January 1780

From the 1st to 4th - In quarters at New York.

The 5th - In quarters at New York.
Private Langfritz, of Captain von Quesnoy's Company of the von Seybothen Regiment, died in the hospital at Vauxhall.

From the 6th to 13th - In quarters at New York.

The 14th - In quarters at New York.
Today the East River is frozen so that many people have crossed from here to Brooklyn on the ice. However, at eleven o'clock, midday, the tide came in and the river immediately opened again.

The 15th - In quarters at New York.
The enemy crossed the Kills River, which is frozen over, from Amboy to Staten Island, with 9,000 men and attacked our troops. One thousand men of the regiments lying in garrison here were detached as a reinforcement. They were embarked at four o'clock in the afternoon, but because of much ice were unable to sail and therefore had to be debarked again.

The 16th - In quarters at New York.
The 1,000 men, who were to have sailed over to Staten Island as a reinforcement, were embarked again this morning and because the ice still prevented them from being shipped over, at eleven o'clock, midday, they were again debarked.

The enemy reportedly remains on the island, but in the area toward Amboy.

The 17th - In quarters at New York.
The enemy, under the command of the American General [William Alexander, Lord] Stirling, withdrew from Staten Island.

The British troops on Staten Island, commanded by the English General [Thomas] Stirling, during this attack, suffered four dead. On the enemy's side, twelve men were made prisoners of war.

The 18th - In quarters at New York.

Today was the birthday of Queen Sophia Charlotte of England. At twelve o'clock noon a 21-gun salute was fired at Fort George. During the evening General [William] Tryon held a dinner and ball, to which all officers were invited. The house, in which the ball was held, was beautifully illuminated.

The 19th - In quarter at New York.

The 20th - In quarters at New York.

At present the North River is frozen so that the detachment at Paulus Hook, about one mile off New Jersey, can cross back and forth on the ice.

The 1st to 4th - In quarters at New York.

The 25th - In quarters at New York.

During the night a strike force, consisting of 400 men from the regiments lying in garrison here, marched across the ice on the North River to Paulus Hook and from there to Bergen, in New Jersey. Beyond this enemy city a rebel picket of thirty men was captured. These troops were brought here during the night, by our forces, as prisoners of war.

From the 26th to 30th - In quarters at New York.

The 31st - In quarters at New York.

The Hessian Staff Captain [Adolf Wilhelm] von Eschwege, of the Landgraf Regiment, was buried this afternoon in the churchyard of the St. Paul's Church. A detachment from his regiment fired the customary three volleys.

February 1780

From the 1st to 4th - In quarters at New York.

The 5th - In quarters at New York.

The English troops sent an expedition out over Kingsbridge, which captured an enemy out-

post. Ninety-five prisoners of war, among whom
many were wounded, were brought back here.
     The enemy had one hundred men killed. On
the English side, however, only five men were
killed.
     From the 6th to 8th - In quarters at New
York.
     The 9th - In quarters at New York.
     Private Katzenwinkel, who had deserted on
10 March 1778, returned again to the von Voit
Regiment.
     From the 10th to 16th - In quarters at New
York.
     The 17th - In quarters at New York.
     Private Katzenwinkel, who had returned to
the regiment on the ninth of this month, despite his desertion, was allowed his freedom.
However, for a time he had used a false name,
Major Ernst von Reitzenstein, for which crime
he was punished by running the gauntlet twelve
times.
     Private [Georg Peter] Beck, of Colonel von
Voit's Company, died in the hospital.
     The 18th - In quarters at New York.
     The 19th - In quarters at New York.
     A packet boat arrived from England.
     The 20th and 21st - In quarters at New
York.
     The 22nd - In quarters at New York.
     The North River remained frozen over from
January 20 until today. During this time all
provisions were carried across the river to
Staten Island with wagons.
     From the 23rd to 29th - In quarters at New
York.

                    March 1780

     From the 1st to 4th - In quarters at New
York.
     The 5th - In quarters at New York.
     The 76th Regiment of Scots and the 80th

                    175

Regiment marched from here for Long Island.

An old warship, on which prisoners were kept, burned today in the harbor, having been set afire by the prisoners, who in part saved themselves and in part were saved by the warships.

The 6th - In quarters at New York.

The 7th - In quarters at New York.

The frigates Thames and Virginia, as well as a privateer, sailed from here this morning. They are going to the Delaware River to cruise for enemy ships which plan to sail out of Philadelphia.

From the 8th to 20th - In quarters at New York.

The 21st - In quarters at New York.

At seven o'clock this evening a 74-gun ship arrived from Georgia. General [James] Robertson, who recently left London, also arrived on this ship.

The 22nd - In quarters at New York.

Private Krieger, of the von Seybothen Regiment, accidently shot and killed himself, between three and five o'clock this morning, while on duty at his post on the Naval Stores watch.

The 23rd - In quarters at New York.

A strike command of 350 men, under the command of Lieutenant Colonel [Duncan] McPherson, was carried over to Jersey last night and, not far from Hackensack, burned down a village.

During this affair the following were made prisoners of war: Private Herterich, of the Colonel's Company, and Private [Christoph] Uhlmann, of the Major's Company, both of the von Voit Regiment, and one private of the von Seybothen Regiment.

Of the Hessians, seven privates of the Leib Regiment, three privates of the Landgraf Regiment, and five privates of the von Donop Regiment were captured.

From the 24th to 30th - In quarters at New

York.
     The 31st - In quarters at New York.
     Today muster was held before Colonel von
Voit's quarters.

                         April 1780

     The 1st - In quarters at New York.
     The following regiments were embarked:
     1)   The 42nd Regiment of Scots
     2)   The Queen's Rangers
     3)   The Prince of Wales' Volunteers
     4)   The Hessian von Ditfurth Regiment.
     The English 22nd Regiment came from Long
Island to Staten Island and the English 37th
Regiment to New York.
     The 2nd - In quarters at New York.
     The fleet, on which troops were embarked
yesterday, sailed from here for Charleston.
     From the 3rd to 16th - In quarters at New
York.
     The 17th - In quarters at New York.
     An expedition to Hackensack in New Jersey
was made by a strike force of three hundred
men. Seventy of the enemy were brought back as
prisoners of war. The Hessians, on the other
hand, had six dead and thirteen wounded.
     From the 18th to 24th - In quarters at New
York.
     The 25th - In quarters at New York.
     A fleet from England, consisting of 95
sail, entered the local seaport this afternoon.
     The 26th and 27th - In quarters at New
York.
     The 28th - In quarters at New York.
     This year's exercises were conducted by
the von Voit Regiment, and executed exceptionally well. General [James] Pattison, as
well as General Robertson and the Brunswick
Major General [Friedrich Adolf] von Riedesel,
attended these exercises and maneuvers with a
large number of officers.

Mail arrived from Europe.

The 29th and 30th - In quarters at New York.

May 1780

From the 1st to 9th - In quarters at New York.

The 10th - In quarters at New York.

Today the von Seybothen Regiment conducted exercises and maneuvers before the Hessian Lieutenant General von Knyphausen and the English Brigadier General Paterson.

The 11th and 12th - In quarters at New York.

The 13th - In quarters at New York.

The English 37th and 43rd Regiments conducted their maneuvers with firing this morning.

The 14th - In quarters at New York.

The 15th - In quarters at New York.

The two English regiments mentioned on the thirteenth of this month conducted their maneuvers and firing this morning, before Brigadier General Paterson, with a great many onlookers in attendance.

The English 44th Regiment and the Hessian von Lossberg Regiment embarked and are to sail to Canada in a few days.

The English 54th Regiment replaced the 44th Regiment at Paulus Hook.

The English 38th Regiment was sent to Jamaica, on Long Island, and entered the camp on the height at Brooklyn Ferry.

From the 16th to 18th - In quarters at New York.

The 19th - In quarters at New York.

The frigate Gaudalupe came from England and brought four captured ships into the harbor, of which two were Spanish, one with 22 cannons, one French, and one American.

One came from the island of Martinique and

was very heavily loaded with all sorts of merchandise.

The 20th and 21st - In quarters at New York.

The 22nd - In quarters at New York.

The two Hessian regiments, the Leib Regiment and the Landgraf, conducted firing exercises this morning.

The 23rd - In quarters at New York.

Again today, two Hessian regiments, Donop and Bose, conducted firing exercises.

The 24th - In quarters at New York.

Mail arrived from Europe.

The 25th - In quarters at New York.

The 26th - In quarters at New York.

Four Hessian Regiments, Leib Regiment, Landgraf, Donop, and Bose, this morning were reviewed at the exercise place on the East River and also fired [their weapons].

The 27th - In quarters at New York.

The 28th - In quarters at New York.

The Hessian Engineer Captain and Deputy Quartermaster General [Wilhelm Reinhard Jakob] Martin died yesterday afternoon and was buried in the churchyard at St. Paul's at six o'clock this evening.

The 29th - In quarters at New York.

The frigate Iris entered the local harbor and brought the news that the Americans had surrendered Charleston to the General-in-Chief Sir Henry Clinton. Six thousand Americans were made prisoners of war, including six generals.

The above frigate Iris was not meant to come here but to go to Halifax. However, as it captured three American ships, it decided to sail here and bring the ships in. They were: one of twelve, one of fourteen, and one of twenty guns.

The 30th - In quarters at New York.

The 31st - In quarters at New York.

The English cannoneers today conducted firing exercises on the large exercise place on the East River.

June 1780

The 1st — In quarters at New York.
The Ansbach Artillery conducted firing exercises today.
The 2nd and 3rd — In quarters at New York.
The 4th — In quarters at New York.
Today was the birthday of His Royal Majesty, George III of Great Britain, who turned 42 years old. A royal 21-gun salute was fired at Fort George. All the armed ships lying at anchor in the harbor fired a salute and, after this occurred, on every ship a very loud hurrah was given.
The 5th — In quarters at New York.
The 6th — Today an expedition consisting of 7,000 men, under the command of the Hessian Lieutenant General von Knyphausen, sailed over to Staten Island in flatboats and schooners and made night camp at Decker's Ferry.
The 7th — At four o'clock in the morning the army moved out and was carried across the Kills River in flatboats.
As soon as the Field Jaegers, who constituted the advance guard, arrived at Elizabethtown, an uninterrupted small arms fire began. The army marched on to Connecticut Farms.
There the enemy was attacked and in the fighting 2nd Lieutenant [Friedrich] Ebenauer, of the Ansbach Jaeger Corps, was killed.
Wounded
1) The English General Stirling, by a musketball in the foot.
2) The Hessian Ensign [Bernhard Wilhelm] Wiederhold, of the Leib Regiment, received two wounds from musketballs.
At twelve o'clock at night, the army retreated back to Elizabethtown and set up night camp close to the Kills River.

The 8th - The 17th Dragoons and the 22nd
Regiment, both English regiments, moved forward
toward Elizabethtown this morning. The first
had entered the small city of Elizabethtown.
The latter, however, marched to the right of
the woods. Although these regiments exchanged
shots with the enemy the entire morning, they
were completely driven back into the lines by
midday. As a result the Ansbach von Voit
Regiment at once moved forward and fired on the
enemy with cannon and small arms, charging
three times, one after the other, and with such
a terrible fire against the enemy from cannon
and small arms that the enemy could no longer
withstand the fire, but had to retreat all the
way back to Elizabethtown.

During this attack the von Voit Regiment
had the following wounded:

1) Grenadier Bach

2) Grenadier Goll

3) Private Schmid, of Lieutenant Colonel
von Reitzenstein's Company, and

4) Private Walter

5) Private Imhaeusser, and

6) Private [Valentin] Grau, of Captain
von Stain's Company.

The enemy losses on the other hand, were
one major, two subalterns, and seventy privates, a total of 73 persons.

After half an hour, the enemy again opened
fire on our outposts. Therefore, every outpost
was reinforced with a field jaeger and by this
means, the enemy was silenced.

The camp for our troops, about a mile from
Elizabethtown, was formed in a square and built
of huts made from various boards and brush.

Two enemy deserters, from the infantry,
entered the camp.

Elizabethtown, a rather uniformly built
little city, is well populated and lively, but
has only one church.

The 9th - In camp near Elizabethtown.

This morning the fire from the outpost was very heavy. However, this afternoon it was less or nothing at all.

Private Abt, of the von Seybothen Regiment, who deserted on 4 October 1779, entered our camp as a deserter from the rebels and brought a horse with saddle and bridle, which he had ridden as a member of the Light Horse, with him.

The 10th - In camp near Elizabethtown.

This afternoon the camp was changed and moved forward toward Elizabethtown, in a line.

An enemy deserter, from the Light Horse, by name of [Michael] Guenther, arrived here in camp with a horse and is already enlisted into the Ansbach Jaeger Corps.

The Jaeger Sergeant [Joseph] Bach was promoted to 2nd lieutenant in the Jaeger Corps.

The 11th - In camp near Elizabethtown.

The enemy had almost completely withdrawn from Elizabethtown and our sailors took a schooner away from near Elizabethtown.

The defenses for our retreat on the Kills River were being strengthened day and night, by our army.

The 12th - In camp near Elizabethtown.

An enemy member of the Light Horse arrived in our camp as a deserter.

Six citizens of Elizabethtown shot from a house and wounded a field jaeger. They were later arrested and sent to headquarters at New York.

An English engineer, who was to map the region near Elizabethtown, was shot from among the ruins near the church at Elizabethtown, and had to have his foot amputated.

The 13th - In camp near Elizabethtown.

There was no firing today.

An expedition by the Field Jaegers was made through Elizabethtown and brought back the report that the enemy had withdrawn.

The 14th - In camp near Elizabethtown.

The 15th - In camp near Elizabethtown.
During our stay here, three defensive po-
sitions have been built on the Kills River.
Also a floating bridge over the Kills River
between Staten Island and Jersey has been
constructed with 29 one and two-masted ships.
A Hessian field jaeger was killed this
evening at an outpost.
The 16th - In camp near Elizabethtown.
During the Jaegers' patrol an enemy ri-
fleman was wounded and taken captive.
The 17th - In camp near Elizabethtown.
The floating bridge across the Kills River
is 270 strides long.
The Ansbach von Seybothen Regiment arrived
here in camp today from New York.
Since the troops have been here near Elizabethtown, the von Voit Regiment has been in
the brigade of the Hessian Major General [Carl
Wilhelm] von Hackenberg. However, now the 2nd
Ansbach Regiment is in the brigade of Colonel
von Voit.
The Hessian regiments, Donop and Bose,
built two small defensive positions during the
night.
Washington's army retreated during the
night to Chatham, but continued firing with
cannons at the workers. However, it was very
quiet at the outposts.
The 18th - In camp near Elizabethtown.
The 19th - In camp near Elizabethtown.
General-in-Chief Clinton arrived at New
York recently from Charleston and today he came
here and observed the army in camp. The regiments moved out without weapons.
Because the English and Hessians conducted
themselves so bravely during the conquest of
Charleston, the General-in-Chief Clinton has
ordered them to wear a plume as a sign of
honor.
The enemy fire on our outposts was fairly
strong.

The 20th - In camp near Elizabethtown.
A strike command from our army, consisting
of fifty men, moved through the woods on our
left wing, but made no contact with the enemy.
The 21st - In camp near Elizabethtown.
This morning the enemy fired at our whale
boat lying in the Kills River, but our cannon
fire forced them to again withdraw.
Twenty-eight enemy deserters arrived in
camp and four prisoners were brought in from
the militia.
The 22nd - In camp near Elizabethtown.
The Queen's Ranger Regiment, which had
been at Charleston, came here to join the
Jaeger Corps and the Hessian Donop Regiment at
the outposts.
This evening an expedition was undertaken
in which a private of the Rangers was killed
and one corporal and one private, of the
mounted jaegers, were wounded.
The 23rd - In camp near Elizabethtown.
Lieutenant General von Knyphausen moved
forward over Springfield this morning, with the
following regiments:
  1)   The 17th Dragoon Regiment
  2)   The Guard Regiment
  3)   The 22nd Regiment
  4)   The 37th Regiment
  5)   The 38th Regiment
  6)   The 57th Regiment
  7)   The Blue Hussars, and
  8)   The Green Hussars, all the above being
English units.
  9)   The Ansbach von Seybothen Regiment
  10) The Jaeger Corps
  11) The Leib Regiment
  12) The Landgraf Regiment, and
  13) The von Bose Regiment, the last three
are Hessian units.
The reserve corps consisted of the following:
The 22nd Regiment [sic]

The 43rd Regiment, and
The Queen's Rangers, English units,
The Ansbach von Voit Regiment
The von Donop Regiment, and
The Buenau Regiment, of Hessians.

The enemy was attacked near Springfield, but withstood the heavy fire very well.

During the evening the [English] army retreated into the lines near Elizabethtown.

During this engagement the following officers were wounded:

1) Captain Norman, of the 38th Regiment
2) Lieutenant Colonel [Ernst Karl] von Prueschenck and
3) Captain [Friedrich Heinrich] Lorey, of the Hessian Jaegers
4) Captain von Roeder and
5) 1st Lieutenant von Diemar, of the Ansbach Jaegers.

The dead and wounded, on the English side, amounted to some seventy men.

Springfield, a rather small place, was laid in ashes.

During the evening, the army received the order to immediately vacate the Jerseys. Therefore, at ten o'clock in the evening, it withdrew, in the best order, across the floating bridge to Staten Island. The outlying pickets formed the rear guard.

Further, the enemy remained quiet during the retreat and nothing more was heard of them.

Deserters during withdrawl from Springfiled

From the von Voit Regiment, Private [Wilhelm] Braun, of Captain von Stain's Company, and Officer's Servant Bauer, servant for Staff Captain von Tritschler.

The 24th - At two o'clock in the morning the regiments arrived at Decker's Ferry on Staten Island.

This morning the English regiments were embarked on schooners and shipped to Philipsburg, on York Island.

185

The 43rd English Regiment and the Hessian
von Donop Regiment were shipped to New York.
The Hessian von Buenau Regiment remained
on Staten Island.
The 25th - Both Ansbach regiments and the
Hessian regiments were also embarked this
morning and were to have gone to Philipsburg.
The wind, during the evening, was very unfavorable and the anchor was dropped in the North
River at Fort Knyphausen.
The 26th - We sailed at four o'clock in
the morning and during the evening sailed in
near Philipsburg, where the camp on the heights
was occupied.
Captain Norman, who was wounded on the
23rd of this month near Springfiled, died at
New York and was buried.
The 27th - The camp was moved forward a-
bout two and one-half miles.
Grenadier [Johann Peter] Seifferlein, of
the von Voit Regiment, deserted from camp.
From the 28th to 30th - In camp near Philipsburg.

July 1780

The 1st - In camp near Philipsburg.
The baggage and tents of the regiments arrived today.
From the 2nd to 4th - In camp near Philipsburg.
The 5th - In camp near Philipsburg.
Deserters from the von Voit Regiment
1) Staff Servant [Johann Adam] Reuter
2) Private [Johann] Stuelpner, of Major
von Seitz' Company,
3) Private Kraus, of Lieutenant Colonel
von Reitzenstein's Company, while on post with
the picket.
The 6th - In camp near Philipsburg.
Grenadier [Georg] Hohenberger, of the von
Voit Regiment, deserted from camp.

The 7th - In camp near Philipsburg.
Grenadier [Michael] Erhardt, of the von
Voit Regiment, deserted from the field watch.
The 8th - In camp near Philipsburg.
Deserters from the von Voit Regiment
1) Grenadier Braun
2) Grenadier [Friedrich] Gossler, from
the camp.
From the 9th to 11th - In camp near Phil-
ipsburg.
The 12th - In camp near Philipsburg.
Private [Johann Heinrich] Rhau, of Colonel
von Voit's Company, deserted from the camp and
was captured by the Jaeger's picket and brought
back in arrest.
The Ansbach Field Jaeger [Adam] Gardelow
deserted from the picket.
From the 13th to 16th - In camp near Philipsburg.
The 17th - In camp near Philipsburg.
An enemy deserter entered camp.
The 18th - In camp near Philipsburg.
Private [Martin] Zollfrank, of Major von
Seitz' Company of the von Voit Regiment, deserted while bathing.
The 19th and 20th - In camp near Philipsburg.
The 21st - At three-thirty in the morning
the two Ansbach regiments marched to Harlem and
entered camp there.
This afternoon the enemy attacked the Refugees in Jersey opposite Harlem and burned
their two vessels. The Refugees not only defended their blockhouse, but during the enemy's
retreat, captured the two cannons which they
had with them.
The 22nd and 23rd - In camp near Harlem.
The 24th - The two Ansbach regiments
marched to New York and entered camp at the
exercise place on the East River.
The 25th - In camp at New York
The 26th - In camp at New York

This morning the following sentence was
pronounced against the recaptured deserter
Rhau, who had deserted on the twelfth of this
month. Because of his having committed disloyal desertion, he was to be punished by hanging. But, as this was an especially severe
punishment, it was changed to death by a firing
squad.

The Hessian Major General [Johann Chris-
toph] von Huyn was buried at six o'clock this
evening in the garrison church, as befitted his
rank.

The burial command consisted of the Grenadier Companies of the Ansbach von Voit Regiment, the Hessian von Donop Regiment, and three
cannons.

The 27th - In camp at New York.

Lieutenant and Auditor Herrnbauer died at
New York during the past night and as he requested, was buried without further ceremony in
the exercise place, where both Ansbach regiments are camped.

The 28th - In camp at New York.

The deserter Rhau, of the von Voit Regiment was executed behind the front at seven
o'clock this morning.

The 29th and 30th - In camp at New York.

The 31st - In camp at New York.

The deserter Glatz, of Captain von Eby's
Company of the von Voit Regiment, who had been
captured, was sentenced to be hanged by a
court-martial, and he was immediately so notified.

August 1780

The 1st - In camp at New York.

The 2nd - In camp at New York.

Private Glatz, of the von Seybothen Regiment, notified of the death sentence by hanging, had the sentence changed to death by a
firing squad, and this morning at seven o'clock

this was carried out behind the front.

From the 3rd to 11th - In camp at New York.

The 12th - In camp at New York.

Today was the Prince of Wales' birthday. All the ships raised their flags and during the evening there was a house illumination at Brooklyn and a fireworks display.

The 13th - In camp at New York.

Major General Pattison, City Commandant of New York, gave up his office because of poor health. General-in-Chief Clinton appointed Lieutenant General Robertson to fill this office.

The 14th - In camp at New York.

The 15th - In camp at New York.

People were pressed onto the warships. Therefore, from ten o'clock in the morning until one o'clock in the afternoon, a line moved out of the city stretching from the East River to the North River.

The 16th - In camp at New York.

Due to the press activity, the line was again employed from four until eight o'clock in the morning.

The 17th and 18th - In camp at New York.

The 19th - Today both Ansbach regiments marched out of New York and into camp at Harlem.

From the 20th to 24th - In camp at Harlem.

The 25th - In camp at Harlem.

The enemy appeared in Jersey close to the North River. They burned some wood and fired a few small cannons.

The 26th - In camp at Harlem.

For conducting the activity in Jersey, the enemy is said to have five thousand men. Today these fired on a row galley.

From the 27th to 31st - In camp at Harlem.

September 1780

From the 1st to 18th - In camp at Harlem.
The 19th - In camp at Harlem.
The four cannons of the Ansbach regiments conducted target practice this morning.
The 20th - In camp at Harlem.
The 21st - In camp at Harlem.
Private [Erhard] Seidel, of Lieutenant Colonel von Reitzenstein's Company of the von Voit Regiment, died on the nineteenth of this month in the hospital in New York of a fever.
The 22nd - In camp at Harlem.
Because of Lieutenant General Cornwallis' victory in Virginia over the army commanded by the American General Gates,[2] which was three times larger than his own, and its complete dispersal, the garrison at New York today fired a feu de joie.
From the 23rd to 26th - In camp at Harlem.
The 27th - In camp at Harlem.
The American General [Benedict] Arnold defected to the English army and arrived at headquarters in New York yesterday with twenty deserters from the enemy.
General Arnold was immediately taken on by the English army as a brigadier general.
From the 28th to 30th - In camp at Harlem.

October 1780

From the 1st to 8th - In camp at Harlem.
The 9th - In camp at Harlem.
The unhappy fate which the English Major [John] Andre, the Adjutant General for the General-in-Chief Clinton, received from the enemy was reported here and made known to the army today.
The 10th - In camp at Harlem.
The 11th - In camp at Harlem.
An expedition under the command of the English Major General [Alexander] Leslie was embarked at Staten Island yesterday. It consists of 3,000 men and is to sail to Virginia.

The 12th - In camp at Harlem.
The 13th - In camp at Harlem.
Mail arrived from Europe.
Recalled from the von Voit Regiment
1) Regimental Quartermaster Model
2) Quartermaster Sergeant Randlein.
The 14th - In camp at Harlem.
The 15th - In camp at Harlem.
A transport fleet from England, including the third recruit transport, which was led by 2nd Lieutenant [Ferdinand] Foerster, arrived in the harbor at New York today.
The 16th and 17th - In camp at Harlem.
The 18th - In camp at Harlem.
The recruits for both Ansbach regiments arrived in camp today and were immediately divided among the companies.
Officers who arrived were:
1) 2nd Lieutenant Foerster, and
2) 2nd Lieutenant [Johann] von Fabrice, assigned to the von Voit Regiment.
3) 2nd Lieutenant [Heinrich] von Mattolay, and
4) Regimental Surgeon [Johann Heinrich] Schneller, who were assigned to the von Seybothen Regiment.
The 19th - In camp at Harlem.
The von Seybothen Regiment entered winter quarters today in the brewery on the North River at New York.
From the 20th to 24th - In camp at Harlem.
The 25th - In camp at Harlem.
Because this was the coronation day of George the III of Great Britain, the warships in the harbor at New York fired their cannons.
The 26th and 27th - In camp at Harlem.
The 28th - In camp at Harlem.
The agreement for the exchange of prisoners by the English side, as well as by the American side, was agreed upon on the 25th of this month, and published for the army today.
The English Major General [William] Phil-

lips commands a corps consisting of the following:
   The English Grenadiers
   The Light Infantry, and
   The 42nd Regiment of Scots.
From the 29th to 31st - In camp at Harlem.

November 1780

From the 1st to 10th - In camp at Harlem.
The 11th - In camp at Harlem.
A provisions fleet containing 61 sail entered the harbor at New York from Cork.
From the 12th to 19th - In camp at Harlem.
The 20th - In camp at Harlem.
Three buildings burned down during the past night in the area of the Naval Stores watch at New York.
The 21st - In camp at Harlem.
The 22nd - The von Voit Regiment moved into winter quarters today in New York and entered the North Church on William Street.
From the 23rd to 30th - In quarters at New York.

December 1780

The 1st - In quarters at New York.
Second Lieutenant von Hohendorf's court-martial was published today. He was cashiered with the loss of honor.
The 2nd - In quarters at New York.
Private [Johann Christoph] Ernst, of Captain von Stain's Company of the von Voit Regiment, was promoted to quartermaster sergeant of the Grenadier Company.
The 3rd - In quarters at New York.
The 4th - In quarters at New York.
An American frigate with 32 guns, which was loaded with silk and wine, was sailing from France to Maryland. It was captured by the English frigate Iris, Captain Dawson, in Chesa-

peake Bay and brought into the local harbor
today. The value of this merchant ship's cargo
amounted to 50,000 pounds sterling.
    The 5th - In quarters at New York.
    Mail arrived on a packet boat from Europe.
    From the 6th to 31st - In quarters at New
York.

January 1781

From the 1st to 5th - In quarters at New York.

The 6th - In quarters at New York.

According to reports, 2,500 men of the Pennsylvania militia have quit Washington's army because they have not been paid for two years.

Supposedly they have spiked the cannons at Morristown and burned the magazines there.

They have built defenses with four cannons on the heights near Amboy, in the Jerseys.

Some troops from the Light Infantry and the English Grenadiers have been sent there and it is believed that they will soon march in here.

From the 7th to 12th - In quarters at New York.

The 13th - In quarters at New York.

The affair noted on the sixth of this month, about some American troops quitting, is true. However, they received their pay in good hard cash from Lieutenant General Washington and have returned to their army.

From the 14th to 16th - In quarters at New York.

The 17th - In quarters at New York.

Private Braun, Jr., of Stain's Company, who deserted on 23 June of the past year at Elizabethtown, and Grenadier Braun, who deserted on 8 July of the previous year at Philipsburg, brothers, arrived here today, as deserters from the Americans.

The 18th - In quarters at New York.

The von Voit Regiment was mustered today by the English Commissary Porter, in Williams Street.

From the 19th to 21st - In quarters at New York.

The 22nd - In quarters at New York.

As people were pressed for the English

warships again today, the von Voit Regiment had
to draw the line around the city.

The 23rd - In quarters at New York.

During the past night there was again such
a frightfully strong storm wind, that the
houses in New York shook.

The 24th - In quarters at New York.

The Ansbach invalids being returned to
Germany were embarked on the transport ship
Minerva today. Regimental Quartermaster Model
had the command over them.

The following non-commissioned officers
from the von Voit Regiment departed:

1) Quartermaster Sergeant Randlein, of
the Grenadier Company

2) Corporal Haehnlein, Sr., and

3) Corporal Blank, of the Colonel's Company

4) Medic Drexler, of the Lieutenant Colonel's Company.

From the 25th to 28th - In quarters at New
York.

The 29th - In quarters at New York.

The fleet for England, consisting of two
hundred sail including two frigates and a
sloop-of-war as escorts, sailed out of the
local harbor this afternoon. The Ansbach
invalids went with them and the frigate Clinton
is the Commodore.

The 30th - In quarters at New York.

The fleet which sailed yesterday anchored
off Staten Island.

The 31st - In quarters at New York.

February 1781

The 1st - In quarters at New York.

The 2nd - In quarters at New York.

The fleet for England, which previously
lay at anchor off Staten Island, set sail.

The 3rd - In quarters at New York.

The 4th - In quarters at New York.

Today the army was informed that the English General Arnold had moved forward to
Richmond, in Virginia, and had captured the
seat of government there. A magazine of munitions and armaments for ships were skillfully
conquered by him and destroyed. Very few
troops were lost during this affair.

From the 5th to 14th - In quarters at New
York.

The 15th - In quarters at New York.
A packet boat arrived which brought mail
from Germany.

The 16th - In quarters at New York.
Again today, a packet boat entered from
England and brought mail from Germany.

From the 17th to 28th - In quarters at New
York.

March 1781

The 1st and 2nd - In quarters at New York.
The 3rd - In quarters at New York.
Private Ahlmann, of the von Voit Regiment,
who was taken prisoner on 23 March 1780, near
Hackensack, died in captivity at Philadelphia.

The 4th - In quarters at New York.
The 76th Regiment of Scots and the Hessian
Hereditary Prince Regiment were embarked. The
Hessian von Knyphausen Regiment was transferred
to Kingsbridge.

The 5th - In quarters at New York.
The expedition consisting of the two regi-
ments [mentioned above] and the English Light
Infantry, under the command of the English
Major General [William] Phillips, departed from
here yesterday.

The 6th - In quarters at New York.
An American colonel, who deserted, arrived
at headquarters.

From the 7th to 19th - At New York.
The 20th - In quarters at New York.
Private [Gottlob] Schulz, of Major von

196

Seitz' Company of the von Voit Regiment,
deserted from the regimental watch today at
three o'clock in the morning.

The 21st - In quarters at New York.

At one o'clock this afternoon a brewery
very close to the Naval Stores watch burned
down.

Private Schulz, who deserted yesterday,
returned to the regiment and was punished by
running the gauntlet eight times.

From the 22nd to 29th - In quarters at New
York.

The 30th - In quarters at New York.

On the sixteenth of this month a naval
battle occurred between Admiral [Marriott]
Arbuthnot and the French fleet, in the vicinity
of Chesapeake Bay. The English drove the
French completely away, so that they again had
to enter Rhode Island and three warships were
taken in there without masts.

The 31st - In quarters at New York.

A boat, which had departed Rhode Island
with dispatches sent from the French General
[Dontien Vimeur, Comte de] Rochambeau to the
American Lieutenant General Washington, was
captured by a Refugee officer near Fishkill.

Near Elizabethtown an American picket was
made prisoners of war by the Refugees and today
brought here to the headquarters.

April 1781

From the 1st to 12th - In quarters at New
York.

The 13th - In quarters at New York.

Yesterday Admiral Arbuthnot arrived at
Sandy Hook with his war fleet. Five warships
of this fleet, which on 16 March, of this year,
were damaged in the battle in the Chesapeake
and must be repaired here, including the
admiral's ship, also, arrived in the harbor and
lie at anchor in the North River.

From the 14th to 18th - In quarters at New York.

The 19th - In quarters at New York.

Private [Sebastian] Brenner, of Colonel von Voit's Company, died in the hospital at Vauxhall, of a rupture and dropsy.

The 20th - In quarters at New York.

Yesterday the warship Roebuck brought the best American frigate, the Confederation, loaded with uniforms, into the local harbor as a captured prize. The value of the items on board is estimated at 75,000 pounds sterling.

The 21st - In quarters at New York.

A provisions fleet from England entered the harbor here.

From the 22nd to 26th - In quarters at New York.

The 27th - In quarters at New York.

Corporal [Friedrich] Prevost, of Colonel von Voit's Company, died here in the hospital.

The 28th - In quarters at New York.

The arrival of His Majesty's Ship Amphitrite with dispatches from Lieutenant General Lord Cornwallis, gives General-in-Chief Sir Henry Clinton the opportunity to make known to this part of the army that the troops under his command won a victory over the American army in North Carolina on 15 March 1781. The news of this victory, expressed in his own words, are as follows:

In camp at Guilford, 17 April 1781

General [Nathanael] Greene was strengthened from Virginia with eighteen-month troops [Continentals] and militia from that province. He advanced with his army, which consisted of from five to six thousand men and four 6-pound cannons, as far as this place. I attacked him on 15 March, and after a very hot battle, routed his army and captured his four cannons.

The reassembling of the troops, the number of wounded, as well as the shortage of provisions, prevented our following up the victory on the afternoon of the action.

Therefore, a feu de joie was fired at eight o'clock this evening by the local garrison.

Vice-Corporal [Georg] Glaenzel, of Colonel von Voit's Company, was promoted to corporal.

The 29th - In quarters at New York.

The 30th - The following regiments were embarked today: the 43rd English Regiment and both Ansbach regiments.

Ships for the von Voit Regiment
1) Alicia, staff ship
2) Providence, Lieutenant Colonel and Major
3) Ocean, Captain von Stain.

Ships for the von Seybothen Regiment
1) Alexander, staff ship
2) Wisk, Major
3) Caladonia, Captain von Eyb.

The Commodore is in the frigate Charon.

May 1781

The 1st - We went under sail; then dropped anchor off Staten Island.

From the 2nd to 5th - At anchor off Staten Island.

The 6th - At anchor off Staten Island.

The warship Roebuck, Captain Douglas, to-day brought the American frigate Protector into New York harbor as a captive. It was loaded with flour and was to have sailed from Chester to the French army at Rhode Island.

The 7th and 8th - Lying at anchor off Staten Island.

The 9th - At nine-thirty both admirals, Arbuthnot and Graves, sailed from Staten Island with the war fleet and the transport ships. They then dropped anchor at one o'clock in the afternoon near Sandy Hook.

The war fleet consists of the following ships:

Nr.	Name	Guns	Men	Captains
1)	London	98	750	Admiral Graves
2)	Bedford	74	600	Commodore
3)	Royal Oak	74	600	Admiral Arbuthnot
4)	Robust	74	600	Philip Cosby
5)	America	64	550	Samuel Thomson
6)	Europe	64	550	Schmit Child
7)	Prudent	64	550	Thomas Burnett
8)	Adamant	50	370	Gideon Johnson
9)	Charon	44	280	Thomas Symonds
10)	Media	28	180	Henry Duncan
11)	Roebuck	44	280	Andrew S. Duncan
12)	Assurance	50	300	W. Sweeney

The transport fleet consisted of 23 sail.

The 10th - At anchor near Sandy Hook.

A merchant ship entered here after an eight week voyage from London.

The 11th and 12th - Lying at anchor near Sandy Hook.

The 13th - At nine o'clock in the morning both fleets went under sail and were soon on the ocean.

At twelve o'clock noon we met the merchant ship Nancy. It was two months out of London.

An enemy ship was seen this evening and the frigate Media gave chase.

The 14th - Sailing on the ocean. The wind however, from the west and was contrary for us.

Midday, at eleven o'clock, the marines and sailors on the warships conducted firing exercises with muskets.

To our right we still saw the land of Jersey where the small seaport of Egg, which the Americans hold, is to be found.

At three o'clock in the afternoon the war fleet again turned toward the north and only the following three ships therefrom, remained with the transport fleet, namely: Roebuck, Assurance, and Charon, on the last of which the Commodore remained.

The 15th - We lost sight of land during the past night and sailed today with a reasonably good wind.

The 16th - With a reasonably good wind, we sailed 47 English miles.

The 17th - At four o'clock in the morning bottom was found at 23 fathoms.

The frigate Charon chased two enemy vessels toward Delaware Bay, which were brought back to the fleet, captive, this evening.

This day the wind was light and contrary. In the night, however, a good wind arose.

The 18th - This morning was calm and the sea was still. During the afternoon a good wind arose, which lasted until twelve o'clock at night.

At six o'clock this evening two merchant ships left the fleet. They sailed for Charleston.

At eleven 'clock tonight, bottom was found at eleven fathoms.

The 19th - The wind was good, but early in the morning such a heavy fog set in that not a single ship of the fleet was to be seen. The ships, therefore, had to signal with musket shots and beating on drums and as there was fear of drawing too close to land, the ships again had to turn north. All but a few sails were lowered and the steering rudder was tied down.

At two o'clock in the afternoon bottom was again found at seventeen and one-half fathoms.

At four o'clock in the afternoon the fog disappeared and the fleet immediately changed course to the west again.

The 20th - At seven o'clock in the morning the Virginia coast was already seen. Toward midday we passed Cape Henry on our left and entered Chesapeake Bay, with Hampton lying on our right. At five o'clock this evening we anchored in Chesapeake Bay, near Hampton Roads, eight English miles from Portsmouth.

Two English frigates, the Thames and the Gaudalupe, lie here at anchor.

At seven o'clock in the evening all the transport ships set sail and entered the James River where they anchored at nine-thirty at night.

Notice should be taken here, that a fathom is six feet and a league is three English miles or one German hour.

The 21st - At four o'clock in the morning the ships sailed up the James River. At one o'clock in the afternoon they anchored near Black Walnut Point.

Underway again at four o'clock in the afternoon, and again at five-thirty, anchored. In this area, the political district of Williamsburg lies on our right and Hog Island on our left.

At seven o'clock in the evening we again sailed and at eight-thirty at night, we anchored near Talbot's Point.

The 22nd - At seven o'clock in the morning we sailed and passed Old Jamestown on our right and New Jamestown, Santee Point, and Branthom on our left. At twelve o'clock noon we anchored at the latter. Nine transport ships, on which is to be found the baggage for Arnold's Corps, lie here at anchor.

News was received that the English Major General Phillips died of a fever at Petersburg.

Cape Henry is the midpoint between Sandy Hook and Richmond and Richmond is ninety miles from here.

The 23rd - At anchor at Branthom.

Near our transport fleet lie the following ships:

1) Apollo
2) Bologne
3) Charming Nancy, transport ships for the 43rd Regiment,
4) Nicholaus and Jane, for the convalescents, and
5) Providence Increase, a provisions ship.

The 24th - At anchor near Branthom.

We learned that Lord Cornwallis has returned with the army to Petersburg.

Major General Leslie arrived here this morning with the fleet.

The James River is already sweet water at this point.

Concerning the land of Virginia, especially in this region: It is completely level and provided with great numbers and truly beautiful woods, and there are no stones to be found.

The houses are all made of brick, as are the most beautiful country manors.

All foodstuffs are especially cheap.

The 25th - The fleet received orders to sail back, which was done immediately, and at seven o'clock in the evening anchored near the political district of Williamsburg.

The 26th - At seven o'clock in the morning the fleet sailed, but at four o'clock in the afternoon, anchored at Willoughby Bay.

At five o'clock in the evening underway again and then anchored a mile from Portsmouth.

The 27th - At seven o'clock in the morning underway and then at twelve o'clock noon we anchored in the harbor at Portsmouth.

Opposite Portsmouth lies the exceptionally beautiful city of Norfolk, which five years ago the English General [John Murray, Earl of] Dunmore, who was on an expedition from Boston, came here and burned down completely.

The Elizabeth River flows between the two small cities of Portsmouth and Norfolk.

The 28th - At four o'clock in the morning we landed near Portsmouth. Both Ansbach regiments paraded through the city and entered the camp outside the line commanded by the English Major General Leslie.

The Hessian Hereditary Prince Regiment was already here and was quartered in Portsmouth, because it had not been provided with tents.

The 29th - In camp near Portsmouth.
Corporal [Conrad] Erlbacher, of the von
Seybothen Regiment, deserted from the picket
this morning.
Portsmouth, in Virginia, is a small but
rather uniformly laid out city.
The local area is pleasant, but during the
summer extremely hot. Therefore, guard mount
had to be held at five o'clock in the morning
and during the rest of the day, the soldiers
stood field watch only in vests.
The 30th - In camp near Portsmouth.
The transport ships which had brought us
here sailed back to New York this afternoon.
The 31st - In camp near Portsmouth.
The English 17th Regiment moved ten miles
forward from here.
General Arnold arrived at Portsmouth and
departed for New York immediately.
Lieutenant General Lord Cornwallis marched
out of Petersburg and moved forward toward
Richmond.

June 1781

The 1st - In camp near Portsmouth.
The 2nd - In camp near Portsmouth.
Grenadier Kalb, of the von Seybothen Regiment, deserted from his post with the picket.
The 3rd - In camp near Portsmouth.
The 4th - In camp near Portsmouth.
An English bombardier, who deserted and
was again arrested, was punished twice, in the
morning and in the afternoon, with nine hundred
lashes and a life sentence aboard a warship as
a sailor.
As it was the birthday of His Royal Majesty, George III of Great Britain, a 21-gun
salute was fired today at the artillery fortifications and likewise by the cannons of all
the ships in the local harbor.
The 5th - In camp near Portsmouth.
Private [Konrad] Betten, of Captain von
Eyb's Company of the von Seybothen Regiment,

deserted on the march of a detachment to Great Bridge.

The 6th - In camp near Portsmouth.

Lieutenant General Lord Cornwallis sent fifty American prisoners of war to Portsmouth to be guarded.

From the 7th to 9th - In camp near Portsmouth.

The 10th - In camp near Portsmouth.

During this night an expedition was made by the 160 man garrison of Fort Great Bridge and 240 English troops, a total of four hundred men, under the command of Major Maxwell of the English 80th Regiment.

These troops marched to Black Swamp to attack the headquarters there of the American General Gregory, sixteen miles from Fort Great Bridge near Baendts on Warrent Swamp. They could not cross the river, which was twelve feet deep, and therefore had to return and re-enter their former camps.

Grenadier [Johann Christian] Kaim, of the von Voit Regiment, deserted during this affair.

From the 11th to 15th - In camp near Portsmouth.

N.B.- The Fort Great Bridge lies nine miles from Portsmouth, on the side toward Norfolk.

The 16th - In camp near Portsmouth.

Quartermaster Sergeant [Johann Friedrich] Salzmann, of Captain von Eyb's Company of the von Seybothen Regiment, died in the hospital at Norfolk, of consumption.

From the 17th to 20th - In camp near Portsmouth.

The 21st - In camp near Portsmouth.

Thirty miles beyond Great Bridge the Refugees made seven Americans prisoners of war and brought them here to Portsmouth.

From the 22nd to 24th - In camp near Portsmouth.

The 25th - Today the English Major Maxwell

again led an expedition against Black Swamp, with a force of two hundred men from the English 76th and 80th Regiments and eighty men of the German command at Great Bridge. The enemy fort, containing eight cannons, was conquered. One colonel, two majors, three captains, eight lieutenants, and forty privates, a total of 54 persons, were made prisoners of war. The enemy cannons were dismounted and spiked. The remaining enemy baggage was burned and the fort demolished.

Private Horn, of Major von Seitz' Company of the von Voit Regiment, was missing after this affair. According to other soldiers, he had gotten stuck in the swamp.

The 26th and 27th - In camp near Portsmouth.

The 28th - In camp near Portsmouth.

Private [Franz] Bischof, of Colonel von Voit's Company, due to carelessness, during the evening when the main watch was being relieved, was shot through the hand.

At five o'clock this evening the Hessian Hereditary Prince Regiment was embarked in the new long boats. This regiment was to be taken to the army of Lieutenant General Lord Cornwallis outside Williamsburg. En route it received the order to turn back and to reoccupy the quarters in Portsmouth.

The 29th and 30th - In camp near Portsouth.

July 1781

The 1st - In camp near Portsmouth.

This morning the 17th Regiment of infantry marched into the city and entered quarters in the church.

This evening an expedition, under the command of Major General Leslie, departed from here in long boats. It consisted of the English 17th, 76th, and 80 Regiments and the

Hessian Hereditary Prince Regiment, 900 men in all. These troops went about two miles up the James River, where they received the order from Lieutenant General Lord Cornwallis that they were to return to Portsmouth.

The 2nd – In camp near Portsmouth.

The expedition that left here yesterday returned today. The 76th and 80th Regiments reentered their former camp at Kemp's Landing. The 17th Regiment and the Hereditary Prince Regiment entered their former quarters in Portsmouth.

The 3rd – In camp near Portsmouth.

This morning the 17th Regiment entered the camp here at Fort Arnold.

From the 4th to 6th – In camp near Portsmouth.

The 7th – In camp near Portsmouth.

A bear, which was shot ten miles from here, was brought to the market at Portsmouth to be sold. A pound of bear meat sells for four coppers or five groschen.

The 8th and 9th – In camp near Portsmouth.

The 10th – In camp near Portsmouth.

A fleet of sixteen empty transport ships entered the local harbor from New York, bringing mail from Germany.

The 11th – In camp near Portsmouth.

The 12th – In camp near Portsmouth.

Ten head of the most beautiful cattle were brought here from the enemy side by the Refugees.

The 13th – In camp near Portsmouth.

The 14th – In camp near Portsmouth.

The 43rd and 76th Regiments, the Queen's Rangers, and both Ansbach regiments received orders to embark.

The 15th – At six o'clock in the evening the two Ansbach regiments embarked on the following transport ships:

The von Voit Regiment

1) **Shipwright** – Colonel von Voit

2) <u>Providence</u> - Lieutenant Colonel von Reitzenstein and Major von Seitz.

<u>The von Seybothen Regiment</u>

1) <u>Houston</u> - Colonel von Seybothen
2) <u>Present Succession</u> - Major von Beust
3) <u>Harmony</u> - Grenadier Captain von Eyb.

The 43rd and 6th Regiments, and the Queen's Rangers arrived here in Portsmouth this morning.

The Light Infantry moved into camp one and one-half miles from Portsmouth.

The Hessian Hereditary Prince Regiment moved twelve miles forward from Portsmouth.

Four hundred Negroes with 347 wives and 223 children were brought here to Portsmouth today and transferred across the Elizabeth River. They are from North and South Carolina and Virginia.

<u>The 16th</u> - At anchor near Portsmouth.

The following regiments were embarked today: the Light Infantry and Queen's Rangers at four o'clock in the morning; the 43rd and 76th Regiments at four o'clock in the afternoon. After this time, because of the great heat, nothing more could be done.

<u>The 17th</u> - Sailed out of the city of Portsmouth and at once dropped anchor.

<u>The 18th</u> - Went under sail at five o'clock in the morning and dropped anchor at Hampton Roads.

<u>The 19th</u> - At anchor at Hampton Roads.

At six o'clock in the evening we had a strong thunder storm.

<u>From the 20th to 23rd</u> - At anchor at Hampton Roads.

<u>The 24th</u> - At anchor at Hampton Roads.

Lieutenant General Lord Cornwallis arrived here at the fleet at eight o'clock this morning and looked over the area in comfort.

He remained on the frigate <u>Richmond</u> until seven o'clock in the evening and then returned to Portsmouth.

Upon his arrival the frigate <u>Richmond</u> fired fifteen cannons. The sailors from the warships climbed into the rigging and shouted a loud hurrah.

The 25th – At anchor at Hampton Roads.

Lieutenant General Lord Cornwallis again this morning arrived at the fleet.

The 26th – At anchor at Hampton Roads.

General Leslie sailed for Charleston this morning with a frigate and is to assume command there.

The following men died of high fever on the transport ships:

1) Grenadier [Jakob] List, of the von Voit Regiment, was buried on land on the Norfolk side.

2) Private [Jakob] Witte, of Captain von Eyb's Company of the von Seybothen Regiment, was buried in the water.

The 27th – At anchor at Hampton Roads.

The 28th – At anchor at Hampton Roads.

Grenadier [Balthasar] Scherrer died on the hospital ship.

The 29th – At nine-thirty in the morning the fleet set sail and at a quarter to eleven, as the wind became contrary, again anchored opposite Hampton.

At a quarter to eight in the evening it sailed again, but immediately dropped anchor.

Lieutenant General Lord Cornwallis today went aboard the frigate <u>Richmond</u>, on which was the Commodore.

The 30th – The fleet sailed at five o'-clock in the morning and dropped anchor at twelve o'clock noon near Cape Henry.

Private [Johann Leonhard] Sauler, of Lieutenant Colonel von Reitzenstein's Company of the von Voit Regiment, pack servant on a horse ship, drowned at twelve o'clock midnight on the nineteenth of this month.

The 31st– Sailed at five o'clock in the morning and anchored at eight o'clock in the morning in Chesapeake Bay.

Sailed again at three o'clock in the afternoon and anchored at eight o'clock in the
evening in Chesapeake Bay.

August 1781

The 1st - Sailed at three o'clock in the
afternoon and anchored at eight o'clock in the
evening on the York River.

The 2nd - Sailed at seven o'clock in the
morning and at nine o'clock in the morning
dropped anchor at Yorktown.

The 80th Regiment debarked yesterday evening at Gloucester, which is a very small place
and lies on the right side of the York River.

Yesterday evening two frigates sailed to
Yorktown and lay at anchor there. When the
enemy saw their approach, he retreated at once
to Williamsburg.

As a result, today the regiments debarked
in the following order:

The Jaeger detachment and the Queen's Rangers to Gloucester and

The Light Infantry, the 43rd, 76th, von
Voit, and von Seybothen Regiments to Yorktown.

Lieutenant General Lord Cornwallis, who
commanded this corps, went to Yorktown with his
headquarters.

The troops entered camp very close to the
city, in a line.

Yorktown, a small but pleasant and well
built little city, close to the river, has an
English Church and a courthouse. This place
has pleasant and beautifully laid out gardens,
which however, during the siege, were destroyed
and because of the very many defensive works,
were completely dug up. The buildings have
been completely ravaged and torn apart.

Upon our arrival the inhabitants fled with
their wives and children, leaving behind all
their furniture and belongings.

The 3rd - In camp near Yorktown.
The regimental baggage was landed.
The 4th - In camp near Yorktown.
The transport ships have sailed for Portsmouth in order to take aboard the troops remaining there.
Privates Braun, Jr., and [Michael] Vogel, of Captain von Stain's Company of the von Voit Regiment, deserted this morning from the camp.
The 5th - In camp near Yorktown.
The 6th - In camp near Yorktown.
Second Lieutenant Foerster, of the von Voit Regiment, died at Norfolk on 30 July, and was buried on 1 August.
Private [Eli] Oettinger, of Colonel von Voit's Company, also died at Norfolk.
Promotions in the von Voit Regiment
First Sergeant [Georg] Beyer to 2nd lieutenant
Second Sergeant [Andreas] Albrecht to 1st sergeant
Corporal [Johann Leonhard] Fickel to 2nd sergeant, and
Vice-Corporal Schuster to corporal.
The 7th - In camp near Yorktown.
Privates [Leonhard] Busch and [Johann Michael] Oed, of Lieutenant Colonel von Reitzenstein's Company of the von Voit Regiment, deserted from the camp.
The 8th - In camp near Yorktown.
The Hessian Hereditary Prince Regiment arrived in the harbor from Portsmouth in long boats and were landed near Gloucester.
Nine vessels entered here this afternoon from Portsmouth, bringing troops and baggage.
9th - In camp near Yorktown.
Today we had two very strong thunderstorms. This morning a ranger on post near the windmill was struck dead by lightning. Lightning also struck the frigate Spitfire, injuring five sailors. This afternoon lightning killed a private and the wife of a

sergeant of the 43rd Regiment.

The 10th - In camp near Yorktown.

Four privates of the von Seybothen Regiment deserted from the camp; three, including Private [Johann] Eberlein, from the Major's Company, and Private Paul, of Captain von Eyb's Company.

From the 11th to 13th - In camp near Yorktown.

The 14th - In camp near Yorktown.

The Queen's Rangers, who had been on the Yorktown side, were transferred across to Gloucester.

The 15th - In camp near Yorktown.

An express ship arrived here in the harbor from New York.

The 16th - In camp near Yorktown.

Private [Simon] Hopfer, of the Major's Company of the von Seybothen Regiment, deserted from the cattle guard.

The 17th and 18th - In camp near Yorktown.

The 19th - In camp near Yorktown.

A fleet entered here from Portsmouth yesterday evening.

The 20th and 21st - In camp near Yorktown.

The 22nd - In camp near Yorktown.

A fleet with the remaining troops from Portsmouth entered the harbor here.

The Hessian von Bose Regiment, which debarked this afternoon, was placed on the left wing of our camp.

The 23rd and 24th - In camp near Yorktown.

The 25th - In camp near Yorktown.

The frigate _Richmond_ and three other vessels sailed for New York this morning.

The 26th - In camp near Yorktown.

Lightning struck in the camp of the Light Infantry.

The 27th - In camp near Yorktown.

The 28th - In camp near Yorktown.

Pack Servant Birngruber, of the Artillery, and Pack Servant [Johann Konrad] Baumann, of

Captain von Stain's Company, both of the von Voit Regiment, deserted from the camp, each with two horses.

The 29th - In camp near Yorktown.

At ten o'clock in the morning the camp was changed. Both Ansbach regiments were transferred to the place of the Light Infantry and the Light Infantry was moved further forward.

The 30th - In camp near Yorktown.

A French war fleet had been seen outside the harbor. Therefore, during the night a battery was thrown up on the water and the fortifying of the line was carried out vigorously.

The 31st - In camp near Yorktown.

September 1781

The 1st - In camp near Yorktown.

The 2nd - In camp near Yorktown.

According to reports, six thousand French landed yesterday near Hampton Roads.

Four French warships lay at anchor this morning at the mouth of the local harbor.

The cannons were unloaded from the frigate Charon lying at anchor here in the harbor and brought into the battery at the water side.

In order to complete the defenses, they are being worked on energetically day and night.

The 3rd - In camp near Yorktown.

The 4th - In camp near Yorktown.

Second Lieutenant Schuchard, of the von Seybothen Regiment, died of a high fever at one-thirty in the afternoon, at Yorktown, and was buried during the evening without ceremony.

The 80th Regiment was brought from Gloucester and entered camp here.

The 5th - In camp near Yorktown.

Today the army changed its camp and the von Voit Regiment was placed in the first line.

Three French ships sailed in and joined those warships lying at anchor at the mouth of the harbor.

Private [Johann] Blind, of Lieutenant Colonel von Reitzenstein's Company of the von Voit Regiment, deserted from his post on the cattle guard.

<u>The 6th</u> - In camp near Yorktown.

Five French ships sailed away this afternoon, leaving only two warships lying at anchor.

<u>The 7th</u> - In camp near Yorktown.

The two French warships still lying at anchor at the mouth of the harbor, sailed away at nine o'clock this morning.

<u>From the 8th to 11th</u> - In camp near Yorktown.

<u>The 12th</u> - In camp near Yorktown.

Two small vessels arrived here from New York.

The French war fleet sailed past, out of the York River, and into Chesapeake Bay, this morning because the English Admiral Graves reportedly had arrived with a war fleet of twenty ships.

<u>The 13th</u> - In camp near Yorktown.

This afternoon two French ships cruised up to the mouth of the harbor and then sailed back into Chesapeake Bay.

<u>The 14th</u> - In camp near Yorktown.

This morning an enemy patrol of about fifty cavalry ran into Lieutenant Colonel [Banastre] Tarleton's outpost and they exchanged shots.

This afternoon three French warships sailed into the mouth of the harbor and dropped anchor there, whereupon the English guard ship had to pull back a long way into the harbor.

Two French warships were seen this evening in the bay.

<u>The 15th</u> - In camp near Yorktown.
<u>The 16th</u> - In camp near Yorktown.

Again this afternoon a French warship was seen in the bay.

Our transport ships were brought very close to the city, all in a line.

Powder magazines were established underground in the city, between the heights.

The 17th - In camp near Yorktown.

One of the French warships lying at anchor set sail and again lay at anchor further out in the bay.

Another French vessel was seen during the afternoon in the bay.

The 18th - In camp near Yorktown.

The 19th - In camp near Yorktown.

The French fleet sailed past the mouth of the harbor and at Baltimore, in Maryland, took on troops and provisions.

The 20th - In camp near Yorktown.

A French warship arrived today and dropped anchor at the usual place.

Therefore, there are now four French warships at the mouth of the local seaport.

Additionally, nine small French vessels have been seen in the bay.

The 21st - In camp near Yorktown.

All of the houses of Yorktown, which were outside of the line, were torn down and work on the fortifications was intensified so that one defensive position after the other appears. Day and night two thousand men are constantly working on the defenses.

The 22nd - In camp near Yorktown.

During the night four fireships were sent out of the harbor against the four French warships lying at anchor. As the fireships were ignited too soon, the French warships were alerted, cut their anchor ropes, and two of them sailed off. The other two ran aground, but were refloated and again are lying at anchor in the former place.

The 23rd - In camp near Yorktown.

The two French warships lying at anchor at

the mouth of the harbor, have pulled back so
far that nothing but the tops of their masts
can be seen.

Our fleet, lying at anchor very close to
the city, again spread out in the harbor.

The 24th - In camp near Yorktown.

Three French warships are again lying at
anchor at the mouth of the harbor.

Four rebels were seen outside the line, in
the woods, and were fired upon by the covering
force of the work command.

The 25th - In camp near Yorktown.

In the region of Yorktown a great amount
of cotton is grown in the fields.

The 26th and 27th - In camp near Yorktown.

The 28th - In camp near Yorktown.

Today the enemy took post a mile from our
camp and fired at us with 4-pound cannons.

The Hessian Hereditary Prince Regiment was
transferred here from Gloucester and assigned
in the second line on the left wing.

Several transport ships were sunk in the
harbor.

The baggage as well as the tents of these
regiments were sent to the city of Yorktown.

The 29th - In camp near Yorktown.

At daybreak the firing against the outposts resumed.

The enemy troops have massed together no-
ticeably on our left wing and constantly attack
our pickets. However, our cannons have strongly resisted them.

Of the Ansbach picket, the dead and wounded were: From the von Voit Regiment -
Grenadier Roetter and Private Gruber wounded;
and from the von Seybothen Regiment - Private
[Egide] Zeilmann shot dead and three privates
wounded.

Two Scots of the 71st Regiment and one of
Tarleton's Light Horse were wounded near the
defensive position of the von Seybothen Regiment.

The 30th - At two o'clock in the morning our army pulled the line back toward the city of Yorktown. As soon as our troops had retreated the enemy entered these camps and attacked our right wing, but our cannon fire, which was well-directed, drove him back within half an hour.

The 80th Regiment was transferred over to Gloucester.

Deserters during the retreat, from the von Voit Regiment, were: Grenadier [Georg Jakob] Mueller and Private [Leonhard] Hartlein, of Captain von Stain's Company, and three privates from the von Seybothen Regiment.

October 1781

The 1st - In camp in the line at Yorktown.

The enemy laid out two positions, which were fired upon from our line, against the workers, day and night.

Prisoners brought in here were an American brigadier general and a French hussar.

The 2nd - In camp in the line at Yorktown.

Today the cannon fire against the enemy workers, was much heavier than yesterday.

Because of a very great shortage of forage it was necessary to cut the throats of most of the horses at the York River.

An express arrived here in the harbor from New York at nine o'clock this evening, which brought the news that an English war fleet of thirty sail and 5,000 troops would soon arrive here.

Note! This ship had to sneak past the four French warships lying at anchor at the mouth of the harbor and they had fired upon it.

The 3rd - In camp in the line at Yorktown.

The cannon fire from our lines on the enemy workers was not as strong today as yesterday and the day before.

The 4th - In camp in the lines at Yorktown.

During the day today there was very little firing with cannons from the English lines.

At nine-thirty tonight the enemy attacked the work detachment from the Light Infantry. At Gloucester, at the same time, the enemy attacked. Within one-half hour the attacks were ended and throughout the night the enemy workers were cannonaded from our lines.

The 5th - In camp in the lines at York-town.

The pickets on our left wing were attacked by the enemy all night and our cannon fire continued without let up against the enemy camp.

The 6th - In camp in the lines at York-town.

Fifteen transport ships, which were in the harbor, were sunk very close to the city.

At eight o'clock in the evening the right wing, specifically the redoubt occupied by the 23rd Regiment, was attacked by the enemy. At once a rocket was fired from this redoubt as a signal to the line, whereupon the ever-present cannon fire from all the places on our line began, and fired continually throughout the entire night. The enemy had to retire after a few minutes.

The 7th - In camp in the lines at York-town.

The cannonading from our lines was not as great today as yesterday.

The enemy constructed redoubts and trenches opposite our lines.

Grenadier [Lorenz] Jacobi, of the von Voit Regiment, deserted from his post on picket.

The 8th - In camp in the lines at York-town.

At five o'clock in the morning the enemy clashed with a few positions on our left wing, which fired upon one another.

There was a small engagement during the

night at Gloucester, between our pickets and
the enemy's.
Grenadier [Johann Georg] Gerlich, of the
von Voit Regiment, died in the hospital.
The 9th - In camp in the lines at
Yorktown.
At three o'clock in the afternoon the enemy opened fire with the cannons in his newly
constructed fort opposite our left wing.
Firing upon the frigate Guadalupe was so
strong that it had to retreat into the harbor.
The English Quartermaster General Barkley
and Lieutenant Robertson, of the 76th Regiment,
were killed by a cannonball in the mess house
while eating.
Grenadier [Johann Georg] Dorsch, of the
von Voit Regiment, and two privates, of the von
Seybothen Regiment, deserted from their posts
on picket.
The 10th - In camp in the lines at Yorktown.
Our line fired very heavily with cannons
during the past night.
At two o'clock in the morning the enemy
fired into our camp from the newly built
positions against our left wing, with bombs and
cannonballs, which caused the greatest damage.
Five men of the von Seybothen Regiment
were wounded this morning, including Private
[Johann Wilhelm] Seewald, who was fatally
wounded by a cannonball and died this afternoon
from his wounds. Private Durer, on the other
hand, had a foot amputated because of his
wound.
The enemy fired bombs at the frigate
Charon this evening which caused it and also a
transport ship in the harbor to be burned
completely.
The English Major Gordon arrived as an express from New York and brought the news that
an English war fleet was near the Chesapeake.
Private Stein, of Captain von Stain's Com-

pany of the von Voit Regiment, died in the hospital of a high fever.

Private Boser, of Colonel von Voit's Company, deserted from the picket.

The 11th - In the lines at Yorktown.

At two o'clock in the morning the Ansbach picket was attacked by the enemy.

This morning two transport ships were set on fire by enemy bombs.

Private [Johann Georg] Bessenecker, of the Colonel's Company, and Private [Nikolaus] Schubert, of the Lieutenant Colonel's Company, of the von Voit Regiment, died in the hospital.

During an attack on the defenses on the left wing, by an enemy detachment, Private Tuerk, of Captain von Stain's Company of the von Voit Regiment, was killed and one private was killed and two privates wounded, of the von Seybothen Regiment.

The following men of the von Voit Regiment were wounded in camp: Grenadier Roser and Private Ferch, of the Major's Company, were wounded by shrapnel, and Sergeant Hoffmann, of Captain von Stain's Company, was wounded on the foot by a cannonball.

Private Kaempf, of the von Seybothen Regiment, was wounded by a piece of wood which had been hit by a bomb.

Deserters from the von Voit Regiment picket: Privates [Johann Michael] Ostertag and Stockmohr, of the Lieutenant Colonel's Company, and Privates [Johann Georg] Escherich and [Johann] Roessler, Sr., of Captain von Stain's Company.

From the von Seybothen Regiment: Private [Ignatius] Laeus.

Tonight the enemy again attacked the position held by the 23rd Regiment, but was driven back by our cannons, which fired heavily into the area from which the enemy attacked.

The picket of the Light Infantry was attacked twice during the night.

The regiment entered the trenches in which our tents were also set up, and are thus protected from the cannonballs, at least.

The 12th - In camp in the trenches at Yorktown.

The enemy cannonade was so strong and so many bombs landed in our camp that it was completely impossible to describe.

Drummer Schindelbauer, of the von Seybothen Regiment, deserted from a patrol.

Wounded from the von Voit Regiment were:
1) Grenadier Wolf
2) Private Lauterbach, of the Colonel's Company, while on work detail
3) Private Schuler, of the Lieutenant Colonel's Company, and
4) Private [Andreas] Cantusch, of Captain von Stain's Company.

The 13th - In camp in the trenches at Yorktown.

The picket of the Light Infantry was attacked this morning.

A cannonade from the enemy was very great and no one in camp was safe from the many bombs which fell therein.

Three 18-pounders were set up on the right wing of our line and the English cannonade was also very heavy this night.

The enemy fired mostly two hundred pound bombs and 42-, 36-, and 24-pound cannonballs into our camp.

On the other hand, the English only had one 24 pounder set up in our line and further, were provided with no heavy bombs.

Wounded in the tents in the trenches, from the von Voit Regiment, were:
1) Privates [Konrad] Koerner and
2) [Kaspar] Appold, of the Colonel's Company, by a bomb which landed in the tent; the first had a foot shot off, and the latter received a wound in his knee.
3) Private Fuchs, of Captain von Stain's

Company, was wounded in the chest by shrapnel from a bomb.

4) Private Wagner, of the Lieutenant Colonel's Company, was instantly killed when a two hundred pound bomb landed in the tent of Corporal Gachstetter. Four others in the tent were not wounded.

5) Corporal Schuster, of the Colonel's Company, while on picket, had his right arm shot off.

Wounded of the von Seybothen Regiment was: Grenadier Nuezel, whose foot was shot off by a bomb.

The 14th – In camp in the trenches at Yorktown.

About eight o'clock at night the enemy attacked our right wing, but was again driven back.

Immediately after this attack, both of our outermost positions on the left wing were attacked and after a short engagement, conquered. The largest, with one hundred men, was under the command of the English Lieutenant Colonel McPherson, and the smaller position was commanded by the English Major Kempel.

After this conquest, the left wing of the line as far as the von Seybothen Regiment, was attacked. However, a terrible cannon and musket fire was delivered from the English lines so that the enemy had to pull back into his defenses.

Wounded of the von Voit Regiment were:

1) First Lieutenant von Reitzenstein, wounded in his left leg by a piece of shrapnel, and

2) Grenadier Riess, of the von Seybothen Regiment, was wounded by a bomb.

Both servants of Captain von Eyb and Captain von Metzsch were wounded by a spent bomb which they were trying to dig up.

Corporal Boser, of the Lieutenant Colonel's Company of the von Voit Regiment, was killed by an exploding bomb while on work detail.

Captain [Hermann Christian] Roll, of the Hessian von Bose Regiment, was killed by a musketball while on picket.

Deserters from picket, of the von Voit Regiment, were: Grenadier Ratlar and Private [Johann Simon] Rueckert, of the Lieutenant Colonel's Company, and Privates [Michael] Vogel and [Johann] Fricker, of the Major's Company.

Two privates of the von Seybothen Regiment deserted from picket.

Private [Matthias] Elias deserted from the watch at the redoubt which was established for the von Seybothen Regiment.

A regimental cannon of the von Voit Regiment was completely destroyed by an enemy bomb.

The 15th - In camp in the trenches at Yorktown.

During the past night the enemy did not cannonade us and only four bombs were thrown into our camp. On the other hand, many bombs were fired by the English side and the cannonade was continuous.

Yesterday afternoon a bomb fell in the mess house of the von Voit Regiment. The wife of an English soldier who lay in childbed, below in the basement of this house, had both feet shot off by a bomb and died therefrom in half an hour. The child, however, due to the bomb's explosion, was shattered so that not the least trace of it could be found.

This afternoon a bomb landed in the regimental bake ovens of the von Voit Regiment, wounding Corporal [Christoph] Schilling and Private [Wilhelm] Auernheimer, of Captain von Stain's Company.

Private [Georg] Prewitzer, of the Major's Company of the von Voit Regiment, died in the hospital.

Private [Michael] Marquart and Private [Johann] Meier, II, of the Major's Company of

the von Voit Regiment, deserted from the
picket. Two privates from the von Seybothen
Regiment also deserted from the picket.
    <u>The 16th</u> - In camp in the trenches at
Yorktown.
    The English Grenadiers and Light Infantry
made a sortie tonight into the enemy camp and
in the greatest haste spiked eleven of the
enemy's cannons. One captain and three
privates of the French army were made prisoners
of war. According to their comments a French
war fleet of 33 sails has arrived again in the
Chesapeake from France and joined the other
French fleet lying at anchor there.
    The French army reportedly amounts to
15,000 men.
    Since yesterday evening four French war-
ships are lying before the local harbor.
    The enemy opened new batteries opposite
our left wing and cannonaded our camp steadily
from today on.
    All the hospitals were moved from here a-
cross to Gloucester.
    Private [Andreas] Eberhart, of Captain von
Stain's Company of the von Voit Regiment, died
in the hospital.
    Grenadier [Johann Martin] Reinhart de-
serted from the picket and Private Schwegler,
of the Lieutenant Colonel's Company, deserted
from a work detail, both of the von Voit Regiment.
    A non-commissioned officer of the Hessian
Hereditary Prince Regiment, had both feet torn
off by a cannonball and a drummer of the same
regiment, lost one foot due to a cannonball.
    English deaths were an engineer killed by
a cannonball through the body and the wife of a
cannoneer also killed by a cannonball through
the body.
    An English sailor was wounded by a can-
nonball which shot off a foot and injured his
hand.

The English Light Infantry and the Guard Regiment were transferred across the York River to Gloucester this evening in order to attack the enemy there. However, as the enemy was as strong on the other side as on this side, this plan remained unfulfilled.

During this time, the Hornwork, in which the Light Infantry had been, was occupied by a detachment from the von Voit Regiment, commanded by Lieutenant Colonel von Reitzenstein.

The 17th - In camp in the trenches at Yorktown.

The cannonade from the enemy continued surprisingly strong this morning.

A flag of truce was sent from the English side into the enemy camp this morning.

Note! As soon as a flag of truce is sent out a halt is immediately made to the firing. However, it continues only until the flag again arrives back in its camp.

The Light Infantry and the Guard Regiment, at noon, arrived back here again from Gloucester and took over their former post.

Private [Johann Simon] Kern, of Colonel von Voit's Company, had taken food to his comrades with the detachment in the Hornwork. As he was about to return, he was killed by a cannonball.

Immediately thereafter, one of the Light Infantry had his head completely shot off.

Private [Georg] Schmelzer, of the Major's Company of the von Voit Regiment, deserted from the detachment [at the Hornwork].

A flag of truce from the enemy entered the outer lines.

This evening a flag of truce was again sent to the enemy from the English side. After which, from five o'clock in the afternoon on, a cease fire resulted.

At eight o'clock at night the powder magazine, due to carelessness of an English ar-

tilleryman, who took a light therein, blew up.
As a result, twelve persons were killed, among
whom was Private [Jakob] Gunckel, of the
Major's Company of the von Voit Regiment, who
just at that time, found himself there as he
went on sentry duty.
   The 18th - In camp in the trenches at
Yorktown.
   Grenadier [Johann Michael] Eberlein, Pri-
vate [Christoph] Maeussner, of the Colonel's
Company, and Corporal Nicole, of the Lieutenant
Colonel's Company, of the von Voit Regiment,
died in the hospital at Gloucester.
   Vice-Corporal Gakstetter, of the von
Voit Regiment, was promoted to corporal.
   Corporal [Johann Heinrich] Popp, of the
von Seybothen Regiment, was promoted to 2nd
lieutenant.
   The 19th - In camp in the trenches at
Yorktown.

[At this point Prechtel includes the surrender
articles in their entirety, filling pages 495
to 511 of the copy of the diary at hand. On
page 511 he resumes his account with an order
from Lieutenant General Lord Cornwallis.]

<u>Order from Lieutenant General</u>
<u>Lord Cornwallis</u>
Headquarters at Yorktown in Virginia
19 October 1781
   Lord Cornwallis can not adequately express
the appreciation he owes the officers and men
of this army for their good conduct at every
opportunity since he has had the honor to
command them, but especially for their
extraordinary courage and determination in
defending this position.
   He sincerely regrets that their exertions
were unable to withstand the superior artillery
which opposed them and that the blood of such
brave people was shed in vain.

Lord Cornwallis had done everything in his power to get the provision enabling the army to be returned to Europe. Since this could not be ratified, he had tried to obtain the best treatment for the troops as long as they would be in captivity. Above all, he wanted to insure that they were always provided with the necessities until their freedom was again obtained.

The tents and remaining supplies were not to be wasted.

At three o'clock in the afternoon the entire English army marched out of Yorktown with music playing and cased flags, and after both defensive positions on the left wing had previously been occupied by American and French troops.

From the enemy trenches onward, the American army stood on the left, before whose middle stood Lieutenant General Washington, and on the right, the French army, before which was Lieutenant General Rochambeau.

Both armies paraded in the finest order and we marched in columns between them. Where they ended, the English army marched up in two lines and at a quarter to five in the evening lay down their weapons.

After this ceremony the troops returned through both armies, which had their weapons grounded, to the city of York and reentered their former camp.

From the 9th to 17th of this month, more than 16,000 bombs were fired into our camp.

The army which Lieutenant General Lord Cornwallis commanded had 5,000 men. The American and French armies, on the other hand, amounted to 40,000 men.

List of dead and wounded
of the British army
Dead

2 Captains
4 Lieutenants
13 Sergeants
4 Drummers
133 Privates
156 Total

Wounded

5 Lieutenants
1 Ensign
24 Sergeants
11 Drummers
285 Privates
326 Total

During the English cannonade the enemy reportedly lost more than 500 men.

The 20th — In camp in the trenches at Yorktown.

Those soldiers of ours who have served by the American and French armies were released today. From the von Voit Regiment these were Grenadier Braun and Private Katzenwinkel, of Captain von Stain's Company.

An American Commissary today conducted a muster of our regiments.

Corporal [Christian] Schuster died in the hospital at Gloucester.

The following officers accompanied the regiments into captivity, having been chosen by lot.

From the von Voit Regiment

1) Captain von Ellrodt
2) Captain von Stain
3) Staff Captain von Koenitz
4) 1st Lieutenant von Marschall
5) 1st Lieutenant von Treschel
6) 2nd Lieutenant Prechtel
7) 2nd Lieutenant Drexel
8) 2nd Lieutenant Baumann, Adjutant
9) 2nd Lieutenant von Fabrice

228

10)   2nd Lieutenant Halbmeier
11)   Artillery Lieutenant Hofmann, and
12)   Regimental Surgeon Rapp.
     From the von Seybothen Regiment
1)   Major von Beust
2)   Captain von Quesnoy
3)   Captain von Metsch
4)   1st Lieutenant von Kruse
5)   1st Lieutenant von Reitzenstein
6)   2nd Lieutenant von Cyriacy
7)   2nd Lieutenant Lindemeier, Adjutant
8)   2nd Lieutenant Weinhart, and
9)   2nd Lieutenant Graebner.

The above listed officers have received permission from General Washington, on their parole, to settle up to five miles from the troops.

The remaining officers went to New York on parole, on the transport ship _Andrew_. During the captivity they were quartered on Long Island.

Second Lieutenant Feder, while having a high fever and while still in the harbor at York, jumped from the ship _Andrew_ and drowned.

The 21st - At twelve o'clock noon the prisoners were escorted out of Yorktown by the American militia consisting of five hundred men with two cannons. Halfway to Williamsburg, night camp was made under the open sky.

The captured officers had to give their blacks to the enemy.

The 22nd - Night camp was made at Williamsburg.

The 23rd - The third march was fifteen miles beyond Williamsburg, where night camp was made.

The 24th - The fourth march was past Longcastle and the troops camped 45 miles beyond York.

The 25th - The fifth march took us sixty miles beyond York.

The 26th - The sixth march was past Newcastle and night camp was made four miles beyond this place; 78 miles from York.

The 27th - The seventh march, night camp was made one hundred miles from York.

The 28th - The eighth march, night camp was made 114 miles from York.

The 29th - The ninth march, night camp was near Fredericksburg, still ninety miles from Winchester.

The 30th - Underway at four o'clock in the afternoon and we marched two and one-half miles beyond Fredericksburg to the Rappahannock River and made night camp.

The prisoners of war from Gloucester were taken on another route and joined us again at Fredericksburg.

The 31st - We remained at the Rappahannock River.

November 1781

The 1st - We crossed the Rappahannock River. The water reached only to the knees of the troops. Just across the river lies Falmouth. Today night camp was made twenty miles beyond Fredericksburg.

Those troops which were to enter captivity at Fort Frederick marched away today without an escort.

The 2nd - We marched twenty miles to the Frak-Weiler Courthouse, from here it is still forty miles to Winchester.

The 3rd - We made night camp thirty miles from Winchester.

The 4th - We passed the Blue Ridge, or the Blue Mountains, and the River Shenandoah and camped for the night fourteen miles from Winchester.

The 5th - We arrived at Winchester. The prisoners of war were transported four miles further into a woods where already two barracks for captive troops had been built. These were

truly very poorly put together and as they were
not half adequate for quartering the troops,
the men had to build new barracks later on, but
already at this time it was very unpleasant and
as cold as in winter.

This place very quickly took on the appearance of a great city and was permanently
occupied by a detachment of 200 American
militia, commanded by a colonel.

The officers had to obtain their quarters
in the city of Winchester, or the surrounding
area, and for their own money. These quarters
cost from six to eight Spanish dollars per
month, each dollar equals two florin and thirty
groschen.

The soldiers are visited by their officers
two or three times per week and to prevent
misconduct a subaltern must daily maintain a
watch in the barracks of the Ansbach regiments.

From the 6th to 8th - At Winchester.

The 9th - At Winchester.

Today the 76th Regiment of Scots entered
quarters in the English and German churches
here.

Winchester, in Virginia, is an old, prima-
tively built city with two churches, one of
which, however, has been completely unusable
due to being constantly occupied by prisoners
of war.

All the houses here are built of wood.

The inhabitants are a mixture of English
and Germans and very poor, money and clothing-
wise.

The land is exceptionally fertile and
mostly Turkish corn is grown, from which much
cognac is made, which is called whiskey.

There is an astonishingly large amount of
poultry here and all kinds can be purchased
very cheaply.

From Winchester it is about fifty miles to
the heathens, or Indians.

From the 10th to 17th - At Winchester.

The 18th - At Winchester.
First Lieutenant von Reitzenstein and Chaplain Wagner, both of the von Voit Regiment, arrived here with the convalescent captives this evening.

Privates [Georg Adam] Wolf and [Georg] Reinwald, both of Captain von Stain's Company of the von Voit Regiment, died in the hospital at Gloucester.

Private [Johann Stephan] Goert, of the mentioned company, deserted there and entered service with the French Grenadiers.

From the 19th to 30th - At Winchester.

December 1781

The 1st - At Winchester.
Regimental Surgeon [Johann Heinrich] Schneller, of the von Seybothen Regiment, arrived here with the second transport of convalescent prisoners of war.

The following members of the von Voit Regiment died in the hospital at Gloucester:

1) Private Koerner, of the Colonel's Company, of his wounds, received 13 October, of this year.

2) Corporal [Johann] Decker, of Major von Seitz' Company, of a high fever

3) Private Schneider, a minor, of Captain von Stain's Company.

Grenadiers [Heinrich] Ockell, Wachler, and [Johann Wilhelm] Rossel, of the von Voit Regiment, deserted there [at Gloucester] and were taken into French service.

From the 3rd to 19th - At Winchester.

The 20th - At Winchester.
A few convalescent prisoners of war arrived here today from Gloucester.

The 21st - At Winchester.
The 22nd - At Winchester.
Private [Benedikt] Kohlschreiber, of Captain von Stain's Company of the von Voit

Regiment, died in the barracks.

The 23rd - At Winchester.

The 24th - At Winchester.

Grenadier [Johann Matthias] Jacob died of consumption in the barracks.

Drummer Hopfer and Private [Konrad] Weiss, of the Major's Company of the von Voit Regiment, deserted from the barracks and then engaged in the American Light Horse at Newtown.

From the 25th to 28th - At Winchester.

The 29th - At Winchester.

Again today a transport of convalescent captives arrived from Gloucester.

The 30th - At Winchester.

Private [Gottlieb] Traeger, of the Lieutenant Colonel's Company of the von Voit Regiment, deserted and joined the American Light Horse.

The 31st - At Winchester.

January 1782

From the 1st to 5th - At Winchester.
The 6th - At Winchester.
Promotions in the von Voit Regiment
Vice-Corporal Preiss, of the Major's Company, and Vice-Corporal Kretchi, of Captain von Stain's Company, to corporal.
From the 7th to 9th - At Winchester.
The 10th - At Winchester.
The following have joined the American Light Horse: Private Bluemlein, of the Lieutenant Colonel's Company of the von Voit Regiment, and Fifer [Johann] Semmelmann, of the von Seybothen Regiment.
From the 11th to 13th - At Winchester.
The 14th - At Winchester.
A transport of convalescent prisoners of war arrived from Gloucester.
Corporal Schilling, of Captain von Stain's Company of the von Voit Regiment, died on the convalescent transport.
From the 15th to 26th - At Winchester.
The 27th - As the order arrived from Congress at Philadelphia that the English prisoners of war should go from Frederick to Lancaster, and the German prisoners of war from Winchester to Frederick, today both Ansbach regiments marched out of the Frederick Barracks at Winchester.
The 28th - The officers and the baggage of the Ansbach regiments left Winchester and had to make their night quarters in the area of the American General Lach's quarters,[2] under the open sky, and at which place they rejoined the regiments.
The 29th - Night quarters were made at Shipperstown, 25 miles from Frederick.
Three English private soldiers froze to death in camp on this night. The soldiers had to camp in the woods on the snow, and then crossed through a river during extremely cold

weather.

The 30th - Passed the Potomac, which divides Virginia and Maryland. This river is heavily traveled and about one-half mile wide. It froze over during the night so that the regiments had to cross over the ice causing us to feel extremely cold.

Night quarters were made in the small Maryland city of Sharpsburg. Most of our soldiers had to camp, during this cold weather, under the open sky, but near fires.

The 31st - The regiments entered Frederick and entered the Frederick Barracks, under guard.

The Frederick Barracks are about one-half mile from Frederick and consist of a barracks with two splendidly constructed wings.[3]

Four German regiments are here in captivity. The Ansbach von Voit and von Seybothen Regiments and the Hessian Hereditary Prince and von Bose Regiments.

February 1782

The 1st - At Frederick.

The English prisoners of war, which have been here in the Frederick Barracks, were led off today to Lancaster, in Pennsylvania.

The local prisoners of war are under the control of Major [Mountjoy] Bailey, who was formerly of the American army.

Frederick, or Fredericks City, in Maryland or Marion land, is a completely new, strikingly beautiful, and uniformly built city. It has existed for about eighty years. It has a courthouse, which stands a short distance outside the city and the American militia has its parade ground by the courthouse.

There are four churches here, namely:
1) The English Church
2) The Catholic Chapel
3) The Reformed Church, and

4) The Evangelical Church,
of which only the last two have bells.
The inhabitants of Frederick, and of all
Maryland, are mostly Germans, and work the land
completely in the German manner.
The city itself is completely flat and a-
bove all, this is a wonderful region.
About two and one-half miles from Frederick the Monocacy River flows; a river which is
about three feet deep. It contains many fish
which are, however, of no value.
Fifty miles from Frederick lies Baltimore,
the capital city in Maryland, with a good harbor on the Chesapeake.
From the 2nd to 12th — At Frederick.
The 13th — At Frederick.
Today Major Bailey mustered the four captive regiments.
From the 14th to 28th — At Frederick.

March 1782

From the 1st to 9th — At Frederick.
The 10th — At Frederick.
It has been learned that Lieutenant Colo-
nel von Reitzenstein, of the von Voit Regiment,
and 1st Lieutenant von Weitershausen, of the
von Seybothen Regiment, left New York on
December 4, 1781, on parole, for Ansbach.
From the 11th to 13th — At Frederick.
The 14th — At Frederick.
Privates [Michael] Proz and [Michael]
Pfund, of Major von Seitz' Company of the von
Voit Regiment, died at Winchester.
From the 15th to 17th — At Frederick.
The 18th — At Frederick.
This morning Major Bailey mustered the
prisoners of war.
The 19th and 20th — At Frederick.
The 21st — At Frederick.
On 19 February, of this year, the island
of St. Christopher, in the West Indies, was

236

surrendered to the French by the English, by
treaty. The garrison, in compliance with the
first article, marched out and laid down their
weapons, except officers, and are to go to
England. During the remainder of the war, they
are not to fight again.

From the 22nd to 25th - At Frederick.

The 26th - At Frederick.

At three-thirty in the morning the dwell-
ing house of the mason, Gibbs, burned down. A
twelve year old boy sleeping there was severely
burned.

The 27th and 28th - At Frederick.

The 29th - At Frederick.

Private Wuehl died at Gloucester and Drummer [Johann Georg] Fleissinger at Winchester.
Both were of Lieutenant Colonel von Reitzenstein's Company of the von Voit Regiment.

Taken from the Baltimore newspaper - The
Commanding General Sir Henry Clinton has been
called back to England and General [Guy]
Carleton has been named Commanding General of
the English army.

The 30th - At Frederick.

Grenadier Roser, wounded on 11 October
1781, died on 5 February, of this year, at
Gloucester, after the arm on which he had been
wounded had twice been amputated.

The 31st - At Frederick.

Grenadiers [Johann Michael] Hadoerfer[4]and
[Johann] Herolt, both of the von Voit Regiment,
enlisted in the American Light Horse.

April 1782

From the 1st to 13th - At Frederick.

The 14th - At Frederick.

Quartermaster Sergeant [Johann Friedrich]
Salzmann, of the von Seybothen Regiment, died
in the hospital and was buried in the English
churchyard.

From the 15th to 17th - At Frederick.

The 18th - At Frederick.

Through letters from New York, dated 4 December 1781, it has been learned that a jaeger company and ninety recruits arrived at New York from Ansbach.[5] The following officers were with the transport:

2nd Lieutenants Deahna and [Johann Wilhelm Christian] von Hiller, both assigned to the Jaeger Companies

Auditors Pflug and [Paul] Frisch, the first assigned to the von Seybothen Regiment and the latter to the Jaegers.

Regimental Quartermaster [Jakob] Kalnek,[6] who has not been assigned to a regiment.

First Lieutenant von Beust, of the von Seybothen Regiment, received his separation.[7]

Artillery Lieutenant Hofmann was promoted to Staff Captain.

Baggage for the Ansbach prisoners of war arrived in the harbor at Baltimore on 9 April, under the supervision of the Regimental Quartermaster [Carl] Meier, of the von Voit Regiment.

The 19th and 20th - At Frederick.

The 21st - At Frederick.

Grenadier Scheller, Jr., of the von Voit Regiment, died at New York on 20 February, this year.

Second Sergeant [Ludwig Friedrich] Schwed, of the vacant Lieutenant Colonel's Company of the von Voit Regiment, died at Winchester of a high fever on 10 March, this year.

The 22nd and 23rd - At Frederick.

The 24th - At Frederick.

Regimental Quartermaster Meier arrived here today with the baggage.

The 25th - At Frederick.

Today the Americans held a penance and fasting day.

Cannoneer [Leonhard] Naehr, of the von Seybothen Regiment, died in the barracks at Winchester on the fifteenth of this month.

238

The 26th and 27th - At Frederick.

The 28th - At Frederick.

Regimental Quartermaster Ludwig, of the Hessian Hereditary Prince Regiment, also arrived here with the baggage for the Hessian prisoners of war.

The following from the von Voit Regiment have been sent from New York to Ansbach with the invalid transport:

1) Medic [Andreas] Meier, of the Grenadier Company

2) Corporal Kreglingen, of the vacant Lieutenant Colonel von Reitzenstein's Company

3) Private Johann] Schlaegel, of Captain von Stain's Company.

The 29th - At Frederick.

First Sergeant [Johann Friedrich] Hauff, of the vacant Lieutenant Colonel von Reitzenstein's Company of the von Voit Regiment, was demoted.

The 30th - At Frederick.

May 1782

From the 1st to 4th - At Frederick.

The 5th - At Frederick.

Second Lieutenant Nagler, of the von Seybothen Regiment, died at New York.

From the 6th to 12th - At Frederick.

The 13th - At Frederick.

Both Regimental Quartermasters, Meier and Ludwig, who came here with the baggage, today began their return to Baltimore, and from there will return to New York on the two single-masted English sloops.

From the 14th to 19th - At Frederick.

The 20th - At Frederick.

The American Major Bailey today mustered the prisoners of war lying here.

From the 21st to 25th - At Frederick.

The 26th - At Frederick.

Promotions in the Jaeger Battalion

1) Quartermaster Sergeant [Leonhard] Hausselt to regimental quartermaster.
2) Medic Arnold to regimental surgeon.
The 27th - At Frederick.
From the American newspapers from Baltimore - Admiral [George] Rodney has captured five French warships-of-the-line in the West Indies. The admiral's ship, on which was Admiral de Grasse, was included. This ship had 110 cannons; on the lowest deck 42-, on the middle 24-, and on the upper deck 18-pounders. Twenty-seven trunks with money were found aboard. The other ships had 74 cannons. After the capture, one of these ships, through carelessness, blew up, causing the deaths of four hundred persons.
From the 28th to 31st - At Frederick.

June 1782

The 1st - The American Major Bailey today mustered the four captive regiments lying here.
The 2nd - At Frederick.
The following legal American order was published for the local inhabitants:
From the 4th instance on, no one in the future should support or provide quarters for a prisoner of war. In the event an inhabitant is caught doing this, he shall be punished with a fine of five hundred pounds local money, and if he is unable to pay, he shall serve three years as a sailor on an American ship. If, due to health, this can not be performed, he shall be punished with 39 lashes.
From the 3rd to 12th - At Frederick.
The 13th - At Frederick.
Private Goert, who deserted on 18 November 1781, yesterday returned to the regiment as a prisoner of war.
From the 14th to 17th - At Frederick.
The 18th - At Frederick.
Today the American Major Bailey mustered

the prisoners of war.
From the 19th to 24th - At Frederick.
The 25th - At Frederick.
Because of the birth of a French prince,
the Americans today held a celebration during
which the local militia fired their weapons
outside the city, on the left side of the road
to Philadelphia.
From the 26th to 30th - At Frederick.

July 1782

The 1st - At Frederick.
Private [Johann Georg Christian] Gaertner,
of Captain von Quesnoy's Company of the von
Seybothen Regiment, was captured today by an
American patrol in the city, and as he tried to
flee, was shot through the body.[9]
From the 2nd to 12th - At Frederick.
The 13th - At Frederick.
The American Major Bailey mustered the
prisoners of war at six o'clock this evening.
From the 14th to 31st - At Frederick.

August 1782

From the 1st to 20th - At Frederick.
The 21st - At Frederick.
Private [Johann] Braun, of the vacant
Lieutenant Colonel von Reitzenstein's Company
of the von Voit Regiment, died in the hospital
in the poorhouse of bilious fever.
The 22nd and 23rd - At Frederick.
The 24th - At Frederick.
At six o'clock in the evening the American
Major Bailey mustered the prisoners of war.
Orders from the American General [Benja-
min] Lincoln in Philadelphia: The captured
officers may go hunting as often as they wish.
The 25th - At Frederick.
The 26th - At Frederick.
It is learned from the newspapers from

Baltimore that a general exchange [of prisoners] is to take place and that the English Lieutenant General Lord Cornwallis has already been exchanged.

The 27th - At Frederick.
Garrison Order
Frederick City, 24 August 1782

Those prisoners of war who wish to remain in this country should immediately receive their freedom and receive a certificate from the war minister which will grant them every freedom of native born citizens, when a sum of eighty dollars is paid.

John Wood, Colonel
Commissary

From the 28th to 31st - At Frederick.

September 1782

The 1st and 2nd - At Frederick.
The 3rd - At Frederick.

All prisoners of war who find themselves on the land, whether from Burgoyne's or Cornwallis' armies, must return to the barracks at once.

The 4th - At Frederick.
The 5th - At Frederick.

Field Jaeger Schweiger and Private [Johann] Liebel, of Major von Seitz' Company of the von Voit Regiment, have enlisted with the American troops.

The 6th - At Frederick.

Private Abt, of Captain von Stain's Company of the von Voit Regiment, enlisted with the American troops.

The 7th - At Frederick.

Grenadier [Johann Georg] Bauer and Private [Johann] Schultheiss, of Major von Seitz' Company of the von Voit Regiment, enlisted with the American troops.

The 8th - At Frederick.

Private [Konrad] Heermann, Jr., of Captain

von Stain's Company of the von Voit Regiment, enlisted with the American troops.

From the 9th to 13th - At Frederick.

The 14th - At Frederick.

Packmaster Thomel, died here in the store-house.

From the 15th to 19th - At Frederick.

The 20th - At Frederick.

Drummer [Georg Nikolaus] Reichart, and Private Goert, of Captain von Stain's Company of the von Voit Regiment, enlisted with the American troops.

The 21st - At Frederick.

An American recruit transport, consisting of about 24 men, all from the four German regiments lying here in captivity, left here today.

The Staff Servant [Karl] Nehrlich, of the von Voit Regiment, again enlisted with the American troops.

The 22nd - At Frederick.

The 23rd - At Frederick.

Private [Johann Peter] Lochner, of the Colonel's Company of the von Seybothen Regiment, enlisted with the American troops.

The 24th - At Frederick.

Promotions in the vacant
Lieutenant Colonel von Reitzenstein's Company
of the von Voit Regiment

1) The sick and having-remained-in-New-York, Corporal [Konrad] Duernhoeffer to 1st sergeant

2) The present here, Corporal [Konrad] Wiederstein to 2nd sergeant.

The 25th - At Frederick.

Private Roedel, of Captain von Stain's Company of the von Voit Regiment, enlisted with the American troops.

From the 26th to 30th - At Frederick.

October 1782

From the 1st to 4th - At Frederick.
The 5th - At Frederick.
The American Major Bailey mustered the prisoners of war.
From the 6th to 15th - At Frederick.
The 16th - At Frederick.
Private [Thomas] Dressel, of the vacant Lieutenant Colonel von Reitzenstein's Company of the von Voit Regiment, enlisted with the American troops.
The 17th - At Frederick
At Winchester the following men, of the von Voit Regiment, have enlisted with the American troops:
    1) Grenadier [Konrad] Stengel[9]
    2) Drummer Abt, of the Colonel's Company
    3) Private [Friedrich Jakob] Schaeffer[10]
and
    4) Private [Konrad] Buttin,[11] of the vacant Lieutenant Colonel von Reitzenstein's Company
    5) Private Lochner and
    6) Private Hiessinger, of Major von Seitz' Company, and
    7) Private [Sophonias] Wannemacher,[12] of Captain von Stain's Company.
From the 18th to 21st - At Frederick.
The 22nd - At Frederick.
Today the second recruit transport for the American army left here and consisted of about twenty men from the four German regiments lying here in captivity.
The 23rd - At Frederick.
The Americans recruiters, who had previously been here, departed. However, immediately other American troops from Armand's Corps took their place. Drummer [Johann Andreas] Wurzbach, formerly of the vacant Lieutenant Colonel von Reitzenstein's Company, who had deserted at Winchester, was with them.
From the 24th to 27th - At Frederick.
The 28th - At Frederick.
Private [Johann Veit] Klein, of the Lieu-

tenant Colonel's Company of the von Voit Regiment, and Cannoneer [Christian Friedrich] Tauber,[13] of the von Seybothen Regiment, enlisted in Armand's Corps.
The 29th - At Frederick.
Private [Peter] Fehr, of Major von Seitz' Company of the von Voit Regiment, enlisted in Armand's Corps.
The 30th and 31st - At Frederick.

November 1782

The 1st - At Frederick.
The recruiters from Armand's Free Corps of Americans left here today for Winchester. All together they had enlisted five men from the four regiments lying here in captivity.
From the 2nd to 4th - At Frederick.
The 5th - At Frederick.
Private Loew, of Captain von Stain's Company of the von Voit Regiment, enlisted in Armand's Free Corps at Winchester.
From the 6th to 25th - At Frederick.
The 26th - At Frederick.
Today the American Major Bailey held muster.
The 27th - At Frederick.
The 28th - At Frederick.
Today the American provinces celebrated a day of humiliation.
The 29th and 30th - At Frederick.

December 1782

The 1st and 2nd - At Frederick.
The 3rd - At Frederick.
Private [Georg] Feile, of Captain von Stain's Company of the von Voit Regiment, died of consumption.
From the 4th to 20th - At Frederick.
The 21st - At Frederick.
The American Armand's Free Corps came from

Winchester and was quartered here. Within this corps there are at least fifty men from the two Ansbach regiments.

Private [Kaspar] Schemig, of Captain von Stain's Company of the von Voit Regiment, enlisted in Armand's American Corps, which is lying here.

The 23rd and 24th – At Frederick.

The 25th – At Frederick.

Today Armand's American Free Corps marched away from here for Philadelphia.

The 26th – At Frederick.

Private [Jobst] Hertlein, of Captain von Stain's Company of the von Voit Regiment, took duty with the grenadiers of Armand's American Corps.

The 27th – At Frederick.

The 28th – At Frederick.

In a letter from the American General Lincoln, it was made known that the baggage for the four German regiments lying here in captivity has arrived in the Delaware, near Wilmington.

From the 29th to 31st – At Frederick.

January 1783

The 1st - At Frederick.
On New Year's Eve, from twelve to one o'-clock in the night, all the bells were rung.
From the 2nd to 6th - At Frederick.
An American detachment to reinforce the prison guard came here from Baltimore. Among them were both musicians, Fifer [Johann Jakob] Messerer and Drummer [Johann Burckhardt] Koehlner, of the Grenadier Company of the von Voit Regiment.
From the 7th to 17th - At Frederick.
The 18th - At Frederick.
A letter to Major von Beust from the Regimental Quartermaster [Johann Georg] Daig, of the von Seybothen Regiment, arrived in which he reported that he was with the baggage at Lancaster, Pennsylvania.
From the 19th to 23rd - At Frederick.
The 24th - At Frederick.
In the Philadelphia newspapers of 14 January, was to be seen, and from New York it was written, on 4 January, that Charleston had been evacuated and the English Lieutenant General Leslie, with his staff, had arrived in New York.
Charleston reportedly was taken over by the American General [Anthony] Wayne three days after the English marched out.
The 25th - At Frederick.
It has been learned that Chaplain Erb, of the von Seybothen Regiment, has departed New York for Europe.
The American Major Bailey today mustered the prisoners of war.
His Serene Highness has made a regiment of the former Jaeger Battalion and therefore three new jaeger companies have been sent to America, which, however, now lie at Halifax.
The 26th - At Frederick.
The 27th - At Frederick.

His Serene Highness has graciously announced the following promotions in his regiments:

1) Lieutenant Colonel von Reitzenstein, of the von Voit Regiment, to be chief and holder of the Jaeger Regiment.

2) Staff Captain von Metzsch, of the von Seybothen Regiment, to captain of the von Voit Regiment and to receive Major von Seitz' Company.

3) [No entry.]

4) Both Staff Captains von Tritschler and von Koenitz, of the von Voit Regiment, to captains in the Jaeger Regiment.

5) 1st Lieutenant von Kruse, of the von Seybothen Regiment, to staff captain of the von Voit Regiment.

6) 1st Lieutenant von Reitzenstein, of the von Voit Regiment, to staff captain of the Jaeger Regiment.

7) 1st Lieutenant von Schoenfeld, of the von Voit Regiment, to staff captain of that regiment.

8) 1st Lieutenant Seidel, of the von Seybothen Regiment, to staff captain of that regiment.

9) [No entry.]

10) [No entry.]

11) 2nd Lieutenants Tunderfeld, Altenstein, and Weinhart, of the von Seybothen Regiment, to 1st lieutenants in that regiment.

12) [No entry.]

13) Both 2nd Lieutenants Prechtel and Guttenberg, of the von Voit Regiment, to 1st lieutenants in that regiment.[2]

Note Well! Lieutenant Colonel von Reitzenstein's Company in the future is the Major's Company.

1st Lieutenant [Ernst Friedrich] von Wurmb, of the Guard du Corps, received a jaeger company and has arrived with it at Halifax.

The 28th - At Frederick.

Recruit Hunger, of Captain von Stain's Company, deserted at New York.

The 29th - At Frederick.

A reinforcement for the prisoner of war guard arrived here.

Order from the American Major Bailey - All prisoners of war who are in this state shall report into the barracks here by 10 February, and those here in the city and surrounding area, likewise.

The 30th and 31st - [At Frederick.]

February 1783

The 1st - At Frederick.

The following officers have come from Ansbach to the Jaeger Regiment:

1) 2nd Lieutenant [Ehrenfried Hans Friedrich] Busch

2) 2nd Lieutenant von Hiller

3) 2nd Lieutenant [Friedrich Adolf Carl] von Eyb

4) 2nd Lieutenant [Christoph Julius] von Massenbach

5) 2nd Lieutenant [Franz], Count von Bubna and Lititz

6) 2nd Lieutenant [Christoph Georg Philipp] Otto

7) 2nd Lieutenant [Albertus Magnus] Frank

8) 2nd Lieutenant [August Wilhelm] Neithardt von Gneisenau[3]

9) 2nd Lieutenant [Johann Caspar] Mory.

The 2nd - At Frederick.

The 3rd - At Frederick.

Order from the American Major Bailey - Officers who wish to enter the barracks will report to the officer of the watch and show their parole. Otherwise they will not be allowed to enter the barracks.

Regimental Quartermaster [Ludwig] Flachshaar, of the Hessian von Bose Regiment, arrived here from Lancaster this evening with the

Hessian baggage for the prisoners of war.
The 4th and 5th - At Frederick.
The 6th - At Frederick.
At Winchester the following men of the von
Voit Regiment have taken an oath to America:
    1) Private Arn, of the Major's Company
    2) Private [Johann Georg] Gareis, of Cap-
tain von Stain's Company
    3) Private [Johann Martin] Geissensieder[4]
and
    4) Pack Servant [Johann] Neuhaueser, of
Captain von Metzsch's Company.
Grenadier [Adam] Hohberger, of the von
Voit Regiment, died at Winchester.
From the 7th to 24th - At Frederick.
The 25th - At Frederick.
The American Major Bailey mustered the
prisoners of war this morning.
From the 26th to 28th - At Frederick.

March 1783

From the 1st to 25th - At Frederick.
The 26th - At Frederick.
Twenty-three wagons with baggage for both
Ansbach regiments were seized in Chester
County.[5]
The 27th - At Frederick.
The French cutter Triumph sailed from
Cadiz to Philadelphia, as an express, in 36
days and brought the news that peace had been
agreed upon on 20 January 1783.
At three-thirty in the afternoon, to the
ringing of all the bells by the oldest citizen,
a parade was held through all the streets of
the city, with Major Bailey participating.
They had a white flag with them, and this
procession was held because of the general
peace.
In the evening a feu de joie was fired in
the upper streets of the city.
The 28th - At Frederick.

Regimental Quartermaster Daig arrived here today with the baggage for both Ansbach regiments.

The 29th - At Frederick.

The 30th - At Frederick.

The American General Goetsch[6] arrived here and brought the news that New York was to be turned over to the Americans and as soon as possible, the prisoners of war were to go to Staten Island, or Long Island, in order to be embarked there for Europe.

The Reformed Pastor Henop preached a Thanksgiving sermon here from Psalms 9, Verse 2, because there was peace.

The 31st - At Frederick.

April 1783

From the 1st to 12th - At Frederick.

The 13th - At Frederick.

Staff Captain [Joachim] Kim of the Hessian Hereditary Prince Regiment cut his throat this morning at four o'clock, in his quarters. This evening he was carried out by six private soldiers and buried behind the barracks.

The 14th and 15th - At Frederick.

The 16th - At Frederick.

Private [Samuel] Schwager, of the Major's Company of the von Voit Regiment, died in the barracks.

From the 17th to 21st - At Frederick.

The 22nd - At Frederick.

At eight o'clock this evening, because of the arrival of the Articles of Peace, a fireworks display prepared by the Ansbach Artillery Captain Hofmann, was held at the Great Place at the courthouse. Afterward, the bells were rung at both churches and the entire city was illuminated. Further, the Continental troops fired volleys by platoons, in all the streets of the city.

The 23rd - At Frederick.

The 24th - At Frederick.
Because of the arrival of peace, the local
Governor Johnson and the gentlemen of the city
held a ball in the markethouse, to which all
the captive officers were invited.
From the 25th to 28th - At Frederick.
The 29th - At Frederick.
Order - The previously prisoners of war shall
all have their freedom, but must always be back
in the barracks by nine o'clock in the evening.
The 30th - At Frederick.

May 1783

From the 1st to 8th - At Frederick.
The 9th - At Frederick.
The American Colonel [James] Wood arrived
here from Winchester and brought the order from
General Lincoln from Philadelphia, that
1) The prisoners of war should be turned
loose, and
2) Their march away from here should take
place as soon as possible.
The 10th - At Frederick.
After the officers of the four German regiments lying here had assembled this morning in
the barracks, the American Colonel Wood sent an
officer to the barracks with the order from
General Lincoln, which stated:
That the previously prisoners of war were
completely released from their captivity. The
American guard therefore, also immediately
departed.
On the march, which is to start Monday, an
American guard consisting of two subalterns and
thirty privates will go with the regiments for
protection.
This afternoon, from the Ansbach regiments, one officer, one sergeant, one corporal,
and 24 privates, 27 men in total, were assigned
guard duty.[7]
The 11th - At Frederick.

The 12th - At Frederick.
Because the Monocacy River ran too high
today, the regiments could not march away from
here.
The 13th - From Frederick we marched
fourteen miles to Gucherlein's house and made
night camp there.
Grenadier [Johann] Berger and Privates
[Johann Kaspar] Fuchs and [Georg] Meier, Sr.,
of Captain von Stain's Company of the von Voit
Regiment, deserted on the march.
The 14th - On the second march we crossed
Pipe Creek and halted at noon in Taneytown,
then we marched through Peterlittletown, in
Pennsylvania, and made night quarters at
Scheermann's house.
The 15th - The third march was through
Hannovercity, to Mekcanster, Potscity, and to
Yorktown, in Pennsylvania, where we camped.
Yorktown is a rather pleasant, newly built
city in an exceptionally beautiful flat region,
such as is not often found.
The 16th - The fourth march carried across
the Susquehanna River, which is one and one-
half miles wide at Wright's Ferry, and then
entered camp at Lancaster.
Lancaster is a large and really well-built
city in Pennsylvania, where many skilled people
live.
The 17th - At Lancaster.
The 18th - The fifth march. We crossed
the Connestoga River and made night camp at the
guest house "Zum Rothen Ochsen",[8] on the main
road to Philadelphia.
The 19th - The sixth march. We passed
both the small and large Brandywine Rivers and
made night camp at the inn at White Horse.
In this region, namely, Brandywine Hills,
the English General-in-Chief Howe fought a
major battle with the Americans in 1777.
The 20th - The seventh march was to White
Lamb, six miles from Philadelphia, where night

camp was made.

The 21st – The eighth march. We entered Philadelphia and the regiment was quartered in the New Jail.[9]

Deserters

1)   Private [Georg] Christhulf,[10] of Major von Seitz' Company of the von Voit Regiment

2)   Private [Johann Salomon] Besserer, of the von Seybothen Regiment.

The 2nd – The ninth march. We passed Kensington and Frankfort and were carried across the Neshamminy Creek. We made night camp near Bristol.

The 23rd – The tenth march. We were carried across the Delaware River, which is almost two and one-half miles wide, past Trenton, and made night camp at Princeton.

Trenton is the place where the Hessian Colonel von Rall, during an enemy attack, died of his wounds and most of his corps were made prisoners of war on 26 December 1776.

The 24th – The eleventh march. We marched through Kingston and over the Raritan River to Brunswick Landing. We made night camp at Piscataway, in Jersey.

At Piscataway some of the officers' horses were stolen from the stalls at night, even though the servants always lay at the stall doors.

The 25th – The twelfth march. We passed Bannontown, Woodbridge, and Elizabethtown, and were carried across the Kills River to Staten Island. We entered night camp at Decker's Ferry.

Lieutenant Pendergast was the commanding officer of the American guard which remained behind at Elizabethtown.

The 26th – In camp at Decker's Ferry.

The 27th – The troops were transferred over to Long Island. We then passed through the localities of Utrecht, Flatbush, and Jamaica. The von Voit Regiment was quartered in

Springfield and Little Plain. The von Seybothen Regiment also entered quarters in the district of Springfield.

Promotions

Second Lieutenants Drexel and Minameier,
of the von Voit Regiment, to 1st lieutenant

Second Lieutenants von Cyriacy and Lindemeier, of the von Seybothen Regiment, to 1st
lieutenant

Staff Captain von Kruse received the Jaeger Company of Captain von Wurmb, who had died
of a wound at Penobscot."

Corporal [Georg Michael] Lochstampfer, of
the von Voit Regiment, was promoted to packmaster.

Chaplain Erb, who arrived from Ansbach,
was assigned to the Jaeger Regiment.

Second Lieutenant Count von Bubna, of the
Jaeger Regiment, died of a wound.

From the 28th to 31st - In quarters at
Little Plain.

June 1783

The 1st - In quarters at Little Plain.

Second Sergeant Schmidt, as 1st sergeant,
and Quartermaster Sergeant Kiestling, both of
Captain von Metzsch's Company of the von Voit
Regiment transferred to Major von Seitz' Company.

Third Sergeant [Johann] Blauhoeffer, of
Captain von Metzsch's Company of the von Voit
Regiment, was promoted to 2nd sergeant.

Private [Johann Gabriel] Stuezel, of the
von Seybothen Regiment, was promoted to quartermaster sergeant of Captain von Metzsch's
Company of the von Voit Regiment.

The 2nd - In cantonment quarters at Little
Plain.

The Regimental Surgeon Rapp, of the von
Voit Regiment, actually accompanied us from
captivity at Frederick to Philadelphia, but

there, with his two servants, Private [Michael]
Gerlinger, of the von Voit Regiment, and a
private of the von Seybothen Regiment, he
remained.

The 3rd - In quarters at Little Plain.

The 4th - In quarters at Little Plain.

At one o'clock this afternoon the birthday
of His Majesty, George III, King of Great
Britain, was celebrated with a salute fired
from all the warships at New York. This
evening, throughout the entire army, a feu de
joie was fired.

From the 5th to 7th - In cantonment
quarters at Little Plain.

The 8th - In quarters at Little Plain.

Private Hartmann, of the Major's Company
of the von Voit Regiment, was promoted to
corporal.

From the 9th to 11th - In quarters at
Little Plain.

The 12th - In quarters at Little Plain.

Promotions in the von Voit Regiment were
Vice-Corporal Klein, of the Grenadiers, and
Private [Kaspar] Schiffermueller, of the Colo-
nel's Company, both to corporal.

From the 13th to 25th - In cantonment
quarters at Little Plain.

The 26th - In quarters at Little Plain.

At one o'clock this afternoon the English
Commissary [William] Porter mustered both
Ansbach regiments at Springfield. The English
General [Alured] Clarke was present.

From the 27th to 30th - In quarters at
Little Plain.

July 1783

From the 1st to 17th - In cantonment
quarters at Little Plain.

The 18th - In quarters at Little Plain.

Chaplain [Johann Christoph] Wagner,[12] of the
von Voit Regiment, received his requested

release and wants to go to Nova Scotia with those favoring England.

From the 19th to 31st - In cantonment quarters at Little Plain.

August 1783

From the 1st to 4th - In cantonment quarters at Little Plain.

The 5th - Both the von Voit and von Seybothen Regiments moved out of Springfield and Little Plain and marched into night quarters at Utrecht.

The 6th - The three Ansbach regiments were embarked on warships near Denys's Ferry, on Long Island, in order to be shipped back to Europe.

1) On the frigate South Carolina, the entire Jaeger Regiment, under the command of Colonel von Voit[13]

2) On the frigate Sibylle, a part of the von Voit and a part of the von Seybothen Regiments, under the command of Colonel von Seybothen

3) On the frigate Quebec, the entire company of Captain von Metzsch of the von Voit Regiment, under the command of Captain von Metzsch

4) On the frigate [Emerald], the entire company of Captain von Quesnoy, of the von Seybothen Regiment, under the command of Captain von Quesnoy.[14]

The 7th - We sailed this morning, but after an hour again dropped anchor.

The 8th - We sailed early and dropped anchor near Sandy Hook.

The 9th - We sailed away from Sandy Hook and had a good wind the entire day. We met an English and a French ship.

The 10th - We sailed with a contrary wind.

The 11th - We sailed with a good wind.

Shortly before our departure from America,

Grenadier Captain von Molitor, of the von
Seybothen Regiment, on request, received his
separation.[15]

Promotions

1) Staff Captain von Reitzenstein, of the
Jaeger Regiment, received the Grenadier Company
of the von Seybothen Regiment.

2) Second Lieutenant Baumann was promoted
to 1st lieutenant in the Jaeger Regiment.

The 12th - Sailed with a good and very
strong wind.

The 13th - Sailed with very strong and
good wind, and at four o'clock in the
afternoon, were already six hundred miles from
Sandy Hook.

Our ships had actually received the order
from the admiral at New York to remain two by
two together and to sail with one another to
Portsmouth in England. Alone! This did not
happen and each ship's captain, as soon as he
was on the open sea, sailed according to his
own pleasure.

The following naval officers were on the
frigate Sibylle: Captain Fischerall and
Lieutenants Philips and Presko.

The 14th - We had calm and contrary wind.

The 15th - Was calm.

The 16th - Sailed with good wind.

We passed the Great Fish Bank of Newfound-
land on the left, but saw nothing and sailed
with the current.[16]

The current is a river thirty miles wide
that runs through the ocean and the ships sail
extraordinarily swift on the current.

The 17th - On the ninth day of our sea
voyage we had calm during the morning and received good wind during the afternoon.

Grenadier [Johann] Fehr, of the von Seybothen Regiment, died this afternoon on the
frigate Sibylle, of consumption, and was buried
at sea during the evening.

The 18th - The tenth day of the sea voyage

had calm in the morning and good wind in the
afternoon.
    The 19th - The eleventh day of the sea
voyage was calm in the morning and a contrary
wind arose during the afternoon.
    A packet boat sailing from England to A-
merica met us.
    The 20th - The twelfth day of the sea
voyage. Sailed with a very good wind.
    The 21st - The thirteenth day of the sea
voyage. We had contrary wind the entire day.
    We met two ships which were coming from
England.
    The 22nd - The fourteenth day on the sea.
We had contrary winds.
    The 23rd - The fifteenth day of our sea
voyage, with very strong and stormy winds, but
we sailed well.
    The middle mast of the frigate Sibylle was
newly installed before our departure from New
York. But it was one which was not meant for a
frigate, but for a large warship. Because of
the great height and weight, the mast began to
sway, causing the rigging, which several times
had to be restrung and tightened with great
effort, to work loose.
    The rolling of the ship today, because of
the strong winds which were very severe,
necessitated lowering the mast onto the
quarterdeck for fear that otherwise it would
break off and place the ship in complete
jeopardy.
    Therefore, at twelve o'clock at night, on
the orders of the ship's Captain Fischerall, it
was chopped down and thrown overboard with all
the rigging and two large sails which were
attached. During this activity, not only was
the top of the aftermast broken, but also the
railings on the ship were severely damaged.
    The rigging of this mast, due to the vio-
lent storm, hung behind on the steering rudder,
so that for half an hour the mast was dragged

by the ship, until finally, through the knowledge and advice of the naval officers, it was
chopped loose from the steering rudder by the
sailors.

The ship <u>Sibylle</u> was formerly a French
frigate which had been captured by the English
during the war.[7] It is covered with a copper
bottom and has 28 guns and two hundred sailors,
plus five hundred troops on board on this
voyage.

Twenty-six officers are living in the cabins and each has had spacious accommodations.

However, this frigate leaked very badly,
so that four times a day, and for two hours
each time, sixty men had to work at the pumps.

The 24th - The sixteenth day on the sea
voyage. During the morning and the afternoon
we had a calm.

The 25th - The seventeenth day on the o-
cean. Contrary wind.

The 26th - The eighteenth day on the o-
cean. We sailed with good wind.

The 27th - The nineteenth day on the ocean
voyage. We sailed with good wind.

Since the middle mast was chopped down, we
have sailed with only one sail on the forward
mast.

Today a middle mast was put up, but very
small, and it is called a jury, or emergency
mast.

The 28th - The twentieth day of the sea
voyage. We sailed with good wind.

The 29th - The 21st day on our voyage. We
again sailed with a very good wind.

The 30th - The 22nd day of our voyage. In
the morning it was calm and in the afternoon we
sailed with a very good wind.

The 31st - The 23rd day of the sea voyage. We sailed with a good wind, but went 31
miles too far to the left.

A great ship was seen at a great distance.

September 1783

The 1st - The 24th day of the sea voyage.
Major von Seitz, of the von Voit Regiment,
after tolerating a fourteen day nerve sickness,
died at eight o'clock this morning on the
frigate Sibylle, in the 43rd year of his life.
Because land would soon be reached, the body
was placed in a coffin, which was made on the
ship.
A small two-masted ship was seen in the
distance.

The 2nd - The 25th day on the ocean. We
sailed with a good wind.
This evening the ship ran aground and was
held fast. The water was frightfully restless
and due to the rolling of the ship, the top of
the aftermast broke off.

The 3rd - The 26th day of our sea voyage.
At twelve-thirty at night a strong storm arose
which lasted throughout the entire day, by
which, however, we sailed with a good wind.
At six o'clock in the evening bottom was
found at sixty fathoms.
We glimpsed a large ship in the distance.

The 4th - The 27th day of the sea voyage.
We sailed with surprisingly stormy, but good
wind.
As the body of the dead Major von Seitz
could no longer be retained, at nine o'clock
this morning, attended by all the officers and
private soldiers, he was buried. Although
several heavy iron balls were tied on the
coffin, he did not sink, but was to be seen as
far as the eye could see, floating away on the
water. Later Staff Captain Seidel, of the von
Seybothen Regiment, gave a short eulogy.
On the frigate Sibylle, the upper part of
the aftermast was again repaired. On the other
hand, the middlemast broke, which injured a
sailor in the chest.
A ship which was going to England met us.

The 5th - The 28th day of the sea voyage.
At midnight a shockingly strong storm arose and
as we were thought to be near land, we again
had to turn out to sea. The storm abated at
twelve o'clock noon, and we were able to
glimpse the Scilly Islands at three o'clock in
the afternoon, where we entered the English
Channel. During the evening we again lost
sight of land.

The 6th - The 29th day of our sea voyage.
At four o'clock in the morning a frightfully
great storm arose which continued until three
o'clock in the afternoon. Also during the
morning, because of the nearness of land, we
had to sail back toward the north. After the
storm, we caught sight of land on our left
side, namely Plymouth, Dartmouth, and Torbay.
During the evening we again lost sight of land.

The 7th - The 30th day of the sea voyage.
At four o'clock in the morning we saw the area
near Portsmouth, where we entered the harbor at
twelve o'clock noon, and anchored at Spithead.

The 8th - We sailed at seven o'clock in
the morning and then anchored two miles from
Portsmouth.

A rifle shot from this place, in the previous year, the Royal George sank.

A Danish warship, on which there is an
admiral, lies here at anchor.

A Prussian two-masted ship sailed out of
the harbor.

Ships' Flags
Denmark
1) Red, with a white cross, and cut out
below.

2) Blue, with a red cross, cut out below,
a white border and in the middle, the coat of
arms.

France
An entirely white flag.
Great Britain
1) Blue

2) Red
3) White, with a red cross.
On each flag, behind, on the upper corner,
the cross of St. George, white on red.
The transport flags are red with three
yellow anchors, and on the upper rear corner,
the cross of St. George, white, red, and blue.

Austria
A yellow flag with double black eagles.

Prussia
White, in the middle, the black eagle.

Sweden
A blue flag with a yellow cross.

Spain
A white flag, in the middle the coat of
arms in various colors.

Holland
Has a flag with three stripes, white,
blue, and red.

Hamburg
Has all red flags, and in the middle, two
decoration crosses.

Bremen
Has a flag with three white and three red
stripes. Behind, on the staff, six white and
six red stones.[18] This was seen on a board at a
dam.

America
A flag with thirteen stripes, red, white,
and blue.[19] Behind, on the upper corner, a blue
square on which there are thirteen white stars,
which represent the thirteen colonies.

The 9th - At anchor at Portsmouth.

The 10th - At anchor at Portsmouth.

A fleet arrived here in the harbor this
noon from Quebec, which had Hessians,
Brunswickers, and Anhalt-Zerbsters on board.
It had been twenty days enroute.

Staff Captain Seidel and Corporal Karl, of
the von Seybothen Regiment, were sent to
London.

The 11th - At anchor at Portsmouth.

The 12th - At anchor at Portsmouth. In place of the frigate Sibylle we received two other transport ships, namely, Eolas and Polly. Colonel von Seybothen is to board the first and Major von Beust the latter. An American brig entered the harbor this evening.

The 13th - On the frigate Sibylle, still lying at anchor at Portsmouth. Colonel von Seybothen embarked on the ship Eolas today.

The 14th - Major von Beust, of the von Seybothen Regiment, and the remaining troops from the frigate Sibylle, embarked on the transport Polly today.

The 15th - As there was absolutely no wind, we remained at anchor at Portsmouth. Staff Captain Seidel returned from London.

The 16th - At anchor at Portsmouth because of contrary wind.

The 17th - Because of contrary wind, still at anchor at Portsmouth.

The 18th - At anchor at Portsmouth. Two English warships came from Jamaica in the West Indies and two Hamburg ships entered the harbor at Portsmouth today.

The 19th - At six o'clock in the evening we sailed from Portsmouth to Spithead and were at once struck by very stormy weather and rain, but we still had good wind.

The 20th - To the left we glimpsed the small English city of Gent, from which very much food comes, but which has no harbor; Dover with a small sea harbor; and Deal, where we anchored at one-thirty in the afternoon. This region is called the Downs.

The water here, even on calm days, is very restless, because the Deal River and the great ocean and the North Sea run together here.

The 21st - At anchor at Deal. This morning the ship Eolas and the two ships with Anhalt-Zerbst troops sailed for

Bremerlehe.

The ship _Polly_ remained here because the ship's Captain Boyd and Mate Patterson are not familiar with the North Sea and no pilot was to be had at Deal for less than sixty guineas. Therefore, one will be brought here from London, who will work for thirty guineas.

Two English men-of-war, which came from the East Indies with merchandise and are to sail to London, arrived in this harbor.

The 22nd - At anchor at Deal.

The 23rd - At anchor at Deal.

A warship with 74 cannons came here this evening with a fleet from London, and sailed on to Portsmouth, where it will remain during the winter.

The 24th - Lying at anchor at Deal.

The coast of France, which is opposite the English coast, is very low. It can be seen clearly from here in bright weather, as can the city of Calais, and it is estimated to be 21 English miles across the Channel.

At four o'clock this afternoon the pilot named Stewart, arrived here from London and at five-thirty we set sail with fresh wind.

Therefore, the [the lack of a] pilot is to blame that we were unable to follow our troops and had to travel alone, under the command of Major von Beust, to Ansbach, even though they had lain at anchor at Hannover Muenden for fourteen days.

The 25th - At four o'clock in the morning we lost sight of the English coast and all land, and entered the North Sea. At ten o'clock in the morning calm set in and at seven o'clock in the evening a contrary wind arose from the east, which lasted all night.

The 26th - The third day on the North Sea voyage, sixty miles from the English city of Armouth. In this region, because of the large herring catches, there are many fishing boats. The wind was still contrary. Therefore, from midnight until midday, we had to tack.

The 27th - The fourth day on the North Sea voyage we sailed with contrary wind.

The 28th - The fifth day on the North Sea voyage, contrary wind and very stormy weather. This morning we were forty miles from the Dutch coast.

The 29th - The sixth day on the North Sea voyage. The wind was constantly contrary, with stormy weather.

A Swedish brig coming from the West Indies and sailing to Stockholm met us.

The 30th - The seventh day on the North Sea voyage. We had fully contrary wind.

The North Sea, during our voyage, generally has a depth of thirty to forty fathoms, and because of many rocky shoals are to be found therein, our trip is rather dangerous.

This afternoon bottom was found at fifteen fathoms.

October 1783

The 1st - The eighth day on the North Sea voyage. During the morning contrary wind and in the afternoon calm.

The 2nd - The ninth day on the North Sea voyage. At three o'clock in the morning good, but very light wind from the north, which lasted until nine o'clock in the morning. Later a calm settled in until two o'clock in the afternoon, when the previously light wind arose. It continued until nine o'clock at night. Then, however, a very good wind from the west arose and bottom was sounded at 21 fathoms.

The 3rd - The tenth day on the North Sea voyage. The good wind continued without let up and during the morning bottom was found at fifteen fathoms.

A Bremen brig, the Victoria, came from London and met us this morning.

At ten o'clock we glimpsed the Dutch islands of Juist, on which there is a tower, and
Nordorney, on which two towers stand. From the
last island it is still 24 miles to the Weser
Bay.

Because the voyage to the Weser Bay is too
long to make today, we sailed further north in
the sea, which continued until eight o'clock at
night, when we began our return.

The 4th - At four o'clock in the morning
we set our course for Bremerlehe. At five
o'clock we saw land, the coast of Holland. In
this region there are many sandbanks, which are
clearly marked, however.

The wind turned contrary at ten o'clock,
from the southwest, and the tide was very
strong. Therefore we anchored in the Weser
Bay.

During the afternoon we sailed with the
Bremen ship _Victoria_ in company and passed the
entrance tower in the middle of the bay. At
six o'clock in the evening, however, we anchored twelve miles from Bremerlehe, at the
mouth of the Weser River.

The 5th - On the eleventh day of our sea
voyage the wind was contrary with a strong
storm. Therefore, we remained at anchor at the
mouth of the Weser River.

On the right the land is called Oldenburg
and belongs to Denmark. On the left, however,
lies Hannover.

The 6th - The twelfth day of our voyage.
We sailed at eleven o'clock, midday. The wind
was very contrary so that we had to anchor at
seven o'clock in the evening in the Weser, two
miles from Bremerlehe.

The 7th - The thirteenth day of our voyage. We sailed at seven o'clock in the morning
and at eight o'clock dropped anchor at Bremerlehe.

Bremerlehe, in Hannover, is a small, very
ancient, built-up place of absolutely no sig-

nificance.

The 8th - At anchor at Bremerlehe.

This morning the English Major Gunn held muster on our ship <u>Polly</u> and at eleven o'clock, midday, the troops began to transfer onto five single-masted Bremen sloops. In the evening the ships went underway and sailed throughout the night, with a contrary wind.

Four miles from Bremerlehe, on this side, the Weser has already changed to sweet water.

The 9th - At three o'clock in the morning, because of continued contrary wind, we anchored on the Weser River. At nine o'clock in the morning we sailed and passed, on the left: Rekum, Renabek, and Vegasack. Here many beautiful ships are built. On the right we passed: Hammel Wharf, Oelschlicht, Taegeland, a large district land which formerly was Danish, but which now belongs to a Dutch prince of Ethin; and Glockenstein, and Langenau, where during the evening we anchored close to land, two and one-half miles from Bremen.

The 10th - We sailed at nine o'clock in the morning and had to have the ships pulled, in part with horses, and in part by soldiers, on the land.

N.B. - In this region boats were to be seen being rowed by women.

At twelve o'clock noon we arrived at the harbor in Bremen.

Bremen is an exceptionally important trade city in the District of Bremen, lying to the left and right of the Weser River, which divides the old and the new towns from one another. There is also a small island between the two Weser bridges. This city is well fortified and has seven city gates. Here there are very many churches, in addition to those noted here.

1) The exceptionally beautiful and large Dome Church, attached to the Evangelical religion and belonging to the King of England.

2) The very large Reformed Church of St. Ancharu.

3) The exceptionally beautiful City Hall.

4) The very new Wheat House.

5) The watchtower outside [the city] with the large waterwheel built in the Weser River, which is built with wood and provides the water for all and every house in the city.

A battalion of five hundred men commanded by a major lies here in garrison and has white and red uniforms.

The herring trade is vigorously conducted here.

The region is entirely flat land and around the city are the most pleasant summer houses and the most productive vegetable gardens. As a rule, the inhabitants are the most pleasant people, very polite and especially knowledgable in commercial dealings.

The 11th - During the afternoon the Ansbach troops were embarked on three Weser ships, which are called Boecke and anchored on the Werder.

The 2th and 13th - At anchor on the Werder.

The 14th - Still lying at anchor near Bremen, on the Werder.

The Hessian Prince Friedrich Regiment marched by on land, near Bremen.

From the 15th to 17th - At anchor near Bremen.

The 18th - During the afternoon we sailed from Bremen and about a mile from Bremen, near the small place, Habenhausen, we anchored for the night on the Weser.

The 19th - We shoved off at seven o'clock in the morning.

Our fleet on the Weser River consisted of eight ships; four of which had one mast each and from Bremen onward were pulled on land by seven horses pulling two ships connected together.

The Prussian citizen and owner of the
ships of the fleet, Casselmann, brings these
troops from Bremen to Hannover Muenden for pay
from the English Crown and at the same time,
commands the fleet as admiral.
     At twelve o'clock noon we stopped and
anchored near Dreye at midday.
     In this region many hundreds of thousands
of geese are to be seen in the meadows.

In the Afternoon

     Underway at two o'clock and we anchored
for the evening on the Weser River, about ten
miles from Bremen.
     The 20th - Underway at seven o'clock in
the morning and passed Issen and Issenburg on
the left bank of the Weser River. About
eighteen miles from Bremen, on the left side of
the Weser, we stopped and landed at noon.

In the Afternoon

     On the right side we passed Inschen, Win-
kel, and Ritzenbergen, where we landed and made
night camp.
     Directly opposite Ritzenbergen is the
mouth of the Aller, which comes from Hannover
and about two and one-half miles from there,
the city Verden lies on the Aller River.
     The 21st - Underway at seven o'clock in
the morning. We passed Hotbergen on the
right. We halted at midday and landed about 24
miles from Bremen.

Afternoon

     We passed Torbaere on the right. During
the evening we anchored near the right bank of
the Weser, about 26 miles from Bremen.
     The 22nd - Underway at seven o'clock in
the morning and we passed Hoya on the right.
     The Weser runs through this city. It has
a very fine bridge, with a drawbridge, built
over the Weser River. The ships passed
through, after lowering their masts.
     This land was named the County of Hoya.
It is Hannoverian and belongs to the King of

England.
    From Bremen to Hoya is about five German
miles.[26]
    On the place where our ships had anchored
the previous night, the Waldeck Major [Chris-
tian Friedrich] Pentzel was shot on his ship.[21]
    As soon as we had passed the bridge at
Hoya, we halted at noon and the ships tied up.
Afternoon
    Underway we passed Aeusterob on the left
and Stendern and Schweringen on the right. We
landed at the latter and made night camp.
    The 23rd - Underway at seven o'clock in
the morning and passed Sebbenhausen on the
right and Drakenburg on the left, where we
halted at midday and tied up.
Afternoon
    We passed Ballie, where we landed in the
evening, about thirty miles from Bremen, and
made night camp.
    The 24th - Underway at seven o'clock in
the morning and on the left we passed the Weser
River's Nienburg. We had to lower our masts
there and passed through the beautiful stone
Weser Bridge, which has five arches.
    Nienburg is a well fortified Hannoverian
city. It has three gates and there is also a
garrison stationed here.
    After the fleet landed at Nienburg during
the noon, then during
The Afternoon
    We went underway and passed Leeseringen,
on the left, where there is a ferry, and on the
right Liebenau. We landed near Liebenau and
made night camp.
    Here it is to be noted that the Hannover-
ian Ridingmaster Kleinschmid took over the
transport and went aboard the staff ship.
    The 25th - Underway at seven o'clock in
the morning and near Liebenau we passed the
dangerous passage where there are very many
rocky shoals in the Weser.

At noon we landed near Landesbergen, which lies on the left side of the Weser.

In the Afternoon

Underway and at evening, near Stolzenau, which is the last Hannoverian settlement, we landed and made night camp.

The 26th - Underway at eight o'clock in the morning and passed Schluesselburg, the first Hessian village, through the middle of which the Weser flows. We halted at noon at Heimhausen, on the left.

Afternoon

We passed Buchholz and Thoren on the right and Ilvese and Windheim on the left. We spent the night in the middle of the stream.

The 27th - Underway at six-thirty in the morning and passed Binn and Petershagen on the right, where we halted at midday.

Afternoon

We passed Loh and Wietersheim on the left and Prussian Minden on the right, where we made night camp.

The 28th - We passed the Weser Bridge at Prussian Minden early. It is built with seven arches. The masts were taken down when passing through.

Prussian Minden is a large and well fortified city. The bridge and the thoroughfare over the Weser are very famous. It has six gates; three Evangelical, one Reformed, and one Catholic Church, the Dome. A Benedictine Cloister is also located here. The infantry regiment Young Waldeck, fifteen hundred men strong, lies there in garrison. It has blue and white uniforms, with red piping and facings of yellow linen. In the Cloisters of the Dome Church drill is held every morning and the parade ground lies immediately in front of the Dome Church.

Close to the Weser Bridge we halted at noon and during the afternoon, at three o'clock, we again went underway. We passed

Ohausen on the right and Neesen and Berghausen on the left. At this latter place, between both of the very beautiful mountains, we spent the night on the Weser River.

The 29th - Underway at nine o'clock in the morning and we passed Holtrup and Vesten on the left and on the right, the former Cloister Woegenstein, Laubasch, and Rehme. Very near this place is the royal Prussian salt works, and Vlotho, where we anchored in the evening and made night camp.

The Prussian village of Vlotho is fully two and one-half miles long and there are three churches here; an Evangelical, a Reformed, and a Catholic Church.

The 30th - Underway at twelve o'clock noon and we anchored and spent the night near Oden, in the County of Lippe.

Through the Prussian land the troops had been led by the Commissary Reverend Dietrich.

From Prussian Minden onward the land on the right side of the Weser belongs to Lippe and everything on the left to Prussia.

The 31st - Underway at seven o'clock in the morning and we passed Velpen, Eisbergen, the last Prussian village, and Dankers, Hesse, on the left; and on the right Huenerhaus, the first Hessian village, and Rinteln, which we entered at noon and where we spent the night.

Rinteln, Hesse, is a secure settlement with a floating bridge of eleven pontoons, across the Weser. This place has two churches, an Evangelical and a Reformed, as well as a university.

The Old Lossberg Regiment, which returned from America already one month ago, lies here in garrison and Lieutenant General von Lossberg is the Governor.

November 1783

The 1st - Underway at eight o'clock in the

morning and on the right we passed Honora. On
the left we passed Ahe, Kohlenstaedt, where a
coal mine and a very large quarry are located,
Kleinenwieden, and Hombeck, where we halted at
noon.

Afternoon

We passed Fuhlen on the right and on the
left Oldendorf, where the castle Schaumberg
sits above on the mountain Inkruckenberg,
Fischbeck, and Wehrbergen, where we landed and
made night camp.

The 2nd - Underway at seven o'clock in the
morning and at nine o'clock in the morning we
arrived at Hameln.

Hameln is a medium size, but well fortified city on the left side of the Weser River,
over which there is a bridge. Because of the
waterfalls, which are in the Weser River, a
lock has been built, through which ships can
and must pass. Therefore, each ship must pay a
toll of twelve dollars.

In the city of Hameln there is a beautiful
armory and two barracks, four churches, two
Evangelical, the Market Church and the Garrison
Church, one Reformed and one Catholic Chapel.

Three battalions of Hannoverian troops lie
here in garrison and the local commandant is
Lieutenant General von Busch.

On the right side of the Weser, on the
very high mountain, lies the famous Fort
George, which is divided into three works;
Number One above, Number Two in the middle, and
Number Three below. Count von der Lippe has
the first, the Hannoverian Major Guns has been
assigned the latter two. In Fort Number Two a
well shaft is to be noted which is more than
five hundred feet above the Weser. In Fort
Number One, is another well which, when
something is dropped in, it takes a minute and
a half before it is heard to drop into the
water.

At one o'clock in the afternoon we

departed from Hameln and passed Hastenbeck (*),
Tuendern, and Hagenohsen on the left, and on
the right Ohr, Emmern, and Osten Aage, where we
landed and made night camp.
     (*) In the year 1759, a battle between
the allies and the French army took place in
which the latter, because they were 124,000 men
strong, gained the victory.   The former's army
had only 24,000 men.
     The 3rd - Underway at seven o'clock in the
morning and we passed Grohnde and Hehlen, of
Brunswick, where we halted at noon.
     Hehlen has a castle which belongs to the
Count of Schulenburg.
                    Midday
     We passed Dastbach, of Brunswick, and Bod-
enwerder, a small Hannoverian city.
     Six miles above the city we landed and
made our night camp.
     The 4th - Underway at seven o'clock in the
morning and on the left we passed Ruehle and
Doelme.   On the right we passed the Devil's
Mill.   Here there are astonishingly large
mountains of bare stone and the Devil's Mill is
built very close to the cliff.   It is driven by
a small stream of water which comes out of the
cliff.   We also passed Preber,[22] which belongs to
Hannover, where very much lime is burned, and
Buhle,[23] where we landed at two o'clock in the
afternoon and made night camp.
     On the 3rd of this month, Quartermaster
Sergeant [Johann Gabriel] Stuezel, of Captain
von Metzsch's Company of the von Voit Regiment,
deserted from the ship.
     The 5th - Underway at seven o'clock in the
morning and on the right we passed Heinsen, a
Hannoverian village, and Stahle, which belongs
to Corvey.   On the left we passed Holzminden, a
small Brunswick city with an iron factory,
where we halted at midday.
                    Afternoon
     We passed Luechtringen on the left and on

275

the right Albaxen, both of which belong to
Corvey, and Corvey, the residence and Benedictine Cloister of the Prince. Here we landed
during the evening and made night camp.

The 6th - Underway at seven o'clock in the
morning and on the right we passed Hoexter, an
Imperial free city with an Imperial garrison of
169 men. There are four churches here, two
Evangelical and two Catholic. Formerly there
was a stone bridge over the Weser, which,
however, at the present time, is completely
unusable.

Many skirmishes took place in this region
in the war prior to the last one, between the
allies and the French army.

On the left we passed Fuerstenberg, an old
Brunswick castle with a porcelain factory on a
very high mountain; and on the right Wehrden,
which belongs to Corvey, where we halted at
midday.

Afternoon

We passed Meinbrexen, of Brunswick, and
Lauenfoerde, of Hannover, on the left and
Blankenau, of Corvey, and Beverungen, of
Paderborn, on the right. We made night camp at
the latter.

The 7th - Underway at eight o'clock in the
morning and passed both difficult sections in
the Weser River, the Juden Kopf [Jew's Head]
and the Schnieber [The Cutter].

Also on the left we passed Wuergassen,
which belongs to Paderborn and Hannover, where
we halted at midday. On the right we passed
Herstelle, of Paderborn, which has a Carmelite
Order Cloister, and Karlshafen, a nicely laid
out Hessian place, which was founded 83 years
ago. There are two very large salt works
here. In the city there is a nice harbor,
which must be entered through a lock from the
Weser River.

The Diemel, which rises in Waldeck, flows
into the Weser here.

Near Karlshafen we landed during the evening and made night camp.   It is 36 miles from
Hannover Muenden.

The 8th - Underway at seven o'clock in the
morning.

At nine-thirty this morning our boat ran
upon a rocky shoal. This caused the helmsman
to be thrown overboard by the rudder. He
righted himself again in the water, but stood
up to his shoulders in the Weser River. He was
picked up later by a boat and brought back to
the ship in an angry mood.

On the right we passed the Hessian Gewis-
senruh, where many French refugees are to be
found; and on the left Wahmbeck, where we
landed and made our night camp.

The 9th - Underway at seven o'clock in the
morning.

Private Saltmann, of Colonel von Voit's
Company, fell into the Weser River this morning
and was recovered again, uninjured.

We passed Bodenfelde, of Hannover, and
Lippoldsberg, of Hesse, on the left; and the
Hessian Gieselwerde on the right, where we
halted at noon.

Afternoon

We passed the Hessian glass factory on the
right.

We landed on the left bank of the Weser
and made night camp.

The 10th - Underway at seven o'clock in
the morning and we passed Oedelsheim on the
left, where we halted at noon, and the Hessian
Franzohsendorf on the right. About one-half
mile beyond this place we landed on the left
side of the Weser River and made night camp.

The 11th - Underway at seven o'clock in
the morning and passed Buschfelden[24]and the
Hannoverian Glashuette on the left. To the
right, on the Weser River, about five miles
from Hannover Muenden, we halted at noon.

Afternoon

We passed on the left Hemeln, of Hannover, and on the right Veckerhagen, of Hesse, with a splendid iron smelter. Here we landed and spent the night.

The 12th - Underway at nine o'clock in the morning. On the right we passed the Hessian Vaake, where we halted at midday, and about one-half mile beyond this place we stopped for the night.

The 13th - Underway at seven o'clock in the morning and had to pass two bad places in the Weser River, Plattenkopf and Steinernwoehr. On the left we passed Juemexe, of Hannover, and on the right Giebertshausen, the Glashuette of Hesse, and Hannover Muenden, where we anchored at twelve o'clock noon.

Near Hannover Muenden the Fulda flows from the right, and the Werra from the left, and below this city the water is called the Weser.

Hannover Muenden lies on the Hessian border and has a good castle.

A battalion of Hannoverian troops lies in garrison here and the commandant is Major General Stokhausen.

A Hessian brigade, which likewise is returning from America, under the command of General [Heinrich Julius] von Kospoth, is in quarters here and tomorrow will resume its march to Kassel, which lies about ten miles from here.

The 14th - At anchor at Hannover Muenden.

It has been learned that Corporal Kolb, of the Grenadier Company of the von Seybothen Regiment, with the first transport, died here.

The rest of the Hesse Hanau Field Jaegers arrived here.

The 15th - Lying at anchor at Hannover Muenden.

The 16th - At anchor at Hannover Muenden.

Private Schoepler, of the Major's Company of the von Voit Regiment, deserted from the

ship.
    The 17th - We debarked in the morning.
Today we began our first march on land and
passed the Hannoverian village of Hedemuenden,
where we were carried over the Werra River and
next arrived in the Hessian villages of
Blickershausen and Ermschwerd, and entered
quarters.
    The 18th - The second march. The quarters
villages were called Uengsterode and
Laudenbach, in Hesse.
    The 19th - The first day of rest.
    The 20th - The third march through Kuec-
hen, Kappel, and then also Bischhausen and into
quarters in Kirchosbach, in Hesse.
    The 21st - The fourth march to Berneburg
and into quarters at Rockensuess, in Hesse.
    The 22nd - The second day of rest.
    The 23rd - The fifth march through Corn-
berg to Weiterode and into night quarters at
Ronshausen, in Hesse.
    The 24th - The sixth march. We passed
Breitenbach, Blankenheim, and Friedlos, and
entered quarters in the two Hessian settlements
of Unterhauen and Oberhauen.
    We crossed over the Fulda Bridge at Breit-
enbach.
    About two and one-half miles from Unter-
hauen lies the Hessian city of Hersfeld. The
garrison is from the Prince Charles Regiment.
Near this city the Huhn River flows into the
Fulda.
    The 25th - The seventh march. Major von
Beust's Company had to march on to Bayreuth
today, apart from us, and entered quarters at
Hausdorf in Fulda. It was commanded by 1st
Lieutenant von Altenstein.
    The troops of the von Voit Regiment were
quartered in the small Fulda city of Huenfeld.
Major von Beust received the order to go with
[the von Voit Regiment] to Ansbach.
    In Huenfeld there are two Catholic chur-

ches, the Parish Church and the Bishopric.

The 26th - The third day of rest.

The 27th - The eighth march. We paraded
through the city of Fulda and were quartered in
the two Fulda settlements of Kohlhaus and
Maretz.

Fulda is an exceptionally beautiful place
on the Fulda River, whose prince writes his
name as von Bibra.

The local garrison has a strength of three
hundred men.

Not far from the city of Fulda lies the
Priory Johannisberg, where the Prior von Zobel
resides.

The 28th - The ninth march through Roth-
emann in Fulda and into quarters at Kothen.

The 29th - The fourth day of rest.

The 30th - The tenth march to Oberthulba
in Wuerzburg and into quarters there.

Through Fulda the troops were led by Herr
von Spiegel, as commissary. Through Wuerzburg
the troops were led as march commissary, by
Sheriff Glaitsmann, from Ebenhausen.

December 1783

The 1st - The eleventh march to Ebenhausen
and Pfersdorf, in Wuerzburg, where we entered
quarters.

Herr von Guttenberg is the Wuerburg magis-
trate at Ebenhausen.

The 2nd - The fifth day of rest.

The 3rd - Through Schweinfurt, where we
passed over the covered Main Bridge, Gochsheim,
in Schweinfurt, then into settled places of
Wuerzburg, Grettstadt, and into quarters at
Ober and Unter Spiesheim.

The 4th - The 13th march through Gerolz-
hofen, in Wuerzburg, and into quarters at
Prichsenstadt, in Ansbach.

The 5th - The sixth day of rest.

The 6th - The fourteenth march through

Wiesentheid, Roedelsee, and into night quarters at Mainbernheim.

The 7th – The fifteenth march over Gollhofen and into night quarters at Uffenheim.

The 8th – The sixteenth march over Rudolzhofen to Neuen Herberg, Pfaffenhoffen, Bachheim, Ottenhofen, and into night quarters at Marktbergel.

The 9th – The seventeenth march through Ober Dachstetten, Graefenbuch, Unter Hessbach, Lehrberg, Neusses, to Ansbach, and then we marched into the barracks at Ansbach with music playing.

NOTES TO INTRODUCTION

1) From A Hessian Diary of the American
Revolution by Johann Conrad Doehla. Translated
by Bruce E. Burgoyne. Copyright c 1990 by the
University of Oklahoma Press. Sources used in
compiling the information are: H. B. Horn
(ed.), British Diplomatic Representatives,
1689-1789, (London, 1932); Eberhard Staedtler,
Die Ansbach-Bayreuther Truppen in Amerikanisch-
en Unabhaengigkeitskrieg, 1773-1783, (Nurnberg,
Germany, 1956); and British Museum Additional
Manuscripts 21807, f. 317 and 21808, f. 196 of
the Haldimand Papers; 23649, f. 9 and 23651,
ff. 73, 122, and 123 of the Rainsford Papers;
29454, ff. 16-27 of the Landsdowne Papers; and
38383, f. 88 of the Liverpool Papers.

2.) The fine appearance of the Ansbach-
Bayreuth soldiers was noted by several diarists
of the period, including the Hessian Captain
Frederick von Muenchhausen, General William
Howe's Aide-de-Camp, who wrote on 23 June 1777,
"The Anspachers are exceedingly tall and hand-
some fellows. Without doubt these Anspach
regiments are the tallest and best looking
regiments of all those here." Friedrich von
Muenchhausen. At General Howe's Side, 1776-
1778: The Diary of General William Howe's Aide
de Camp, Friedrich von Muenchhausen. Translated by Ernst Kipping and annotated by Samuel
Steele Smith, (Monmouth, NJ, 1974), p. 19.

3.) Although the German word "Feldscher"
translates surgeon, because each company had an
individual of this designation, I have used the
American term "Medic".

NOTES TO THE ANONYMOUS DIARY

1777

1.) As noted in the Preface, the first and second pages of the original diary are partially damaged. However, those pages are available in the "True Copy" now in the Nuernberg City Archives. The initial diary entries prior to 11 March 1777 translate as follows:
"March 1777 - March from Ansbach to Marktbergel.
"The 8th of March 1777 - March to Uffenheim.
"The 9th of March - March to Ochsenfurt where the regiments was embarked.
"The 10th of March 1777 - During the morning both regiments rebelled. They wanted to leave the ships and did so. During the afternoon they were to return aboard the ships, which the Eyb Regiment did, but the Voit Regiment refused to do so and instead fled from the spot. As the Field Jaegers were sent after them an attack occurred during which one man of the Voit Regiment was killed and two were wounded. Following this, orders were received for the regiments to march back to Uffenheim, but the men allowed themselves to be talked into returning aboard the ships."
This entry should be compared with the entry for the 10th of March in the Prechtel Diary following, in which all references to a rebellion have been removed. The account by Doehla, of the Voit Regiment, is to the effect that the Eyb Regiment began the rebellion. A jaeger officer, Lieutenant Carl Philipp von Feilitzsch recorded that the Voit Regiment Grenadier Company started the rebellion. As a result of the rebellion and the suppression of the same by the Jaegers, the Jaegers sailed down the river to the Dutch port a few days after the infantry regiments and Colonel William Faucitt, the

English Commissary, recommended that once in
America the regiments should not be allowed to
serve together. Doehla, A Hessian Diary, pp.
4-5; Carl Philipp von Feilitzsch. "Tagebuch
des markgraeflichen Jaeger-leutnant Carl
Philipp von Feilitzsch", a manuscript in the
archives of the University of Bayreuth, Germany, entry for 1777; an anonymous manuscript
(Ms. hist. Nr. 485 - "True Copy" of the
Prechtel diary in the Huntington Library) in
the State Archives, Nuernberg, Germany.
     2.) Doehla noted that the infantry sol-
diers continued to have bad feelings toward the
Jaegers as a result of the incident at Ochsenfurt and that the Prince talked to the men in-
dividually to get them to continue their march,
after extra ships were provided. Doehla, A
Hessian Diary, p. 5.
     3.) A more detailed list of cities passed
and the description of some of them is to be
found in the Prechtel Diary following.
     4.) The ships for the Ansbach-Bayreuth
troops, loaded at Holland, were: Diana, 298
tons; Durand, 330 tons; Friendship, 255 tons;
Hopewell, 329 tons; Juno, 236 tons; Myrtle, 309
tons; Providence (2), 310 tons; Stag, 317 tons;
and Sumetry, 281 tons. Hesse-Cassel jaeger
recruits were on the Apollo, 361 tons, and
Providence (1), 366 tons. Hesse-Hanau recruits
were on Favorite, 221 tons and Mediator, 181
tons. The Ansbach-Bayreuth contingent was
given another ship, Aurora, before the convoy
sailed from England. Public Record Office,
C.O. 5/141, f. 91; Doehla, A Hessian Diary, p.
17.
     5.) Incidents which occurred at sea are
more fully noted in the Prechtel Diary
following.
     6.) A German mile equals six English
miles.
     7.) This and subsequent mention of church
calendar terminology is not used in the

Prechtel Diary following, for which I can give
no explanation.
    8.) A fathom equals six feet.
    9.) Illumination was created by placing
candles, or lamps, in the windows of houses.
Often more than one such light would be placed
in a single window.
    10.) Apparently the soldiers served on
the gun crews as the ship's crew could not have
sailed the ship and manned the guns.
    11.) This sounds like luxury and is quite
contrary to the comments of other Hessian
diarists. Carl Philipp Steuernagel of the
Waldeck Regiment described the berthing as
follows: "Our bunks were so tightly arranged
that we had to lay pressed against one another
and no one could move let alone turn over. Six
by six. In general there was space for a board
which was five feet long and six feet wide.
When we were tired of lying on one side in this
narrow holder, the senior, or one in command,
gave a signal so that all could turn on the
other side at the same time, and without this,
since we were so closely packed, we often ended
up with our heads where our feet had been."
Valentin Asteroth, of the Hessian von Huyn
Regiment wrote on 5 August 1776, "The wind
moved the ship so violently that three berths
collapsed and as three were arranged one above
the other and six persons occupied each one,
eighteen men fell out. Carl Philipp Steuernagel. "Ein kurze Beschreibung" (A brief
Description), a manuscript in the Bancroft
Collection of the New York Public Library, f.
7; Valentin Asteroth. Tagebuch aus dem Amerikanischen Unabhaengigkeitskrieg, 1776-1783
(Diary of the American War of Independence,
1776-1783), (Treysa/Ziegenhain. Germany, 1966),
entry for 5 August 1776.
    12.) The summary of rations is similar to
that reported by other Hessian diarists. As a
rule, six to eight women, plus their children,

were allowed to travel with each company.

13.) The Somerset was a 64-gun ship, Captain George Ourry. Muenchhausen, At General Howe's Side, p. 14.

14.) This was the first Ansbach-Bayreuth contact with the American military and the first casualty.

15.) This movement was an effort to create a diversion in behalf of General John Burgoyne who had invaded the colonies from Canada and found himself nearly surrounded near Saratoga, New York.

16.) York Land is used to mean mainland New York as opposed to York (Manhattan) Island.

17.) Burgoyne capitualted on 17 October 1777

18.) Charles, Earl Cornwallis had crossed into New Jersey with a force from General William Howe's command at Philadelphia for a planned attack, in conjunction with General Thomas Wilson's troops, against Forts Billingsport and Redbank. Both forts were evacuated by the Americans without a fight.

19.) Although the German word "Matrosen" translates as sailors, it is also a term applied to artillerymen.

1778

1.) Colonel von Eyb had been so ill when the regiment was in New York that he had not sailed up the Hudson River in October 1777 nor traveled with the regiment to Philadelphia the following month. He arrived in Philadelphia on 27 March 1778. His recall orders may have arrived from England by the same packet that delivered General Howe's recall. Feilitzsch, "Tagebuch", entry for 27 March 1778; Doehla, A Hessian Diary, p. 73; Muenchhausen, At General Howe's Side, p. 50.

2.) Von Sichart is known to have kept a diary during his stay in America, but its present location, if it still exists, is unknown. Doehla, <u>A Hessian Diary</u>, p. xiii.

3.) This was the Mischianza, a spectacular organized in part by Major John Andre. It was put on to show General Howe that he was held in high esteem and affection by his subordinates.

4.) The English had developed a series of twelve redoubts as a defensive line to protect the city of Philadelphia from the Americans.

5.) This movement was to counter the Marquis de Lafayette who had taken post at Barron Hill with a large American force. When the English army approached, however, he withdrew.

6.) The dictionary defines Turkish music as "crude, noisy music produced by shrill wood instruments, various drums, triangles, and other percussion instruments."

7.) The peace commissioners were Frederick Howard, Earl of Carlisle; George Johnstone, formerly Governor of West Florida; and William Eden, later Lord Auckland, who had come from England, plus General Henry Clinton. Their attempt to arrange a peace settlement with the American colonies failed. Carl Leopold Baurmeister. <u>Revolution in America: Confidential Letters and Journals, 1776-1784, of Adjutant General Baurmeister of the Hessian Forces</u>. Translated by Bernhard A. Uhlendorf. (New Brunswick, NJ, 1957), p. 76.

8.) Doehla noted that as a result the unit coined the phrase "the devil drowned in Hell" as the German "Teufel" translates devil in English. Doehla. <u>A Hessian Diary</u>, p. 76.

9.) The Ansbach-Bayreuth regiments were sent to New York by ship. Even so, it seems strange that the author made no reference to the Battle of Monmouth Courthouse, on 28 June 1778, fought by the English and Hessian troops marching overland from Philadelphia.

10.) The designation "fifth house" is not clear.

11.) These were actually enlisted men of a company of New Hampshire volunteers who pretended to be officers. Frederick Mackenzie. Mackenzie Diaries: Diary of Frederick Mackenzie, Giving a Daily Narrative of His Military Service as an Officer of the Regiment of Royal Welsch Fusilers During the years 1775-1781 in Massachusetts,, Rhode Island, and New York. 2 vols. (Cambridge, MA, 1930), 2:346-48; Doehla, A Hessian Diary, p. 80.

12.) Some, if not most, of the desertions at this time from the English, Hessians, and Ansbach-Bayreuth units were to avoid the hard work of constructing defensive lines across the entire island. Ibid., p. 85.

13.) The diarist wrote "Dominic Hill".

14.) In the Battle of Rhode Island American losses were 211 men; English and Hessian, including Ansbach-Bayreuth, losses were 260 men. Howard W. Preston. The Battle of Rhode Island - August 29th, 1778, (Providence, RI, 1928). p. 43.

15.) The cavalry rank of riding master is the equivalent of the infantry rank of captain.

16.) These recruits had been mustered in Frisdorf in Ansbach on 25 October 1777 and began their march to the port at that time. Prussia refused them permission to pass through Prussian territory on the Rhine River. Therefore they spent nearly two months living in open boats at Bensdorf, which belonged to Hesse-Hanau, before being allowed into winter quarters in Hanau. In the following February they began a fifty day march overland to Bremerlehe, where they boarded ships for America. The total time for the trip to America was eleven months. When mustered at Bremerlehe on 5 April 1778 the shipment included two second lieutenants, one medic, one sergeant, five corporals, and 103 jaegers, plus one major, two 2nd lieutenants, two medics, one sergeant, five corporals, three drummers, and 187 recruits.

British Museum Additional Manuscripts, "Hard-
wicke Papers", vol. 35378; Public Record
Office, C.O., 5/11 f. 58.
17.) This weather was later known as the
"Hessian Winter". The cold, snow, and rain
created many problems and even deaths. Stephen
Popp. "Popp Journal, 1777-December 1783",
Pennsylvania Magazine of History and Biography.
Translated by Joseph G. Rosengarten. (Phila-
delphia), vol. 26 (1902), p. 33.; Mackenzie,
Diaries, 2:435-36.

1779

1.) This is cornmeal as we understand the
term today.
2.) This may have been due to frostbite
caused by the extreme weather of late 1778.
3.) This is a type of hemlock, extremely
poisonous.
4.) Minor may be used to indicate someone
under a certain age; to reflect the son of
another member of the unit; or, more likely, an
individual who joined the unit with the same
last name as another person already in the
unit.
5.) As noted in the Preface, the author
used various spellings when referring to the
Raisonable and the Renown.
6.) The Refugees were Loyalists.
7.) The author noted this ship as the
Hundert.
8.) As will be noted in the pages which
follow, Abt returned to his unit after
deserting from an American unit. Following his
capture at Yorktown he again joined the
American army.
9.) Mertschery seems an unlikely name for
the ship and the author used a spelling of
Schip Wricht for the Shipwright.
10.) The inhabitants were also warned to
stay indoors during this time "on pain of

death.[11]   Samuel Greene Arnold. _History of the State of   Rhode Island   and Providence   Planta-tions_, (Spartanburg, SC, 1970), 2:446.

11.) The 1779 recruit shipment totaled 157 men of   all ranks   when mustered   at Dordrecht, Holland, on 29 March 1779. K.G. Davies (ed.). _Documents   of   the American   Revolution, 1770–1783_. Colonial Office Series, 21 vols. (County Dublin, Ireland, 1973-80), 16:64.

12.) The English did not capture Savannah at this   time, but had successfully   resisted a combined American and French siege of the city.

13) These units   were employed by General Clinton to   capture   Charleston,   SC, which surrendered on 11 May 1780.

14.) This was the _Pan_. Some of the sur-vivors   went aboard   the _Anna_,   which lost   its masts en   route to Charleston.   That   ship then drifted to   England where the   men were   put on still another   ship and   resumed their   trip to Charleston.   An   interesting   account   of   the incident   is in   Johann   Ewald.   _Diary of   the American War: A Hessian   Journal_.   Edited   and translated   by Joseph P.   Tustin. (New   Haven, Conn., 1979) pp. 190-91.

1780

1.) This   was   a   reinforcement sent   to General Clinton in South Carolina.

2.) The _Royal American Gazette_ carried an article of   about 700   words reporting   this 16 April incursion into New   Jersey. _Royal Ameri-can Gazette_.   (New York, 20 April 1780).

3.) The   sentence   is   unfinished in the German text.

4.) Apparently hanging was a   death for criminals,   while   facing a   firing   squad   was considered a more proper death for a soldier.

5.) This means   that the regiment contin-ued to   list him   as a   deserter and   not as   a prisoner of war.

6.) Apparently this was necessary because many ships were kept on the American coast and impressment was the only means of replacing crew members who died or deserted. Even in England men were pressed into the British Navy and the English practice of stopping American ships, which continued after the Revolution, in order to press men onto English ships, was a major cause of the the War of 1812.

7.) The Battle of Camden, in South Carolina, was fought on 16 August 1780.

8.) Because of over-crowding on the transports there were more deaths than usual among the 152 Ansbach-Bayreuth recruits. Baurmeister, _Revolution in America_, p. 386; Doehla, _A Hessian Diary._ p. 139.

9.) He was charged with having committed acts of fornication two years earlier in Bayreuth with Colonel von Seybothen's wife, who had remained in Bayreuth. _Ibid._, p. 141.

1781

1.) The Flagstaff was a defensive position on Staten Island.

2.) Although the Chatham is listed, only the Charon is mentioned in later entries.

3.) To the best of my knowledge no one has ever made an in depth study of how the Revolution affected the lives of the slaves nor the institution of slavery.

4.) This is probably a reference to Colonel Alexander Scammel. St. George Tucker. "St. George Tucker's Journal of the Siege of Yorktown, 1781", William and Mary Journal, (Williamsburg, VA), Series 3, vol. 3 (1948), p. 381.

5.) St. George Tucker noted on 2 October 1781, "I discovered with the Assistance of a Glass from seventy to an hundred horses dead on the shore of York or floating about in the River.". Ibid., 382.

6.) Completely different names, Barkley and Robertson, appear in the Prechtel Diary. I attribute this to copying errors, or use of phonetic spelling, when first heard, but corrected at a later date.

7.) (Johann) Michael Ostertag (Easterday, Eisterday, Yesterday) settled near Jefferson, MD, as a miller. He was naturalized on 24 March 1794. He died 23 August 1837, at the age of 93, having fathered eleven children during two marriages. Nancy Rice Kiddoo, "Of Revolutionary Memory: German Mercenaries Who Immigrated to Western Maryland", Journal of the Pennsylvania German Society, (Philadelphia), vol. 23, (1989), p. 67.

8. (Johann) Simon Rueckert (Rickert) married Anna Margreth Staub in Frederick County, MD, on 1 January 1784, and fathered three children. He was buried 11 February 1793, in Loudoun County, VA, age 40. Ibid., p. 69; Nancy Rice Kiddoo. A printed list "Marshalling

Traces of Hessian Soldiers of the American
Revolution Who Marched As Prisoners-of-War to
Frederick County, Maryland, Recruited Local
Brides, and Joined the Ranks of American
Citizens", (Whippany, NJ, n.d.)

9.) The soldiers were given a reward for
salvaging cannonballs.

10.) These redoubts are generally referred to as 9 and 10. Number 9 was attacked by
the French and Number 10 by the Americans.
Henry P. Johnston. The Yorktown Campaign and
the Surrender of Cornwallis, 1781, (Yorktown,
VA., 1975), pp. 142-43.

11.) Michael Marquart (Marquardt, Mar-
quert, Marquet, Marquett, Marckwart, Marck-
wardt, Murquet), born 1 January 1758 in
Greuelsheim, Germany, settled in Frederick
County, MD, where he married Anna Huber in 1786
and fathered four children. Naturalized on 24
March 1794, he died 8 November 1831, age 74.
Kiddoo, "A Revolutionary Memory", pp. 65-66;
Kiddoo, "Marshalling Traces".

12.) For an excellent account of the
march into captivity see James L. Carpenter.
The Yorktown Prisoners, a master's thesis
submitted to the College of William and Mary,
(Williamsburg, VA, 1950).

13.) The official English report lists
156 killed, 326 wounded, and 79 missing.
Davies, Documents, 19:208.

NOTES TO PRECHTEL DIARY

1777

1.) Preceding the copy of the diary in the Bavarian State Archives, there is a supplement written by a Captain Helmes, one-time archivist, containing a number of entries from the original (Huntington version) of the diary which differ from the copy in the Bavarian State Archives. The supplement has not been included with this translation as I have included almost the entire Huntington version of the diary here. There is also a brief "Glossary" which has not been included as it adds nothing to the value of the diary or the translation.

2.) This list of officers, not in the original, is a valuable addition to this copy of the diary.

3.) According to the initial treaty, Ansbach-Bayreuth placed only one company of jaegers in English service.

4.) References to the mutiny on this date were recorded in all the other known Ansbach-Bayreuth diaries covering the march to the port.

5.) Little Providence and Great Providence are listed as Providence (2) and Providence (1), respectively, in official reports. Public Record Office, C.O. 5/140, f. 91.

6.) This type of entry, noting events which transpired at a later date, clearly indicates editing after the original entries were recorded.

7.) Many Hessians used the term plantation to describe the American farms.

8.) Actually the attack was made early in the morning on 26 December 1776.

9.) This is the author of the diary. The Ansbach-Bayreuth soldiers seem to have advanced more easily to commissioned status than the men of the other German states.

10.) Verplanck's Point.

11.) This appears to be the individual mentioned in Captain Friedrich von Muenchhausen's diary . On 4 June 1777 he wrote that the newly arrived Ansbachers were causing him much trouble because they spoke only German. However, next day he wrote, "I have found an adventurer who speaks German, French, and English, and have had him transferred to the Anspachers." Muenchhausen, At General Howe's Side, p. 13.

12.) The attack on Redbank took place on 22 October 1777.

13.) Muhlenberg had served in the Ansbach-Bayreuth military forces during his youth in Germany.

1778

1.) This sounds as if it had been the city's bowling green before the war, or an assembly area where military organizations would pitch their camp.

2.) The author of this diary.

1779

1.) In the original diary Prechtel had written that this was the Raisonable.

2.) Because of the way this is written, it sounds as if the Restoration were a privately owned frigate, and, as it is not listed with the ships of the English navy at the end of the diary, it may have been.

3.) According to the account in Lieutenant Feilitzsch's diary, the returnees traveled to Ansbach-Bayreuth by way of Holland and then sailed down the Rhine and Main Rivers.

1780

1.) Several times during the war German deserters were offered amnesty if they would return to duty. This may have been the case with Katzenwinkel.

2.) This is obviously a reference to the English victory at Camden, South Carolina, on 16 August 1780.

1781

1.) I have used the term shrapnel to mean pieces of bombs although shrapnel, as such, was not invented until later.

1782

1.) Prechtel used Frederick, Frederic-town, and Frederick City at various times in his diary. In general, I have used the simple Frederick.

2.) I have not been able to identify this individual.

3.) One wing of the Barracks, still in use, is on the grounds of the Maryland School of the Deaf.

4.) Either John Odorfer or Michael Hol-dorfer is believed to be John Michael Hadorfer. Each was a member of the first partisan legion commanded by Brigadier General Armand, Marquis de la Rouerie, discharged on 15 November 1783 and entitled to land from Virginia and from the United States. Louis A. Burgess, Virginia Soldiers of 1776, (Spartanburg, SC, 1973) vol. 3, p. 1253.

5.) On 4 May 1781, William Faucitt, then a major general, writing from Bremerlehe, noted that the Ansbach recruits "were very fine". These undoubtedly included a third company of jaegers, which had been approved by England on 22 January 1781. The reinforcement arrived in

New York on 11 August 1781. Davies, Documents,
XIX, pp. 24, 107, and 166.
    6.) Kalnek, or Calnec, born 1745 in Sax-
on-Coburg-Gotha, settled in Nova Scotia after
the war and brought his wife and four children
over from Berlin in 1784. He died in 1831 at
age 86. Staedtler, Die Ansbach Bayreuther
Truppen, p. 72.
    7.) Lieutenant von Beust was released for
insulting his colonel. He later settled in
Nova Scotia, having altered his name to De
Beust. Ibid, p. 151
    8.) Gaertner had deserted previously and
claimed to be married to an American. Because
of his wound he may have been left behind in
Frederick when the Ansbach-Bayreuth troops
marched away in the spring of 1783. Ibid., p.
157; Doehla, A Hessian Diary, p. 221.
    9.) Conrad Stengel, listed by Burgess as
being entitled to land from Virginia and from
the United States for his service in Armand's
Legion, was discharged at York, Pennsylvania,
and settled in that area. He married a girl
named Catherine and had at least two children. He died prior to 1826. The artist Lewis
Miller has given us a sketch of "Old Stengel,
ein Hess 1777". Burgess, Virginia Soldiers of
1776. p. 1253; Lion G. Miles, The Hessians of
Lewis Miller, (Millville, PA, 1983), pp. 59-60.
    10.) Friedrich Jakob Schaefer, listed by
Burgess as having served in Armand's Legion,
married a Gertraut Krebs and had at least one
son, born in Frederick County, Maryland.
Burgess, Virginia Soldiers of 1776, p. 1253;
Kiddoo, "Of Revolutionary Memory", p. 70.
    11.) Conrad Budding, sketched by Lewis
Miller, was born in 1754 and after deserting at
Winchester, Virginia, served in Captain John
Sharp's Company of Armand's Legion as Conrad
Pudding. Discharged in York, Pennsylvania, in
1783, he joined the York County Militia, having
married Elizabeth Sechrist in April 1783. They

had three children. He died at York on 30
April 1837, age 83. A list in the Pennsylvania
Archives gives the year of his death as 1828,
at age 74. Miles, The Hessians of Lewis
Miller, pp. 4-6; Samuel Hazard (Comp.), Pennsylvania Archives, (Philadelphia, 1852), Series
4, vol. 3, p. 880.
    12.) Burgess lists John Wannenmaker as a
member of Armand's Legion, discharged on 15
November 1783 and entitled to 200 acres of land
from Virginia and 100 acres from the United
States. Burgess, Virginia Soldiers of 1776. p.
1253.
    13.) Christian Tawbert, listed as a cor-
poral in Armand's Legion, was discharged on 15
November 1783 and entitled to 400 acres of land
from Virginia and 100 acres from the United
States. Ibid.

1783

    1.) On 8 August 1783 Lord North wrote to
General Sir Guy Carleton, commanding English
forces in America, that the Margrave of
Ansbach-Bayreuth had proposed a regiment of
jaegers consisting of six companies. Because
the number of jaegers was only enough for five
companies, approval had been withheld. Now,
however, because of the peace treaty, because
only one field officer had been appointed for
the regiment, and because the Margrave had done
everything possible to help the English cause,
the King had given his consent to the immediate
formation of the new regiment. Davies,
Documents, XXI, pp. 201-202.
    2.) Prechtel received another promotion.
    3.) Later Gneisenau was a field marshall
in Prussian service. Staedtler, Die Ansbach
Bayreuther Truppen, p. 35.
    4.) Martin Geisensieder was also entitled
to land for his service in Armand's legion. He
was listed under the name Keizenzeder as having

died in Crawford County, Pennsylvania, on 15 December 1819. Burgess, Virginia Soldiers of 1776, p. 1253; Hazard, Pennsylvania Archives, Series 4, vol. 3, p. 880.

5.) There is a vast amount of correspondence concerning the supplies seized and detained in Chester County, Pennsylvania, on 1 January 1783 by Sheriff John Gardner. The actual value of the Ansbach-Bayreuth clothing was 61 pounds, 5 shillings, but for all the English, Hessian, and Ansbach items the value was in excess of 6,000 pounds. On 6 March 1783 Gardner was ordered by the Pennsylvania Supreme Executive Council to surrender the detained items to the Secretary of War, but most of the clothing had been embezzled. That of the Ansbachers was valued at 2,906 pounds, 5 shillings, 11 pence in Pennsylvania currency at that time. As noted in the Introduction, the seized items included a sword for Prechtel and a sewing chest for his wife. Davies, Documents, XIX, pp. 386-87; Hazard, Pennsylvania Archives, Series 2, vol. 10, pp. 6-9; Series 4, vol. 3, pp 875-76; Hazard, Pennsylvania Collected Records, vol. 13, pp. 484, 491, 525-26, 539-40.

6.) I have not been able to identify this individual. Possibly General Horatio Gates is meant.

7.) Doehla noted in his diary on this date, "For the first time I again went on guard duty." Doehla, A Hessian Diary, p. 222.

8.) While this translates "At the Red Oxen", because of the many Germans in the area, the name of the inn could have been in either English or German.

9.) The men of the regiments did not like being quartered in the jail because they were locked up to prevent desertion. Ibid, p. 226.

10.) A Georg Christhulf, formerly of the 4th Company of the Ansbach Regiment, was listed in the 6th Company, 4th Battalion, Philadelphia

County Militia on 10 April 1784. He was apparently a musician and had surveyed 400 acres of land in Luzerne County. On 8 September 1785 Georg Christhilf married Sabrina Schneider. They had three children. Georg died during a yellow fever epidemic in Philadelphia in 1793. A son, Heinrich, fought against the English in the Battle of Baltimore in 1814. From a typed Christhilf family genealogy, dated 14 November 1986, owned by Nicholas Christhilf of Annapolis, MD.

11.) This would seem to indicate that the men of the 1782 recruit shipment had been sent to reinforce the Penobscot garrison.

12.) Initially Wagner had remained behind at Frederick where he had been promised work and planned to marry. He traveled to Nova Scotia with Molitor's group in 1783 with four children, but no wife, and received 400 acres of land in Annapolis County. Wagner returned to Germany after a dispute over who would be the local preacher. Staedtler, Die Ansbach Bayreuther Truppen, p. 71.

13.) Prechtel makes if sound as if all the Ansbach-Bayreuth jaegers had been assembled in New York, including those previously landed in Nova Scotia.

14.) The Emerald was a 42-gun frigate, Captain Sir Shipper. There were 148 sailors and 52 marines on board plus the English General Browne, Colonel Emmerich, and several English and Hessian staff officers. Doehla, A Hessian Diary, p. 232.

15.) After the war Molitor led a group of Ansbach soldiers to settle in Clements Township, Annapolis Royal, Nova Scotia, where he received 700 acres of land. His own family group included his wife, six children, and ten servants. Other soldiers in the group were Regimental Surgeon Friedrich Arnold, and Privates Konrad Herterich, Adam Barth, Friedrich Ensenberg, and Karl Horneber, and Lieutenant Stephen von Molitor. I have translated a short anonymous diary in The New York Public Library, probably written by Captain Molitor, and hope to publish it in a subsequent volume containing other Ansbach-Bayreuth diaries. Staedtler, Die Ansbach Bayreuther Truppen, pp. 71-73, 151; Maxwell Sutherland, "Case History of a Settlement", The Dalhousie Review (Halifax) vol. 41 (Spring 1961) pp. 65, 71.

16.) This is a reference to the Gulf Stream.

17.) The Sibylle had been captured by the British frigate Hussar, Captain Thomas M. Russell, in late 1782 or early 1783. Baurmeister, Revolution in America, p. 547.

18.) The word in the German text is Steine [stones]. This appears to be a copying error which should be Sterne [stars].

19.) This appears to be an American flag with blue, as well as red and white stripes.

20.) As a German mile equaled six English miles, it was thirty miles from Bremen to Hoya.

21.) Major Pentzel committed suicide about 55 miles south of Bremen. Other details are missing. Born 12 March 1733 in Helsen, he was a professional soldier who had risen from the ranks and was a great story teller and the life of the party. He had suffered several periods of illness while in America and may have committed suicide due to poor health. Philipp Waldeck, "Tagebuch", a manuscript in the Bancroft Collection of The New York Public Library, passim; Algemeen Rijksarchief, Raad von State, nr. 1969, "1744-1793", The Haag, Netherlands; Bruce E. Burgoyne, Waldeck Soldiers of the American Revolutionary War, (Bowie, MD, 1991), p. 107.

22.) This may be present day Brevoerde.

23.) This may be present day Polle.

24.) This may be present day Bursfelde.

BIBLIOGRAPHY

Note - Only those references actually
cited in the translation have been listed in
this bibliography. Any library can furnish the
reader with extensive lists of documents,
books, and articles dealing with the
Revolution, War, Hessians, Battles, or any
other related subject.

ALGEMEEN Rijksarchief, Raad von State, nr.
1969, "1744-1793", The Haag, The Netherlands.
ANONYMOUS (Probably Johann Ernst Prech-
tel). "Tagebuch", Ms. hist. nr. 485, Staats-
archiv Nuernberg, Germany.
ARNOLD, Samuel Greene. History of the
State of Rhode Island and Providence Plan-
tations, 2 vols. (Spartanburg, SC, 1970).
ASTEROTH, Valentin. Tagebuch aus dem A-
merikanischen Unabhaengigkeitskrieg, 1776-1783,
(Treysa/Ziegenhain, Germany, 1966).
BAURMEISTER, Carl Leopold. Revolution in
America: Confidential Letters and Journals,
1776-1784, of Adjutant General Major
Baurmeister of the Hessian Forces, translated
and edited by Bernhard A. Uhlendorf, (New
Brunswick, NJ, 1957).
BRITISH Museum Additional Manuscripts,
"Haldimand Papers", nr. 21807, f. 317, nr.
21808, f. 196; "Hardwicke Papers", nr. 35378;
"Landsdowne Papers", nr. 29454, ff. 16-27;
"Liverpool Papers", nr. 38383, f. 88; and
"Rainsford Papers", nr. 23649, f. 9, nr. 23651,
ff. 73, 122-23.
BURGESS, Louis Alexander. Virginia Sol-
diers of 1776, (Spartanburg, SC, 1973).
BURGOYNE, Bruce E. (Comp.). Waldeck
Soldiers of the American Revolutionary War,
(Bowie, MD, 1991).
CARPENTER, James L. The Yorktown Prison-
ers, A master's thesis submitted to the College
of William and Mary (Williamsburg, VA, 1950).

CHRISTHILF, Nicholas. A typed script copy of a Christhilf family genealogy, (n.p., 1986).

DAVIES, K.G. (Ed.). Documents of the American Revolution, 21 vols., (County Dublin, Ireland, 1973-80).

DOEHLA, Johann Conrad. A Hessian Diary of the American Revolution, translated and edited by Bruce E. Burgoyne, (Norman, OK, 1990).

EWALD, Johann. Diary of the American War, A Hessian Journal, translated and edited by Joseph P. Tustin, (New Haven, CT, 1979).

FEILITZSCH, Carl Philipp von. "Tagebuch des markgraeflichen Jaegerleutnant Carl Philipp von Feilitzsch", a manuscript in the archives of the University of Bayreuth, Germany. A copy is in the War Archives of the Bavarian State Archives in Munich, Germany.

HATCH, Charles E., Jr. Yorktown and the Siege of 1781, (Washington, DC, 1954).

HAZARD, Samuel. Pennsylvania Archives (Philadelphia, 1852).

HAZARD, Samuel. Pennsylvania Collected Records, (Harrisburg, 1852).

HORN, H.B. (Ed.). British Diplomatic Representatives, 1689-1789, (London. 1932).

JOHNSTON, Henry P. The Yorktown Campaign and the Surrender of Cornwallis, (New York, 1975).

KIDDOO, Nancy Rice. "Marshalling Traces of Hessian Soldiers of the American Revolution who Marched as Prisoners-of-War to Frederick County, Maryland, Recruited Local Brides, and Joined the Ranks of American Citizens", a printed list, (Whippany, NJ, n.d.).

KIDDOO, Nancy Rice. "Of Revolutionary Memory: German Mercenaries who Immigrated to Western Maryland", Journal of the Pennsylvania German Society, (Philadelphia) vol. 23, (1989).

MACKENZIE, Frederick. Mackenzie Diaries. Diary of Frederick Mackenzie, Giving a Daily Narrative of His Military Service as an Officer of the Regiment of Royal Welsh Fusiliers during

the Years 1775-1781 in Massachusetts, Rhode
Island, and New York, (Cambridge, 1930).
    MILES, Lion G. The Hessians of Lewis
Miller, (Millville, PA, 1983).
    MUENCHHAUSEN, Friedrich von. At
General Howe's Side, 1776-1778, translated by
Ernst Kipping and annotated by Samuel Steele
Smith, (Monmouth Beach, NJ, 1974).
    POPP, Stephen. His Journal 1777 - Decem-
ber 1783", The Pennsylvania Magazine of History
and Biography, translated by Joseph P. Rosengarten, (Philadelphia), vol. 26 (1902).
    PRESTON, Howard W. The Battle of Rhode
Island - August 29th, 1778, (Providence, RI,
1928).
    PUBLIC Record Office, "Colonial Office Pa-
pers", 5/11, f. 58; 5/140, f. 91; 30/55, no.
7133.
    ROYAL American Gazette. (New York, 20 A-
pril 1780).
    STAEDTLER, Erhard. Die Ansbach Bayreuther
Truppen in Amerikanischen Unabhaegigkeitskrieg,
1777-1783, (Nuernberg, Germany, 1956).
    STEUERNAGEL, Carl Philipp. "Ein kurze Be-
schreibung", a manuscript in the Bancroft
Collection of The New York Public Library.
    SUTHERLAND, Maxwell. "A History of a Set-
tlement", The Dalhousie Review, (Halifax), vol.
41, (Spring 1961).
    TUCKER, St. George. "St. Georg Tucker's
Journal of the Siege of Yorktown, 1781",
William and Mary Quarterly Historical Magazine,
(Williamsburg, VA), series 3, vol. 3 (1948).
    WALDECK, Philipp. "Tagebuch", a manu-
script in the Bancroft Collection of The New
York Public Library.

INDEX

305

BLECKER (cont.)
18 94 135
BLIND, Johann 78 214 Pvt 78 214
BLUEMLEIN, Pvt 234
BONN, Heinrich 94 Pvt 94
BOSE, 53 77 85 179 183
BOSER, Cpl 85 222 Pvt 82 220
BOYD, Capt 265
BRAUN, Grenadier 54 88 187 194
228 Grenadier Sr 61 Johann
241 Johann Wilhelm Sr 61 Pvt
94 185 241 Pvt Jr 48 53 56 61 76
194 211 Pvt Sr 22 143 Wilhelm
185 Wilhelm Jr 48 53 56 61 76
BRAUNING, Pvt 66
BRENNER, Pvt 198
BREY, Andreas 91 Musketeer 91
BROEGEL, Johann 90 Musketeer
90
BROWN, 39 156 166
BROWNE, Gen 300
BRUMMER, Johann 16 94 132 Pvt
16 94 132
BUDDING, Conrad 297 Elizabeth
297
BUENAU, 37 38 53 149 150 164
185
BURGESS, 297-299 Louis A 296
BURGOYNE, 242 Bruce E 301
Gen 121 122 John 121 286
BURNETT, Thomas 200
BUSCH, Ehrenfried Hans
Friedrich 249 Leonhard 76 211
Lt 249 Pvt 76 211
BUTTIN, Konrad 244 Pvt 244
BYRON, Adm 28 153 John 28 153
CALNEC, 297
CANTUSCH, Andreas 83 221 Pvt
83 221
CARLETON, Gen 237 Guy 237
298
CARPENTER, James L 293
CASSELMANN, 270
CHARLES, Earl Of Cornwallis
125 286 Prince Of ?? 64
CHARLOTTE, Queen Of England

CHARLOTTE (cont.)
45
CHILD, Schmit 200
CHRISTHILF, Georg 300 Heinrich
300 Nicholas 300 Sabrina 300
CHRISTHULF, Georg 254 299 Pvt
254
CLARKE, Alured 256 Gen 256
CLINTON, Gen 10 27 41 58 120
121 150 169 183 189 190 290
Henry 10 49 52 56 120 139 150
179 198 237 287
COMTEDEROCHAMBEAU,
Dontien Vimeur 65 Gen 197
CORNWALLIS, 242 Charles 13
Gen 125 Gen Lord 13 18 57 71-
75 87 88 136 Lord 66 70 72 87
198 203 226 227 Lt Gen 66 190
198 Lt Gen Lord 204-210 226
227 242
COSBY, Philip 200
COUNT, Of Schulenburg 275
CYRIACY, Lt 26 148
DAIG, Johann Georg 100 247
Quartermaster 100 247 251
DAVIES, 293 297-299 K G 290
DAWSON, Capt 60 192
DEAHNA, Lt 238
DEBEUST, 297
DECKER, Cpl 232 Johann 232
Vice-Cpl 41 170
DEGRASSE, Adm 240
DELAFAYETTE, Marquis 287
DELAROUERIE, Marquis 296
DEUER, Grenadier 90 Johann 90
DIETLEIN, Johann Ludwig 94 132
Pvt 94 132
DIETRICH, Rev 273
DILL, Jakob 94 Johann Jakob 24
146 Pvt 24 94 146
DITFURTH, 27 34 47 150 160
DOEHLA, 284 286 287 291 297
299 300 Johann Conrad 282
DOEHLEMANN, Cpl 27 151
Johann Christian 27 Johann
Christoph 151

DOERRER, Grenadier 90
Nikolaus 90
DONOP, 52-55 179 184
DORN, Johann Friedrich 42 171
Sgt 42 171
DORSCH, Grenadier 82 219
Johann Georg 82 219
DOUGLAS, Capt 67 199
DRESCHEL, Pvt 94
DRESSEL, Pvt 244 Thomas 244
DREXEL, Friedrich 49 55 62
Johann Christian 27 151 Lt 89
228 255 Medic 49 55 62 Pvt 102
Sgt 27 151
DREXLER, Medic 195
DUERNHOEFFER, Cpl 243
Konrad 243
DUNCAN, Andrew S 200 Henry
200
DUNMORE, Gen 71 203
DURER, Pvt 82 219
DUTCH, Prince Of Ethin 268
EARL, Of Carlisle 287 Of
Dunmore 71 203
EBENAUER, Friedrich 50 180 Lt
50 100 180
EBENEAUER, Friedrich 100
EBERHART, Andreas 224 Pvt 224
EBERLEIN, Grenadier 87 226
Johann 212 Johann Michael 87
226 Pvt 212
ECKER, Carpenter 103
ECKERT, Carpenter 94 Johann
Michael 94
EDEN, William 287
EGLER, Johann Adam 72 Pvt 72
ELIAS, Matthias 223 Pvt 223
ELMAJER, Grenadier 93 Johann
Georg 93
EMMERICH, Col 300
ENSENBERG, Friedrich 300
ERB, Chaplain 28 152 247 255
Georg Christoph Elias 28 152
ERHARDT, Grenadier 54 187
Michael 54 187
ERLBACHER, Conrad 71 204 Cpl

ERLBACHER (cont.)
71 204
ERLWEIN, Johann 24 94 146 Pvt
24 94 146
ERMERT, Georg 26 91 94 148
Musketeer 91 Pvt 26 94 148
ERNST, Johann Christoph 60 192
Pvt 60 192
ESCHERICH, Johann Georg 220
Pvt 83 220
ETTMEIER, Grenadier 149 Johann
Georg 26 149
EWALD, Johann 290
EYB, 101 102 283
EYRISCH, Georg 91 Musketeer 91
FANNING, Col 35 159 161
FAUCITT, William 283 296
FEDER, Ferdinand 152 Lt 40 152
168 229
FEEH, Musketeer 90
FEHR, Grenadier 258 Johann 258
Peter 245 Pvt 245
FEILE, Georg 245 Pvt 245
FEILITZSCH, 286 Lt 295
FERCH, Pvt 83 220
FICKEL, Cpl 76 211 Johann
Leonhard 76 211
FISCHER, Johann Christoph 91
Musketeer 91
FISCHERALL, Capt 258 259
FLACHSHAAR, Ludwig 249
Quartermaster 249
FLECHTNER, Johann Christoph
91
FLECTNER, Musketeer 91
FLEISSINGER, Drummer 64 237
Johann Georg 64 237
FLOHR, Cpl 42 170 Johann 42 170
FOERSTER, Ferdinand 58 191
Johann 91 Lt 58 76 191 211
Musketeer 91
FOERTSCH, Johann 90 Musketeer
90
FRANK, Albertus Magnus 249
Grenadier 9 118 Karl 9 118 Lt
249

FRICKER, Johann 84 223 Pvt 84
223
FRIEDERICI, Gottlob 18 135 Pvt
18 135
FRIEDRICH, Gottlob 94 Pvt 94
FRISCH, Auditor 238 Paul 238
FROHMUELLER, Grenadier 90
Jakob 90
FRUEH, Grenadier 93 149 Johann
Michael 26 93 149
FUCHS, 84 Johann Christian 99
Johann Christoph 92 Johann
Kaspar 253 Pvt 57 221 253
Quartermaster 92 99 135
FUEKENTSCHER, Johann Adam
92 Musketeer 92
FUERST, Cpl 157 Georg 157
GACHSTETTER, Cpl 222
GACKSETTER, Vice-Cpl 87
GACKSTETTER, Pvt 41 170
GAERTNER, 297 Johann Georg
Christian 241 Pvt 241
GAKSTETTER, Vice-Cpl 226
GAMBIER, Adm 31 156 James 31
156
GARDELOW, Adam 54 187
Jaeger 54 187
GARDNER, John 299
GAREIS, Johann Georg 250 Pvt
250
GATES, Gen 57 190 Horatio 57
299
GEISENSIEDER, Martin 298
GEISSENSIEDER, Johann Martin
250 Pvt 250
GEITZ, Grenadier Sr 90 92 Johann
Nikolaus Sr 90 92
GEORGE III, King Of England 18
33 72 105 113 123 136 159 180
191 204 256
GERLICH, Grenadier 219 Johann
Georg 219
GERLINGER, Michael 256 Pvt 256
GIBBS, 237
GLAENZEL, Georg 60 199 Pvt 60
Vice-Cpl 199

GLAITSMANN, Sheriff 280
GLATZ, 188 Joseph 56 Pvt 56 188
GNEISENAU, 298
GOERT, Johann Stephan 157 232
Pvt 157 232 240 243
GOETSCH, Gen 251
GOLL, Grenadier 50 181
GOLLWITZ, 38 Friedrich 37 93
Medic 37 93 163 Pvt 38 40
GORDON, Maj 82 219
GOSSLER, Friedrich 54 187
Grenadier 54 187
GOV, Of West Florida 287
GRAEBNER, Carl 39 167 Cpl 39
167 Lt 44 89 229
GRAU, Pvt 50 181 Valentin 50 181
GRAVES, Adm 67 68 78 199 200
214 Thomas 67
GREENE, Gen 66 198 Nathanael
66 198
GREGORY, Gen 205
GREINER, Johann Wolfgang 156
Medic 156
GRUBER, 94 Grenadier 24 Pvt 80
146 216 Simon 24 94 146
GUENTHER, Michael 51 182
GUNCKEL, Jakob 87 226 Pvt 87
226
GUNN, Maj 268
GUNS, Maj 274
GUTTENBERG, Georg Friedrich
121 Lt 248 Sgt 121
HADOERFER, Grenadier 237
Johann Michael 237
HADORFER, John Michael 296
HAEHNLEIN, Cpl 123 Cpl Sr 62
195 Georg 62 Johann Andreas
123 Pvt 42 171 Vice-Cpl 42 171
HAEUFELEIN, Michael 40
HAHN, Field Jaeger 65
HALBMEIER, Lt 89 229
HALBMEYER, Georg Simon
40 Sgt 40 168
HAMMERTER, Musketeer 91
Wendel 91
HARTLEIN, Leonhard 217

HARTLEIN (cont.)
Leonhard Jr 80 Pvt 217 Pvt Jr
80
HARTMANN, Heinrich 58 Pvt
256
HARTUNG, Heinrich 57 Pvt 57
HAUFF, Johann Friedrich 239 Sgt
63 239
HAUSSEL, Leonhard 240
HAUSSELT, Leonhard 42 170 Sgt
42 170 240
HAZARD, 299 Samuel 298
HEERMANN, Konrad Jr 242 Pvt
Jr 242
HELMES, Capt 294
HENOP, Pastor 251
HEPPE, Ridingmaster 126
HERMANN, Sgt 60
HEROLT, Grenadier 237 Johann
237
HERRNBAUER, Auditor 188 Lt
100 188
HERTERICH, Andreas 31 93 155
Konrad 300 Musketeer 93 Pvt
31 46 155 176
HERTLEIN, Jobst 246 Pvt 246
HERZOG, Georg 36 Pvt 36
HEUMANN, Christian Felix 90
Grenadier 90
HIESSINGER, Pvt 244
HILLER, Bartholomai 157 Pvt 157
HILPERT, Ludwig Theodor 41
170 Sgt 41 170
HIPSCH, Johann Peter 92
Musketeer 92
HIRSCH, Lt 40 168
HOCHWEIN, Grenadier 92
Johann Georg 92
HOEHL, Cpl 64 Grenadier 40
HOEPF, Pvt 157
HOFFMANN, Christian 91
Michael 83 Sgt 83 220
HOFMANN, 238 Capt 251 Lt 20
89 99 106 139 229 Michael 42
170 Nikolaus Friedrich 99 Sgt
42 170

HOHBERGER, Adam 250
Grenadier 250 Johann Adam
132 Musketeer 92 Pvt 132
HOHENBERGER, Georg 54 186
Grenadier 54 186
HOLDORFER, Michael 296
HOPF, Johann 64 Pvt 64
HOPFER, Drummer 233 Pvt 36 76
212 Simon 36 76 212
HORN, Pvt 206
HORNEBER, Karl 300
HOWARD, Frederick 287
HOWE, Gen 9 17 118 119 123 129
134 253 286 287 295 William 9
17 117 134 135 139 282 286
HUBER, Anna 293
HUNGER, Peter 24 94 146 Pvt 24
94 146 Recruit 249
HUSSARS, 53
HUYN, 26 34 39 161
IMHAEUSER, Pvt 50
IMHAEUSSER, Pvt 181
JACOB, Grenadier 233 Johann
Matthias 233
JACOBI, Grenadier 82 218 Lorenz
82 218
JAEGER, Christoph 36 Pvt 36
JOHNSON, Gideon 200 Gov 252
JOHNSTON, Henry P 293
JOHNSTONE, George 287
KAEMPF, Pvt 83 220
KAIM, Grenadier 205 Johann
Christian 205
KALB, Grenadier 204
KALNEK, 297 Jakob 238
Quartermaster 238
KARL, Cpl 263
KASSEL, Pvt 24 94 146
KATZENWINKEL, 296 Heinrich
16 46 132 Pvt 16 46 88 94 132
KATZENWINKLE, Pvt 175
KATZENWINKEL, Pvt 228
KAUFMANN, Grenadier 31 93
155 Jacob 31 Jakob 93 155
Musketeer 91
KEIZENZEDER, Martin 298

KEMPEL, Maj 85 222
KERN, Cannoneer 92 Georg 92
  Johann Simon 225 Johann
  Simon Sr 86 Pvt 225 Pvt Sr 86
KIDDOO, 293 297 Nancy Rice 292
KIESTLING, Sgt 255
KIM, Capt 251 Joachim 251
KING, Of England 4 7 11 12 49 59
  270 271 298
KIPPING, Ernst 282
KIRSCH, Musketeer 91
KLEIN, Cpl 94 102 Friedrich 93
  Johann 57 Johann Veit 244
  Musketeer 93 Pvt 32 57 158 244
  Vice-Cpl 256
KLEINSCHMID, Ridingmaster
  271
KLING, Jakob Ernst 156 Johann
  Ernst 31 Sgt 31 156
KNYPHAUSEN, 63
KOEHLER, Drummer 64 Johann
  Burkhardt 64
KOEHLNER, Drummer 247
  Johann Burckhardt 247
KOERNER, Grenadier 92 Johann
  92 Konrad 84 221 Pvt 84 221
  232
KOHLSCHREIBER, Benedikt 232
  Pvt 232
KOLB, Cpl 278
KRAUS, Pvt 54 186
KREBS, Gertraut 297
KREGER, Pvt 37
KREGLINGEN, Cpl 239
KRETCHI, Vice-Cpl 234
KRETSCH, Pvt 170
KRETSCHI, Pvt 42
KREYER, Quartermaster Guard
  164
KRIEGBAUM, Grenadier 90 92
  121 Johann Michael 90 121
KRIEGER, Pvt 176
KUBLAN, Lt 90 99 119
LACH, Gen 234
LAEUS, Ignatius 83 220 Pvt 83
  220

LANDGRAF, 27 30 34 35 47 53
  150 155 160 161 174 176 179
  184
LANGFRITZ, Pvt 173
LAUTERBACH, Adam 36 Pvt 36
  83 221
LEHNERT, Commissary 163
  Mister 164
LEHR, Cpl 91 Johann 91
  Musketeer 93
LEIB, 50 53 176 179 180 184
LEIKAM, Johann 149 Pvt 149
LENKUM, Johann 93 Musketeer
  93
LESLIE, Alexander 58 190 Gen 58
  70 71 73 74 209 247 Maj Gen
  190 203 206
LIEBEL, Johann 242 Pvt 242
LINCOLN, Benjamin 241 Gen 241
  246 252
LINDEMEIER, Lt 89 229 255
LIST, Grenadier 209 Jakob 209
LITITZ, Lt 249
LOCHMUELLER, Johann Georg
  23 144 Pvt 23 35 144
LOCHNER, Johann Peter 243 Pvt
  243 244
LOCHSTAMPFER, Cpl 255 Georg
  Michael 255
LOEW, Pvt 245
LORENZ, Grenadier 10 92 120
  Matthias 10 92 120 Michael 24
  94 145 Pvt 24 94 145
LOREY, Capt 53 185 Friedrich
  Heinrich 53 185
LOSSBERG, 48
LUCK, Johann 18 94 135 Pvt 94
  135
LUDWIG, Quartermaster 239
LUTZ, Grenadier 90 Johann
  Michael 90
MACKENZIE, 289 Frederick 288
MADER, Georg 90 Musketeer 90
MAEUSSNER, Christoph 226 Pvt
  226
MALTZ, Grenadier 90 Leonhard

310

SALAMON, Pvt 157 Thomas 157
SALTMANN, Pvt 277
SALZMANN, Johann Friedrich
205 237 Sgt 205 237
SAULER, Johann Leonhard 209
Pvt 209
SCAMMEL, Alexander 292
SCHAEFER, Friedrich Jakob 297
Gertraut 297
SCHAEFFER, Christian 33 36 159
Friedrich Jakob 244 Pvt 33 36
95 159 162 244
SCHALLER, Capt 26 149 Georg
Friedrich 26 149
SCHARD, Johann 16 132 Pvt 16
94 132
SCHELLER, Grenadier Jr 238
SCHEMIG, Kaspar 246 Pvt 246
SCHERRER, Balthasar 209
Grenadier 209
SCHERZ, Heinrich 157 Pvt 157
SCHIFFERMUELLER, Kaspar 256
Pvt 256
SCHILLING, Christoph 85 223
Cpl 85 223 234 Samuel 63 Sgt
63
SCHINDELBAUER, Drummer 84
221
SCHIRMER, Johann Christoph 41
170 Vice-Cpl 41 170
SCHLAEGEL, Johann 239 Pvt 239
SCHMALZ, Cpl 42 171 Johann
Georg Friedrich 42 171
SCHMELZER, Georg 86 225 Pvt
86 225
SCHMID, Cpl 151 Field Jaeger 63
Grenadier 50 Paul 42 149 171
Pvt 181 Sgt 41 42 149 170 171
SCHMIDT, Musketeer 91 Peter
Paul 91 Pvt 32 Sgt 255
SCHNEIDER, Cpl 42 171
Leonhard 42 171 Pvt 64 71 157
232 Sabrina 300
SCHNELLER, Johann Heinrich 58
191 232 Surgeon 58 191 232

SCHOENEL, Johann Balthasar
148 Pvt 148
SCHOENELL, Johann Balthasar
26 94 Pvt 26 94
SCHOEPF, Dr 99 Johann David
99
SCHOEPLER, Pvt 278
Quartermaster 63 Sgt 63 Vice-
Cpl 41 170
SCHORR, Johann 91 Musketeer
91
SCHREINER, Heinrich 90 Sgt 90
SCHUBERT, Nikolaus 83 220 Pvt
83 220
SCHUCHARD, Lt 40 78 168 213
SCHULER, Pvt 83 221
SCHULTHEISS, Cpl 93 Grenadier
93 155 Johann 242 Johann
Georg 93 155 Pvt 242 Vice-Cpl
30 31 154 155
SCHULZ, Gottlob 64 196 Pvt 64
196 197
SCHUSTER, Christian 84 228 Cpl
84 88 222 228 Vice-Cpl 76 211
SCHWAGER, Pvt 251 Samuel 251
SCHWED, Ludwig Friedrich 238
Sgt 238
SCHWEGLER, Pvt 224
SCHWEIGER, Field Jaeger 242
SEC, Of War 299
SECHRIST, Elizabeth 297
SEEHART, Georg Friedrich 157
Pvt 157
SEEHAUSEN, Musketeer 91
Wolfgang 91
SEEWALD, Johann Wilhelm 82
219 Pvt 82 219
SEFFERT, Pvt 50
SEIDEL, Capt 261 263 264
Christoph 100 Erhard 57 190
Lt 100 Pvt 57 190 Recruit 41
169
SEIFFERLEIN, Grenadier 54 186
Johann 54 Johann Peter 186
SEIFFERT, Georg 65 Pvt 65

314

VONADELSHEIM (cont.)
    Karl Friedrich 98 99 Lt 98-100
    135
VONALTENSTEIN, Andreas Karl
    100 Lt 100 279
VONARNBERG, Karl Gottlieb 35
    161 Maj 35 161
VONBEUST, Capt 99 106 133
    Friedrich Ernst Carl 99 Lt 100
    106 238 297 Maj 73 89 208 229
    247 264 265 278 279 Philipp
    Otto Heinrich 100
VONBIBRA, Prince 280
VONBOSE, 184 212 223 235 249
    Carl Ernst Johann 30 155 Maj
    Gen 30 155
VONBUBNA, Count 249 Franz
    249 Lt 249 Lt Count 255
VONBUENAU, 53 166 186
VONBUSCH, Lt Gen 274
VONCRAMON, 98 Capt 21 100
    107 139 Christoph 100
VONCYRIACY, Lt 89 229 255
VONDERHEYDE, Lt 39 98 Moritz
    Wilhelm 98
VONDERHEYDTE, Lt 168
VONDERLIPPE, Count 274
VONDIEMAR, Justus 6 Lt 6 39 53
    185 Lt Jr 100 Lt Sr 99 111 168
VONDIESKAU, Ridingmaster 27
    150
VONDITFURTH, 39 166 177
VONDONOP, 47 176 185 186 188
    Col 9 125 Karl Emil 9 125
VONELLRODT, Capt 16 88 90 98
    106 121 128 129 131 228
    Christian Philipp 98
VONERCKERT, Capt 90 92 98 106
    121 Ludwig Heinrich Vollrath
    90 98
VONESCHWEGE, Adolf Wilhelm
    174 Capt 174
VONEYB, 9 17 98 106 116-122 124
    128-133 135 Capt 37 56 67 73
    84 99 106 164 188 199 204 205
    208 209 212 222 Col 17 98 106

VONEYB (cont.)
    123 133 134 286 Friedrich
    Adolf Carl 249 Friedrich
    Ludwig 99 Friedrich Ludwig
    Albrecht 98 Lt 249
VONFABRICE, Johann 58 191 Lt
    58 89 191 228
VONFEILITZSCH, Carl Philipp
    283 284 Heinrich Carl Philipp
    100 Lt 40 42 100 168 171
VONFORSTNER, Karl 100 Lt 100
    123
VONGUTTENBERG, Herr 280
VONHACHENBERG, Gen 52
    Karl Wilhelm 52
VONHACKENBERG, Carl
    Wilhelm 183 Maj Gen 183
VONHEISTER, Gen 9 Leopold 9
    117 Lt Gen 117 118
VONHERRNBAUER, Johann
    Friedrich 100
VONHILLER, Johann Wilhelm
    238 Lt 238 249
VONHOHENDORF, Georg 59 60
    Lt 40 59 60 168 192
VONHUYN, 149 166 285 Johann
    Christoph 55 188 Maj Gen 55
    188
VONKELLER, Friedrich 99 Lt 17
    44 99 129 131
VONKNYPHAUSEN, 116 196
    Gen 48 Lt Gen 50 115 178 180
    184 Wilhelm 50 115
VONKOENITZ, Adjutant 168
    August Christian Friedrich 98
    Capt 44 88 228 248 Lt 98 168
VONKOSPOTH, Gen 278
    Heinrich Julius 278
VONKRUSE, Capt 255 Friedrich
    100 Lt 89 100 229 248
VONLOSSBERG, 178 Lt Gen 273
VONMARDEFELD, Johann
    Wilhelm 99 Lt 21 99 139
VONMARSCHALL, Lt 21 88 140
    228
VONMASSENBACH, Christoph

VONMASSENBACH (cont.)
Julius 249 Lt 249
VONMATTOLAY, Heinrich 58
191 Lt 191
VONMETSCH, Capt 229
VONMETZCH, Capt 257
VONMETZSCH, Capt 84 89 222
248 250 255 275 Christoph 98
Lt 21 98 133 140
VONMOLITOR, Capt 17 20 34
129 133 138 160 258 Christian
Theodor Sigismund 99 Johann
Sebastian 100 Lt 99 100 119
Stephen 300 301
VONMUENCHHAUSEN,
Frederick 282 Friedrich 282
295
VONMUHLENBERG, John Peter
Gabriel 128 Pastor 128
VONPRUESCHENCK, Ernst Karl
53 185 Lt Col 53 185
VONQUESNOY, 34 Capt 21 32 34
89 140 145 151 158 160 173 229
241 257 Georg Heinrich 100 Lt
100 129
VONRALL, Col 254
VONREITZENSTEIN, Capt 258
Christoph Ludwig 98
Christoph Ludwig Baron 91
Col 94 190 Ernst 46 175 Lt 24
85 89 121 131 145 222 229 232
248 Lt Baron 98 100 Lt Col 38
73 86 94 168 170 181 186 208
209 211 214 225 236 237 239
241 243 244 248 Ludwig 100
Maj 8 34 106 116 120 121 123
133 135 140 146 151 160 Maj
Baron 98 Wilhelm Friedrich
Ernst 98
VONREYHER, Andreas Friedrich
99 Capt 99 119
VONRIEDESEL, Friedrich 122
Friedrich Adolf 48 177 Gen 48
Maj Gen 177
VONROEDER, Capt 39 53 185
Capt Lt 167 Friedrich Wilhelm

VONROEDER (cont.)
98 Lt 17 98 133
VONSCHOENFELD, Friedrich 98
Lt 98 248
VONSEITZ, Capt 99 106 160
Grenadier Capt 34 Maj 73 94
170 186 187 196 197 206 208
232 236 242 244 245 248 254
255 261 Philipp Friedrich 99
VONSEYBOTHEN, 20 26 28 32 34
37 39-41 44 46 48 51 55 56 58 66
67 71 80 82-85 133 138-140 149
152 156 158 160-162 164-169
171 173 176 178 182-184 188
191 199 204 205 208-210 212
213 216 217 219-224 226 229
232 234-239 241 243 245 247
248 254-258 261 263 264 278
Col 37 42 52 73 78 80 82-84 87
89 208 257 264 291 Johann
Heinrich Christian Franz 99
Maj 17 99 106 133
VONSICHART, 286 Capt 17 134
Lt 17 129
VONSODEN, Friedrich 99 Lt 99
VONSODON, Lt 135
VONSPIEGEL, Herr 280
VONSTAIN, 22 42 83 84 Capt 7 16
23 31 32 35 36 42 48 67 71 76 77
80 83 88 91 94 98 106 121 124
132 140 143 144 146 148 149
155 157 159 170 171 181 185
192 199 211 213 217 219-221
223 224 228 232 234 239 242-
246 249 250 253 Maj 163
VONSTEIN, Capt 98
VONSTEITZ, Capt 140
VONSTRAHLENDORF, Adolf
Daniel 100 Lt 40 42 168 171
VONSTREIT, Lt 17 100 129
Maximilian 100
VONTRECHSEL, Lt 40 88 168
VONTRESCHEL, Lt 228
VONTRITSCHELER, Capt 185
VONTRITSCHLER, Capt 40 53
168 248 Ernst Ludwig 98 Lt 34

316

VONTRITSCHLER (cont.)
98 161
VONTUNDERFELD, Georg
Gustav Lebrecht 100 Lt 100
VONVOIT, 23 24 28 34 37 39 42 46
48 50 52 62 63 66 67 80 98 106
120 122 129 131 133 135 136
139 140 143-146 148 149 151
152 154 155 157-161 163 165-
168 170 171 175-177 181 183
185-188 190-192 194-197 199
205-207 209-211 213 214 216-
226 228 232-239 241-248 250
251 253-257 261 275 278 279
August Valentin 99 Col 12 17
26 47 52 58 73 78 83 84 88 90 94
98 99 106 124 133 143 144 169
171 172 175 177 183 187 198
199 206 207 211 220 225 277
Mrs 58
VONWALDENFELS, 16 18 140
Capt 21 91 98 106 128 130 132
133 136 140 Christoph
Friedrich Joseph 98
VONWEITERSHAUSEN, Karl
Alexander 100 Lt 100 140 236
VONWITZLEBEN, Lt 100 136
VONWOELLWARTH, Karl
Friedrich Eugen 99 Lt 21 99
139
VONWURMB, Capt 255 Ernst
Friedrich 248 Lt 248
VONZOBEL, Prior 280
WACHLER, Grenadier 232
WAEGER, Cannoneer 92
WAGNER, 300 Chaplain 89 232
256 Johann Christoph 256 Lt
100 Philipp Christian 100 Pvt
84 222
WALDECK, Philipp 301
WALDENFELS, Capt 135
WALKER, William 7
WALTER, Pvt 50 181
WANNEMACHER, Pvt 244
Sophonias 244
WANNENMAKER, John 298

WASHINGTON, 52 61 183 194
Gen 61 65 197 229 Lt Gen 123
194 227
WAYNE, Anthony 247 Gen 247
WEIANT, Andreas 57 Musketeer
92 Pvt 57
WEINHART, Heinrich 100 Lt 89
100 229 248
WEISS, Cpl 42 171 Johann Adam
42 Konrad 233 Pvt 233
WEITERSHAUSEN, Lt 21
WENDER, Georg 90 Musketeer
90
WETSCHELL, Christian 48 157
Pvt 48 157
WIEBEMANN, Musketeer 91
WIEDENER, Grenadier 57 Mrs 57
WIEDERHOLD, Bernhard
Wilhelm 50 180 Ensign 50 180
Johann Heinrich 42 171 Sgt 42
171
WIEDERSTEIN, Cpl 243 Konrad
243
WIENNER, Field Jaeger 63
WIESS, Johann Adam 171
WILSON, Brigadier Gen 12 Gen
124 Thomas 12 124 286
WINKLER, Johann Georg Michael
42 170 Vice-Cpl 42 170
WINTERMANN, Musketeer 91
WIRTH, Cpl 90 Ernst Abraham 90
WITTE, Jakob 209 Pvt 209
WOLF, Georg Adam 232
Grenadier 83 221 Pvt 232
WOOD, Col 252 James 252 John
242
WUEHL, Pvt 237
WUESTENDOERFER, Johann
Leonhard 90 Musketeer 90
WURZBACH, Drummer 244
ZEDER, Cannoneer 92 Constable
10 Gunner 120 Michael 10 92
120
ZEILMANN, Egide 80 216 Pvt 80
216
ZELLER, Jakob 91 Musketeer 91

317

ZINK, Cannoneer 92 Johann 92
ZINN, Heinrich Wilhelm 91
　　Musketeer 91

ZIPFEL, Pvt 18 136 Pvt Jr 94 Pvt
　　Sr 94
ZOLLFRANK, Martin 55 187 Pvt
　　55 187

Other Heritage Books by Bruce E. Burgoyne:

A Hessian Officer's Diary of the American Revolution
Translated from an Anonymous Ansbach-Bayreuth Diary and the Prechtel Diary

Canada During the American Revolutionary War: Lieutenant Friedrich Julius von Papet's
Journal of the Sea Voyage to North America and the Campaign Conducted There

CD: A Hessian Diary of the American Revolution

CD: A Hessian Officer's Diary of The American Revolution

CD: A Hessian Report on the People, the Land, the War of Eighteenth Century
America, as Noted in the Diary of Chaplain Philipp Waldeck, 1776-1780

CD: Ansbach-Bayreuth Diaries from the Revolutionary War

CD: Canada During the America Revolutionary War

CD: Diaries of Two Ansbach Jaegers

CD: The Hessian Collection, Volume 1: Revolutionary War Era

CD: They Also Served. Women with the Hessian Auxiliaries

CD: Waldeck Soldiers of the American Revolutionary War

Defeat, Disaster, and Dedication

Diaries of Two Ansbach Jaegers

Eighteenth Century America (A Hessian Report on the People, the Land, the War)
as Noted in the Diary of Chaplain Philipp Waldeck (1776-1780)

Enemy Views: The American Revolutionary War as Recorded by the Hessian Participants

English Army and Navy Lists Compiled During the American Revolutionary War by
Ansbach-Bayreuth Lieutenant Johann Ernst Prechtel

Georg Pausch's Journal and Reports of the Campaign in America, as
Translated from the German Manuscript in the Lidgerwood Collection in the
Morristown Historical Park Archives, Morristown, New Jersey

Hesse-Hanau Order Books, a Diary and Roster: A Collection of Items
Concerning the Hesse-Hanau Contingent of "Hessians" Fighting
Against the American Colonists in the Revolutionary War

Hessian Chaplains: Their Diaries and Duties

Hessian Letters and Journals and a Memoir

Journal of a Hessian Grenadier Battalion

Journal of the Hesse-Cassel Jaeger Corps

Journal of the Prince Charles Regiment
Translated by Bruce E. Burgoyne; Edited by Dr. Marie E. Burgoyne

Most Illustrious Hereditary Prince: Letters to Their Prince from Members of Hesse-Hanau
Military Contingent in the Service of England During the American Revolution

Notes from a British Museum

Order Book of the Hesse-Cassel von Mirbach Regiment

www.ingramcontent.com/pod-product-compliance
Lightning Source LLC
Chambersburg PA
CBHW071636270326
41928CB00010B/1944